Ship To:

**VALENTINA RAMIA**
**356 GREENE AVE APT 4F**
**BROOKLYN, NEW YORK 11216-1193**

---

## Order ID: 107-3211068-1087409

Thank you for buying from Boomerangs Books on Amazon Marketplace.

| | | | |
|---|---|---|---|
| **Shipping Address:** | | Order Date: | Nov 9, 2015 |
| VALENTINA RAMIA | | Shipping Service: | Standard |
| 356 GREENE AVE APT 4F | | Buyer Name: | Valentina Ramia |
| BROOKLYN, NEW YORK 11216-1193 | | Seller Name: | Boomerangs Books |

| Quantity | Product Details | Price | Total |
|---|---|---|---|
| 1 | **Pharmaceutical Reason: Knowledge and Value in Global Psychiatry (Cambridge Studies in Society and the Life Sciences) [Paperback] [2006] Lakoff, Andrew**<br><br>**SKU:** HX-7DWN-N6P1<br>**ASIN:** 0521546664<br>**Listing ID:** 0528PZL9MGY<br>**Order Item ID:** 24057124981194<br>**Condition:** Used - Good<br>**Comments:** Small crease on bottom right corner of front cover. Light crease in spine on front cover. Some writing and underlining in pen throughout first ten or so pages. Binding is tight. Ships same day or next business day. We allow returns within two weeks of the receipt of your purchase. 100% of the proceeds from your purchase directly benefit the AIDS Action Committee of Boston, Massachusetts. The mission of AAC is to stop the epidemic by preventing new HIV infections and optimizing the health of those already infected. | $20.00 | Subtotal: $20.00<br>Shipping: $3.99<br><br>Total: $23.99 |
| | | | **ORDER TOTAL: $23.99** |

**Returning your item:**
Go to "Your Account" on Amazon.com, click "Your Orders" and then click the "seller profile" link for this order to get information about the return and refund policies that apply.
Visit http://www.amazon.com/returns to print a return shipping label. Please have your order ID ready.

**Thanks for buying on Amazon Marketplace**. To provide feedback for the seller please visit www.amazon.com/feedback. To contact the seller, go to Your Orders in Your Account. Click the seller's name under the appropriate product. Then, in the "Further Information" section, click "Contact the Seller."

## Pharmaceutical Reason

When a French biotechnology company seeks patients in Buenos Aires with bipolar disorder for its gene discovery program, they have unexpected trouble finding enough subjects for the study. In Argentina, the predominant form of mental health expertise – psychoanalysis – does not recognize the legitimacy of bipolar disorder as a diagnostic entity. This problem points to a broader set of political and epistemological debates in global psychiatry. Drawing from an ethnography of psychiatric practice in Buenos Aires, Andrew Lakoff follows the contested extension of novel techniques for understanding and intervening in mental illness. He charts the globalization of the new biomedical psychiatry, and illustrates the clashes, conflicts, alliances, and reformulations that take place when psychoanalytic and biological models of illness and cure meet. Highlighting the social and political implications that new forms of expertise about human behavior and thought bring, Lakoff presents an arresting case study that will appeal to scholars and students alike.

ANDREW LAKOFF is Assistant Professor of Sociology and Science Studies at the University of California, San Diego.

CAMBRIDGE STUDIES IN SOCIETY AND THE LIFE SCIENCES

**Series Editors**

Nikolas Rose, *London School of Economics*

Paul Rabinow, *University of California at Berkeley*

This interdisciplinary series focuses on the social shaping, social meaning and social implications of recent developments in the life sciences, biomedicine and biotechnology. It places original research and innovative theoretical work within a global, multicultural context.

**Other titles in series**

Adam Hedgecoe, *The Politics of Personalised Medicine: Pharmacogenetics in the Clinic*

Amade M'Charek, *The Human Genome Diversity Project: An Ethnography of Scientific Practice*

Monica Konrad, *Narrating the New Predictive Genetics: Ethics, Ethnography and Science*

# Pharmaceutical Reason

## Knowledge and Value in Global Psychiatry

ANDREW LAKOFF

CAMBRIDGE
UNIVERSITY PRESS

CAMBRIDGE UNIVERSITY PRESS
Cambridge, New York, Melbourne, Madrid, Cape Town, Singapore, São Paulo

Cambridge University Press
The Edinburgh Building, Cambridge CB2 8RU, UK

Published in the United States of America by Cambridge University Press, New York

www.cambridge.org
Information on this title: www.cambridge.org/9780521546669



First published 2005
Reprinted 2007

Printed in the United Kingdom at the University Press, Cambridge

*A catalogue record for this publication is available from the British Library*

ISBN-13 978-0-521-83760-6 hardback
ISBN-13 978-0-521-54666-9 paperback

For my parents
George Lakoff
and
Robin Tolmach Lakoff

# Contents

# Acknowledgments

Like its subjects, this book is the product of its intellectual milieu. I am indebted to the teachers, friends, and colleagues who have nurtured it along the way. In the Berkeley anthropology department, I was fortunate to encounter an environment that encouraged engaged reflection, and where the stakes of thought were high. My thesis advisor, Paul Rabinow, provided a model of intellectual curiosity and conceptual rigor. Lawrence Cohen, Stephen Greenblatt, Stefania Pandolfo, Nancy Scheper-Hughes, and Thomas Laqueur provided early and ongoing inspiration for this effort. Conversations with Stephen Collier have continually challenged me to rethink the implications of my work. Liz Roberts, Natasha Schull, and Kate Zaloom are friends and colleagues who have generously engaged with this material over a number of years. Ivan Ascher, Jennifer Fishman, Duana Fullwiley, Frederick Keck, William Mazzarella, and Tobias Rees provided incisive comments on earlier drafts of this book. Randolph Starn was extremely generous in his support over the course of my years at Berkeley.

As a dissertation, this work would never have moved beyond the glimmer of an idea without the support and creative inspiration given by Julia Svihra. At multiple junctures, spiritual and intellectual sustenance has come from good friends: special thanks go to Miles Becker, Jon Eldan, Tal Lewis, Tanya Pearlman, Josh Siegel, Kurt Strovink, and Rebecca Plant. George Lakoff and Kathleen Frumkin have been extraordinary sources of cheer and inspiration. Robin Tolmach Lakoff was, as ever, unmatched in her wit, wisdom, and culinary prowess.

I must express my gratitudc to the many Argentine psychiatrists and psychoanalysts who allowed me into their world of impassioned thought and practice. Following ethnographic convention, they receive pseudonyms in the book. Upon my arrival in Buenos Aires,

I encountered several seasoned anthropologists who became close friends and guides to the city. Adriana Stagnaro, Laura Ferrero, Axel Lazzari, and Juan Manuel Obarrio introduced me to the *porteño* intellectual and cultural worlds. Scholars of Argentine social thought were extremely gracious in linking me to the *mundo-psi* and teaching me about its history. I am grateful to Eduardo Keegan, Mariano Plotkin, Hugo Vezzetti, and Sergio Visacovsky. Mireille Abelin's personal warmth and spirited engagement with Argentina nourished this work immensely.

Early conversations with Allan Young and Tanya Luhrmann helped convince me that I was going in the right direction. My hosts at the Department of Social Medicine at Harvard, Byron Good, Mary-Jo Good, and Arthur Kleinman, along with Michael Fischer, brought me into a unique setting of ethically engaged reflection on the social dimensions of healing. In Cambridge and after, I have been lucky to have as interlocutors and friends Joe Dumit, Jenny Reardon, and Kaushik Sunder Rajan. In San Diego I encountered a fruitful place for interaction with colleagues and graduate students in Sociology and Science Studies. I would especially like to thank Jim Holston, Teresa Caldeira, Steven Shapin, Andy Scull, Steve Epstein, Geof Bowker, John Evans, John Skrentny, and Amy Binder for making me feel at home.

Thanks to Sarah Caro and Cambridge University Press for their excellent work in bringing the project to fruition. The project has been nurtured all along by Nikolas Rose, whose interventions at many stages have been of great help. Toward the end, Talia Dan-Cohen graciously helped shape the manuscript into its final form.

I am grateful to the institutions that have provided material and institutional support in my research and writing. Graduate study was funded by a National Science Foundation Graduate Fellowship. My research in Argentina was assisted by an NSF Dissertation Improvement Grant. Upon my return, I was fortunate to receive the financial support and stimulating company provided by a fellowship from the Townsend Center for the Humanities at UC Berkeley. At Harvard I was supported by a NIMH training grant in Medical Anthropology.

Chapter 1 appeared in modified form as "Diagnostic Liquidity: Mental Illness and the Global Trade in DNA," in *Theory and Society* 34 (2005); a portion of Chapter 3 appeared as "The Lacan Ward: Pharmacology and Subjectivity in Buenos Aires," in *Social Analysis* 47:2 (2003); and modified versions of Chapter 5 were published as "The Anxieties of

Globalization: Antidepressant Marketing and Economic Crisis in Argentina," in *Social Studies of Science* 34:2 (2004), and as "The Private Life of Numbers: Pharmaceutical Marketing in Post-Welfare Argentina," in Aihwa Ong and Stephen J. Collier (eds.), *Global Assemblages: Technology, Politics and Ethics as Anthropological Problems.*

# Introduction: specific effects

> "To want to be human has no scientific basis. It amounts to sheer dilettantism."
>
> *Niklas Luhmann.*[1]

It is a Thursday morning in the psychopathology ward of Hospital Romero, and potential DNA donors have come in for their appointments. Romero is a public hospital in a working-class neighborhood of Buenos Aires, serving poor patients from outlying areas of the city. The psychopathology ward is taking part in a collaborative investigation with a French biotechnology company to find genes linked to bipolar disorder. The doctors are to make diagnoses and gather blood samples from two hundred patients, in exchange for a hundred-thousand-dollar donation from the biotech company. DNA is extracted from these samples at a nearby laboratory, and then sent by courier to the company's research campus outside of Paris. There, the company will seek to find and patent genes linked to susceptibility to the disorder. But the immediate problem for doctors at the hospital is how to know who has the disorder, in the absence of physically measurable signs and symptoms.

Gustavo Rechtman, a staff psychiatrist, is screening potential subjects. In one examination, a young woman does most of the talking, rapidly and in disjointed bursts. She is a psychoanalyst, she explains, and so she does not believe in genetic explanations for mental illness. But a patient of hers who had read about the study in the newspaper told her that she had certain characteristics that seemed like they could be "bipolar," so she decided to come – just in case, out of curiosity. She does not want to give her name: professionally, she says, it would be bad for her reputation if it were known that she had come to find out about her genetic makeup. It soon becomes apparent that the woman thinks that there is already a genetic test available for bipolar disorder, and she has come to Romero to take it. She is not sure whether she really wants to know, or even if it would be possible to know such a thing through a blood test. When the doctor finally makes it clear that in fact there is not yet a genetic test, but the hospital is collecting samples in the hopes of finding genes for bipolar disorder, she begins to protest the very premise of the study.

"But how can you possibly know a person's diagnosis if you haven't been treating them?" she demands. She cuts off Rechtman's response, explaining that in psychoanalysis, you have to establish a transferential relationship with the patient in order to see the psychic structure. Rechtman tries to calm her, explaining the rationale for diagnosis: "there are certain signs of the disorder – for instance, what was it that your friend noticed?" The woman lists a few symptoms: insomnia, cocaine use, depressions, an eating disorder. "My analyst says that I'm an obsessive," she says.

"But the psychoanalytic clinic has its limits," she says. "Perhaps if there were something physical?" They debate further, back and forth, until finally Rechtman tries to close off the examination: "I wouldn't include you in the study, because it's not clear what you have." "But what else could it be?" she asks, now almost wanting to be convinced. "Maybe it's what your analyst says, obsessive neurosis," he suggests. "But I suspect that it is bipolar disorder." She muses for a moment, then poses another question: "What does Prozac have to do with all this?" Rechtman throws up his hands. At last, they reach a labored conclusion, agreeing to disagree. Her DNA will not be among the samples sent by courier to Paris. She has rescued her professional pride, and declined to take on a new illness identity.

Despite her protestations, the woman's presence at the hospital indicates a certain urge to transform her conception of herself, to try new explanations and interventions. Because the experience of psychiatric disorder dynamically interacts with the ways that experts recognize and name it, its diagnosis is a moving target. Psychiatry, whose objects of knowledge emerge in the encounter between patients' subjective reports and clinicians' interpretive schemes, has had a difficult time shifting the disorders under its purview into stable things in the world. The search for genes related to mental illness is, among other things, an attempt to turn mental disorders into more durable entities. However, as we will see, the setting of the gene hunt in Argentina posed distinctive challenges, which highlight the uncertain and heterogeneous character of psychiatric knowledge.

It turned out that despite the estimates of transnational epidemiology, there were very few diagnosed cases of bipolar disorder in Argentina. It was not simply a question of finding the "missing patients." Rather, bipolar disorder was not recognized as a valid entity by most Argentine mental health experts. "A concept vanishes when it is thrust into a new milieu, losing some of its components, or acquiring others that transform it," as Deleuze and Guattari write.[2] What did it mean that bipolar disorder "vanished" when thrust into this milieu of expertise? The question of how to recognize disorder points to the two broad problems that structure this book.

First, to what extent is scientific knowledge about mental disorder universally valid? One quality attributed to the natural sciences is the independence of their established facts from local contexts: a given chemical element or a chromosome is the same "thing" whether studied in San Francisco or São Paulo. Work in the social studies of science has shown that such universality is a tenuous achievement: the solidification of a fact requires the ongoing stabilization of the network of actors and techniques through which the fact is produced.[3] Psychiatry is a field that has not achieved such stabilization. Perhaps, as Ian Hacking argues, this instability is inherent to the human sciences because the classifications scientists use to study humans interact with and transform the very objects they are studying.[4] Recent developments in the life sciences such as genomics promise the achievement of universal validity. Whether they can do so remains uncertain. As we will see, given the heterogeneity of its epistemic forms, the Argentine *mundo-psi* (psy-world) is an apt site for studying the challenges faced by a "global" technique such as genomics in assimilating mental disorder.

Secondly, the interaction raised the question of the salient aspect of the human that is at stake in expertise about mental disorder. This encounter between biotechnology research and psychoanalytic self-identity in a marginal hospital in Buenos Aires was exemplary of a broader contemporary conflict over where to locate mental illness: is it in the psyche or in the organism? Can it be recognized and treated through purely technical means, or must one account for the particular life trajectory of the subject? To ask about the site of disorder is to ask about ways of knowing – and working on – the human. The early life history in which a subject is formed; the social surroundings in which a person sustains relationships; the neurochemical fluctuations that alter an organism's behavior: all of these name possible sources of disorder and possible targets of intervention. Such controversies over models of the human are significant beyond the narrow confines of debates among experts. The psy-sciences are key sites in which selves are constituted as beings of a certain kind, where individuals come to understand the sources of their actions and adopt techniques for transforming themselves.[5] The analysis of current transformations in expert knowledge about human behavior, then, is also a way of studying what kind of humans we are becoming. Such a study is not a matter of seeking to discover the truths about ourselves – whether through cathartic self-exploration or genomic technology – but rather involves an analysis of the historically situated process in which experts come to recognize humans as beings of a certain kind.

I situate this analysis at a point of encounter between a globalizing apparatus for understanding and intervening in mental illness according to the norms of biomedicine, and a distinctive epistemic milieu, the Argentine *mundo-psi*. At this conjuncture, the implications of diverse forms of knowledge about the human become palpable in the everyday practice of expertise. Globalizing forms of cosmopolitan science are confronted by a unique combination of political and ethical elements. Predominant models of the human among Argentine mental health experts are bound up with both a political project of social modernity and an ethical task of self-formation. This milieu forms a unique experimental setting in which to track the contested extension of potentially universalizing forms of knowledge and technique.

The backdrop to this study is the rise of a new biologically oriented set of understandings and interventions in North American psychiatry over the past two decades, heralded by President George H. W. Bush's declaration of the 1990s as "The Decade of the Brain." The advent of the new biomedical psychiatry has typically been either celebrated as the result of scientific discovery that will lead to medical breakthroughs, or criticized as a sinister form of social control linked to a loss of personal autonomy and responsibility.[6] By analyzing the specific conflicts that emerge around the practice of expertise in the Argentine *mundo-psi*, I show that predominant ways of understanding this transformation – either as scientific triumph or as dangerous medicalization – are insufficient. Indeed, such understandings are themselves parts of an assemblage that includes both technical innovation and the responses it provokes.[7]

What is most concretely at stake in recent transformations of knowledge about abnormal behavior, I argue, is the emergence and consolidation of a linked set of techniques and practices for reconfiguring the human and its ills. The recent "molecular" turn in psychiatry is best understood by examining how technical innovations, regulatory guidelines, professional norms, and bureaucratic demands crystallize in a novel apparatus for understanding and intervening in disorder. In this book I describe the operations of this apparatus, and follow the responses that it incites in a distinctive epistemic milieu.

## Pharmaceutical reason

The absence of bipolar disorder in the mental health world of Argentina pointed to a broader phenomenon: the ongoing prevalence of psychoanalytic understandings of mental illness among experts. This was not a matter of an incomplete "diffusion" of knowledge from center to periphery, but rather of an unfriendly ecology of expertise – one in which the politics of knowledge militated against the adoption of a model of mental illness that was associated with biological reductionism, with the dismantling of public health, and with North American hegemony.

The new biomedical psychiatry is the most recent in a long series of efforts to fully integrate psychiatry into medicine. As historian Gladys Swain writes, in response to the question of whether psychiatry can be considered a legitimate medical discipline, "the entire history of psychiatry since Pinel could be reinterpreted in the light of this question and of the oscillations in the response."[8] Born in asylums, places of exclusion as much as of cure, psychiatry has long struggled to separate itself from its association with the custodial administration of deviance.[9] Is the field a site for the treatment of illness or for the pathologization of the abnormal?

The philosopher of science Georges Canguilhem evinced a strong suspicion of forms of knowledge that claimed to emulate the natural sciences in discovering the norms of human conduct. He thought that questions concerned with how humans should act were the proper concern of philosophy rather than the natural sciences. Thus, he argued, behaviorist psychology forgets to situate its specific conception of human behavior in relation to the historical circumstances and social milieu in which it is led to propose its methods and techniques: it strives only to be an instrument, without being able to ask of whom or what it is an instrument. Noting these tendencies toward social control, Canguilhem warned prospective experts in human conduct: upon exiting the Sorbonne, one can either go uphill toward the immortals of the Pantheon, or downhill in the direction of the prefecture of police.[10]

Ongoing debate over the definition of psychiatry's task points to the ambiguous epistemic status of its subject matter, the "psyche" or "soul," in secular modernity. Two centuries after its invention, psychiatry's illnesses have neither known causes nor definitive treatments. The field's difficulty in stabilizing its forms of knowledge and intervention has contributed to its problematic position within contemporary biomedicine. In a 1997 editorial in the *American Journal of Psychiatry* entitled "What is Psychiatry?" the influential schizophrenia specialist Nancy Andreasen expressed frustration at her medical colleagues' sense of the role of psychiatry.[11] She told the story of a typical encounter: "a neurologist with whom I was having dinner defined psychiatry as the discipline that deals with syndromes of unknown cause, while neurology is the discipline that discovers the causes of syndromes, turns them into 'real diseases,' and then assumes responsibility for studying and treating them." And even worse: the other psychiatrist who was dining with them agreed with the neurologist.

In the editorial, Andreasen tried to respond, defending psychiatry in a manner that, while assured, nonetheless pointed to two key problems for the field in legitimating its interventions: the amorphous quality of its object and the ambiguity of its task. "Psychiatry is the medical specialty that studies and treats a variety of disorders that affect the mind – mental illnesses. Because our minds create our humanity and our sense of self, our specialty cares for illnesses that affect the core of our existence ... Psychiatry is defined by its province, the mind."[12] Andreasen was quick to clarify that this province was a material one: "What we call mind is the expression of the activity of the brain." She sought, finally, to define the discipline by its task – by what its practitioners *do*: they "modulate the psyche," either through psychotherapies that also affect the brain, or by medications that also affect the mind. The question remains, however: according to what norms should this psychic modulation take place? What exactly counts as a disorder of the mind, and what as cure? How, in other words, to scientifically treat pathologies that strike "the core of our existence"?

The intangibility of its objects and the ambiguity of its task have doomed psychiatry to a marginal status within medicine, characterized by the pathos Andreasen expresses around this never-ending question, "What is psychiatry?" One response to this pathos is to suggest that conditions have not yet been ripe for the field's "take-off" into normal science, and to cite current developments as signs of impending advance. The recent movement in North American psychiatry towards more biological models of mental disorder is, among other things, an attempt to more securely locate the field within medicine as a viable technical practice – that is, one with well-defined aims and clearly measurable treatments.

The new biomedical psychiatry seeks to find organic correlates for behavioral disorders and hone targeted pharmaceutical interventions whose efficacy can be tested through clinical research. Its goal is to restore normal psychic functioning by linking intervention – typically, but not exclusively through drug therapy – directly to specific brain-based disorders. The norm that guides intervention is one of "specificity" of effect: thus, for example, "depression" should be treatable by an "anti-depressant." However, since both the putative effects of a given medication and the characteristics of its target illness population are subject to interpretation, the achievement of specificity involves a process of mutual adjustment between illness and intervention. Illness comes gradually to be defined in terms of that to which it "responds." The goal of linking drug directly to diagnosis draws together a variety of projects among professionals, researchers, and administrators to craft new techniques of representation and intervention. These projects range from diagnostic standardization and the generation of clinical protocols to drug development and molecular genetics. This constellation of heterogeneous elements is joined together by a strategic logic I call "pharmaceutical reason." The term "pharmaceutical reason" refers to the underlying rationale of drug intervention in the new biomedical psychiatry: that targeted drug treatment will restore the subject to a normal condition of cognition, affect, or volition.

## The medicated person

While pharmaceutical treatment is central to the new biomedical psychiatry, it is important to emphasize that the development of psychopharmaceuticals did not lead directly to the institutionalization of pharmaceutical reason. The latter was as much a result of efforts to normalize professional practice as it was the product of technical innovation. The "specific effects" that are attributed to psychotropic medication in contemporary biomedical psychiatry are not built into the medication itself; rather, they are the product of a complex interaction between chemical substance, psychiatric expertise, and health administration.[13] This becomes apparent in looking at the recent history of the uses and understanding of chemical intervention into the psyche.

In 1949, John Cade stumbled upon lithium salts as a means to treat manic depression, a finding that remained relatively obscure for two decades. More prominently, in 1952 a French team described the antipsychotic properties of chlorpromazine. And in 1957 the first tricyclic antidepressant was developed, which would eventually contribute to a radical increase in the diagnosis of depression.[14] In the transnational context of overcrowded mental hospitals and the widespread critique of psychiatric institutions, these drugs – especially the anti-psychotics – were the answer to a number of needs and their use spread rapidly. It became possible to transfer patients from asylums to community-based care and to expand the use of psychotherapy to psychotic patients.[15] In this moment of institutional reform, experts saw both psychopharmacology and psychoanalysis as medical techniques that could be used to move mental illness out of the asylum.[16]

The development of the first generation of psychotropic medication thus promised a certain relief from psychiatry's pathos. But the new drugs did not immediately shift psychiatric knowledge toward the biomedical model of targeted chemical intervention into organic disorder. Rather, medication was initially folded into the task of providing social and psychodynamic therapies. For social psychiatry, the new drugs were tools that were of use in developing forms of group therapy as part of the larger goal of reintegrating institutionalized patients into communities.[17] Meanwhile, psychoanalytic work on psychosis flourished, as delusional symptoms could now be managed by medications that left patients' consciousness intact so that analysis could be practiced with them.[18]

Soon after their introduction, the new drugs began to generate expert reflection on the relation between chemical intervention and human subjectivity. The predominance of psychoanalysis in cosmopolitan psychiatry at the time sparked an initial attempt to integrate these substances into dynamic models of the psyche. The key question was: could such medications affect psychic structure in a way that would render even the most intractable of patients amenable to psychoanalysis? In a 1957 conference in Zurich, innovators in the emerging field of psychopharmacology met to compare notes on their results with the new drugs. The organizer of the conference, Nathan Kline, was a psychodynamic psychiatrist and clinical drug researcher. "Are pharmacologic theories in contradiction to everything we have learned about psychodynamics?" asked Kline in his introduction to the conference volume.[19] "All the evidence is in the opposite direction," he emphatically responded. "What is needed," he continued, "is integrating concepts that might provide possible pathways of linkage between the two sets of facts."

The diverse contributions to the conference volume illustrate Kline and his colleagues' broad-minded attempt to integrate the effects of the new drugs into psychodynamic models. For instance, in "A Psychoanalytic Study of Phenothiazine Action," William Winkelman wrote: "It is time for us to treat [the patient's] personality and character structure with knowledge of the effects of drugs on the structures to be treated."[20] Drugs, wrote Winkelman, did not have direct effects on the ego, but affected the energy available to the psychic structure. He told an anecdote about a patient who, feeling better after the administration of medication, wanted to discontinue psychotherapy. "It was explained to him that the relief was in symptoms only, and would not and could not eliminate the cause."[21] Drugs operated on the surface, not on the depths of the condition – but work on the depths, which depended on the transference relation, might be facilitated by the medication. Under the influence of these new drugs, Winkelman argued, the relationship between the ego, the superego and the id had to be reevaluated. One immediate result, he reported, was that the administration of tablets, whether drugs or placebo, fostered stronger transference.

For both Winkelman and Kline, the new psychoactive medications assisted in the task of working on psychic structure through the intensive relationship between analyst and analysand. In his own contribution, Kline wrote of the varying psychodynamic effects of these drugs: while reserpine allowed for the breakthrough of fairly deep material, chlorpromazine strengthened repressive mechanisms. However, both were useful as disciplinary tools in the effort to perform psychoanalysis with psychotic patients: "chlorpromazine and reserpine make it possible to quiet the schizophrenic sufficiently so that he can enter into psychoanalysis and tolerate the temporary threats of id interpretations."[22] As for the relation of surface to depth, "the drugs do not qualitatively alter the dynamic structure nor do they interfere with the analytic process." But this did not mean that the operations of the two techniques were completely separate: for Kline, the effect of the drugs was to reduce the quantity of instinctive drive, or psychic energy, and so lessen the necessity of defense against unacceptable impulses. Thus drug dosage could be manipulated in order to further the analytic process: "When the analysis loses its momentum the dosage can be reduced until sufficient psychic pressure once again builds up. In this way the rate of analytic progress can be regulated by the analyst."

This moment of conceptual transaction between psychopharmacology and psychoanalysis proved short lived, as the two disciplines diverged in the ensuing years. But Kline's volume points to the under-determined character of these medications' effects, from the vantage of expertise. As these early speculations indicate, the ideal of the contemporary biomedical paradigm, in which chemical interventions directly treat brain-based disorders, was only one way the use and understanding of these drugs could unfold. There was no direct line from the discovery of psychopharmaceuticals to the rise of a "neuroscientific" psychiatry two decades later. Rather, the drugs provoked questions that were answered in terms of existing forms of expertise.

Investigation of how these drugs operate in diverse clinical situations points to the ambiguous effects of these interventions, as well as the resilience and adaptability of entrenched epistemic forms. As will become clear in the Argentine setting, the effects that a given drug produces depend, at least in part, upon the milieu of expertise into which it enters. In this sense these drugs are instruments whose function is shaped by the form of rationality in which they are deployed; they are the means to various possible ends. Tracing differences in their use and meaning provides a window into broader differences in regimes of health and forms of governance. As we will see, the achievement of "specificity" requires the adoption of a set of concepts and techniques that reconfigure both the object of expert knowledge and the self-conception of the expert.

## DSM-III and the rise of specificity

Kline's dynamic understanding of how psychopharmaceuticals worked on the psyche is strikingly different from the premise of biomedical psychiatry, in which medication targets a specific neurochemical deficiency in order to correct a brain-based illness. How, then, did cosmopolitan psychiatry adopt the logic of specificity? The story involves two interlinked processes: on the one hand, governmental regulation required that pharmaceuticals be proven to have targeted effects in order to circulate in the biomedical system; on the other hand, in order to demonstrate such effects, researchers had to be able to classify disorder in a standardized way. Thus, both intervention and illness had to be reconfigured in order to achieve specificity.

In 1962, the US Congress amended FDA legislation to require that all new medications be tested for safety and efficacy according to randomized, placebo-controlled trials.[23] This was a key event in shaping psychopharmaceuticals into agents with specific effects. For the drugs to be proven effective according to biomedical criteria, they had to target clearly definable illnesses. As Thomas Hughes notes, for a radical invention to circulate widely within a technical system, it must "embody" the economic, political, and social characteristics that will enable its survival in use.[24] To operate within the regulated system of biomedicine, the new drugs had to embody the system's model of the relation between illness and intervention.

Charles Rosenberg calls this the model of "disease specificity."[25] According to this model, illnesses are understood to be stable entities that exist outside of their embodiment in particular individuals, which can be explained in terms of specific causal mechanisms located within the sufferer's body. Disease specificity is a tool of administrative management. This model of illness makes it possible to gather populations for large-scale research, to mandate clinical practice through the institution of treatment protocols, and more generally, to rationalize health practice.[26] At the intersection of individual experience and bureaucratic administration, disease specificity "helps to make experience machine readable," writes Rosenberg.[27]

Under the new FDA legislation, to be marketed to and prescribed by physicians, chemical interventions had to be measurable in terms of efficacy across populations of comparable patients. Clinical psychopharmacology researchers thus needed groups of homogeneous patients on whom to test the new substances. However, diagnostic practice was notoriously unreliable between clinical observers: what one psychiatrist read in the symptoms of a patient might be understood quite differently by another. This hampered efforts to measure the efficacy of interventions: without consistent diagnostic practice, there was no way to ensure that clinical studies were being applied to the same type of patient. In response to the need for homogeneous patient populations for research, clinical psychiatry researchers designed rating scales and questionnaires that would codify illnesses along the model of specificity – as discrete entities that corresponded with targeted therapeutic interventions. As the creators of the Research Diagnostic Criteria (RDC) wrote, "a major purpose of the RDC is to enable investigators to select relatively homogeneous groups of subjects who meet specified diagnostic criteria."[28] Thus, once the regulation of pharmaceuticals according to the guidelines of randomized clinical trials was put in place, the development of diagnostic standards became necessary.[29]

This process of standardization was initially important for research purposes rather than in the clinic. Clinicians in the United States – most of whom were working according to individualizing psychodynamic models – could ignore such diagnostic criteria and rating scales. However, in 1972 a widely publicized comparative study of diagnostic practices indicated that US psychiatrists were significantly out of sync with international norms.[30] And shortly thereafter, third-party payers began to demand that doctors defend their treatment strategies with consistent protocols whose effectiveness had been demonstrated according to professionally sanctioned criteria. Such pressures, as well as a desire to improve psychiatry's status within medicine, led the American Psychiatric Association to set limits to the interpretive autonomy of its members.[31] Diagnostic procedures were the initial focus of this effort.

The 1980 agreement by the APA on a new edition of the *Diagnostic and Statistical Manual of Mental Disorders* (DSM) put in place a set of standards regulating diagnosis according to the model of disease specificity. The change had been set in motion at least six years earlier, when disaffected psychoanalyst Robert Spitzer was named to head the association's DSM-III steering committee and given free rein to determine its membership. Spitzer – who, significantly, was also one of the authors of the Research Diagnostic Criteria – sought like-minded theorists who would base diagnosis on purely descriptive or "phenomenological" traits rather than using theoretical explanations, such as psychodynamic etiology, as a basis for classification.

With the enactment of DSM-III, the APA indicated that the psychoanalytic clinic was moribund in the American psychiatric profession.[32] For the dynamic psychiatry of the 1950s and 1960s, knowledge had been accrued and diagnoses proffered through example and analogy: the expert's authority relied on his or her exegetical prowess. Now the psychiatrist, using DSM-III, became a measurer rather than an interpreter. Unlike the individual case, the diagnostic population had no particular history, no tale of relations with parents or rejections at school – rather, its members shared a set of answers to given questions, and these answers placed them together in an illness category.

As a standards regime, DSM-III sought to produce functionally comparable results across disparate domains.[33] Its primary goal was reliability: if the same person went to two different clinics, he or she should receive the same diagnosis at each site. Based on directly observable traits, and ostensibly atheoretical, the new diagnostic standards structured a broader system of communication. While the epistemology underlying the new manual was positivistic – disorders were out there in the world to be found – its categories were honed according to pragmatic principles: the pathological could best be defined by the dysfunctional. Rating scales based on questionnaires were refined to measure norms of functionality, making it possible for different observers to use the same criteria in coming to a diagnostic evaluation.

Advocates of a renewed biomedical psychiatry hoped that the clear protocols of DSM-III would liberate psychiatry from the idiosyncrasies of subjective judgment. This rapprochement between psychiatry and biomedicine was reflected in the increasing centrality of "evidence-based" research in the discipline's publications, conferences, and academic teaching in the years following the adoption of the new standards. Although the manual professed to suspend the question of etiology, its development was premised on the hope that organic correlates would eventually be found to correspond with well-defined illness categories.

DSM-III was a standardizing but also a dynamic system: its categories were evolving rather than fixed, and its authors set up a committee-based structure within the profession for testing and revising its definitions. The authors did not claim that the standards that emerged from this process were the final description of their object; rather, they were the best compromise among various interests. The point was to delimit a set of rules for the negotiation of future standards. In this Spitzer and his fellow reformers were successful, as DSM in its newly revised versions has continued to evolve and to attain strength.

The enactment of this system for generating and refining standards can be understood as a process of professional normalization. As François Ewald defines it, "normalization produces not objects but procedures that will lead to some general consensus regarding the choice of norms and standards."[34] Normative procedures – in this case, the development of novel ways of defining and regulating illness – do not only constrain; they also generate new objects of knowledge and forms of identity. As Pierre Macherey notes, the norm "'produces' the elements on which it acts as it elaborates the procedures and means of this action."[35] In this case, a process of mutual adjustment between drug and diagnosis, intervention and illness, has generated new definitions of pathology, and thus of normality as well.

DSM-III extended to new sites because of its ability to make behavioral pathology transferable across professional domains. Its standards have multiple possible uses: in gathering epidemiological data, in the development of treatment algorithms, and in claiming insurance benefits. They also form part of protocols for scientific research – for example, for homogenizing patient populations in clinical trials. DSM standards are "boundary objects," in Bowker and Star's terms: "Objects that both inhabit several communities of practice and satisfy the informational requirements of each of them. In working practice, they are objects that are able both to travel across borders and maintain some sort of constant identity."[36] This constant identity – of "disease specificity" – is what enables DSM to function as a connective tissue for biomedical psychiatry, linking populations as they are forged in multiple domains: the clinic, insurance, scientific research. As we will see, however, it is also what provokes resistance to DSM among experts whose thought and practice are incommensurable with the biomedical model. Indeed, a major theme of this book concerns the obstacles faced in the extension of these standards to an unwelcoming professional setting. As became clear in this context, the movement of standards not only carries technical implications, but also poses new ethical and political dilemmas.

To explain why different expert practices predominate across diverse settings, it is necessary to examine the political and administrative contexts that structure the adoption of new knowledge and techniques. In North America, the understanding and treatment of mental illness has been transformed in recent decades by a rationality of health administration – managed care – geared toward managing risk at the individual level through the most efficient possible means. Professional normalization has, to varying degrees of success, enforced the use of diagnostic standards and treatment protocols among psy-professionals. While the biomedical ideal of linking discrete illness entities to measurable intervention may not match actual practice, this gap is the target of ongoing research efforts, such as genomics.

In Argentina, a health system oriented toward public provision rather than the measurement of efficiency has enabled a relatively autonomous professional culture to thrive within medical institutions. Psychoanalysis remains strong in public hospitals and clinics, not only as a health intervention but also as an aspect of a broader political project of social inclusion. Thus resident training and hospital administration are not oriented toward the specificity model and standardized diagnosis. Indeed, this professional culture is explicitly opposed to such normalization. Because the administrative structures that serve to regulate professional practice in the North are not in place in Argentina, experts are able to resist the incursion of pharmaceutical reason.

## Technology and the human

Max Weber noted that the task of medicine, "a practical technology," is to maintain life, but that it does not ask what a good life is. "Natural science gives us an answer to the question of what we must do if we wish to master life technically," he wrote, "but it leaves quite aside ... whether we should and do wish to master life technically and whether it ultimately makes sense to do so."[37] The sciences of the psyche seem to reside precisely on this border between the ethical question of how one should live and the technical question of how to sustain life. As we will see, experts in the Argentine *mundo-psi* insisted on keeping these tasks separate. They defended against the encroachment of biomedical standards, which they saw as part of a dehumanizing process. What brought these experts to worry that as it becomes more medical, psychiatry becomes less human?

There were two related kinds of opposition to the extension of pharmaceutical reason. One involved the perceived need to defend the individual uniqueness of patients. For many psychoanalysts, the statistical rationality of biomedicine struck them as a kind of abstraction that stripped patients of their uniqueness, and thus of their humanity. They argued that the subject matter of their expertise is inherently different from that of biomedicine: that the inability to enforce scientific norms is built into the field, since it is concerned with pathologies of the individual psyche and therefore must operate on the basis of the particular case. As a physician-analyst in Hospital Romero told me, "People are not animals. A mouse can have heart disease, but it cannot be hysteric." A second objection concerned the perceived connection between DSM and the market, in the form of managed care and the pharmaceutical industry. For socially oriented psy-professionals, the rise of biomedical psychiatry seemed to coincide with changes in the role of the state in providing for its citizens' well-being. They associated the new biological psychiatry with the decline of the welfare state, with encroaching neoliberalism and savage capitalism.

The development and extension of potentially universalizing techniques that reorder life – such as DSM or genomics – provokes problematic situations in local settings. The responses that emerge are key sites for analyzing the fraught extension of modern forms of reason – their limits and the transformations they undergo in a new milieu. In such settings the observer does not find a homogeneous project of rationalization or the outright rejection of new forms. Rather, one encounters the construction of novel combinations of ethics, politics, and technique.[38] In Argentina such elements include a distinctive form of psychoanalytic thought, a vision of social modernity that guarantees the public provision of health, and an anti-imperialist politics grounded in the violence and tragedy of recent Argentine history.

The practice of psychoanalysis in Buenos Aires is not limited to offices and couches, but is also widespread in the city's public hospital psychiatric wards – and this is a product of recent political history. Psychoanalysis first entered public hospitals in the 1960s as part of *salud mental* – a "social" vision that sought to extend access to contemporary mental health interventions to marginal urban populations. Under the military dictatorship period beginning in 1976, this socially oriented psychoanalysis was brutally repressed. Excluded from institutions, psychoanalysis sustained itself through the institutional form of the "study group." Then, with the return to democracy in 1983, psychoanalysis again flourished in the city's hospitals and the number of analysts in the city skyrocketed. The work of Jacques Lacan was especially influential. By the late 1990s, however, there was a sense that psychoanalysis was in decline due to an over-supply of experts and a fall of demand. As one article describing the situation put it, there was a "Crisis in Villa Freud" – the upper-middle-class neighborhood of Buenos Aires known for its large population of psychoanalysts.[39]

## Peripheral modernity

At an *asado* with some of my psychiatrist friends, one of them remarked: "He could have studied native ritual on an island in the South Pacific, but he chose to come to Buenos Aires to study the psychiatrists here instead!" It was not an atypical joke for an ethnographer among modern "natives" to hear. The reaction, of amusement but not surprise, was telling: there was something exotic about the *mundo-psi* of Buenos Aires, even to its members. It was not "cultural" difference, however, that was the axis of reflection or mode of self-differentiation – on the contrary.

As a cosmopolitan setting at the outskirts of the modern West, urban Argentina is characterized by a unique tension with respect to Europe and North America. Literary critic Beatriz Sarlo describes the distinctive position of cultural producers in the country as a "peripheral modernity."[40] This term refers to an ongoing tension between modernization and traditionalism, the vanguard and the *criollo*: according to Sarlo, residual defensive elements have historically been in conflict with programs of cultural renovation. She understands this system of response and adaptation in terms of the "versatility and permeability" of Argentine culture.

What is local is precisely its non-locality. As Borges wrote, "the Argentine cult of local color is a recent European cult which the nationalists ought to reject as foreign."[41] In this attack on the invented national tradition of the *gauchesque* movement, he argued: "What is our Argentine tradition? I believe we can answer this question easily and that there is no problem here. I believe our tradition is all of Western culture, and I also believe we have a right to this tradition, greater than that which the inhabitants of one or another Western nation might have."[42] Borges' point was that there may be a positive aspect to this unlocatedness: "I believe the fact that certain illustrious Argentines write like Spaniards is less the testimony of an inherited capacity than it is a proof of Argentine versatility."[43] As Sarlo glosses it, "our marginal situation can be the source of our true originality. It is not based on local color ... but on the open acceptance of influences."[44]

Borges' text signals a pan-European sensibility that I encountered in many of my subjects, cosmopolitan intellectuals who sometimes rued their sense of distance from the metropole. The uneasy relationship to originality and authenticity that this position implies is a continuing subject of reflection for Argentine intellectuals. As one of my informants told me, "in Argentine psychiatry we haven't had many original personalities – but we've had good copies." To describe this site as peripheral while at the same time modern is to use the self-understanding of actors I encountered there, who both identified with and felt peripheral to a more powerful center. As we will see, one point of contention among members of the *mundo-psi* was whether this "center" was located in Europe or North America; was it a source of cultured literati or technocratic expertise? What was at stake in debates over the proper treatment of mental illness was not indigenous knowledge versus universal science, but rather what constituted a modern way of understanding and intervening in psychic suffering.

My approach to this setting builds on a body of research in the social sciences on the relationship between knowledge and social order in sites of scientific controversy. This work has shown that epistemic positions are linked to broader forms of life grounded in communities of knowledge-producers.[45] Conflicting forms of knowledge may prove incommensurable not only in terms of their proponents' respective epistemic commitments but also in terms of their visions of social order and notions of the good. Ethnographic inquiry provides further insight into these dynamics by considering expertise as a situated practice – that is, an activity that is embedded in a social milieu and governed by shared principles of regulation.[46] I extend this analytic rubric beyond the question of the norms of social actors and the demands of institutions by looking at the contested extension of techniques that embed forms of life. Such techniques are abstractable, but link up to local situations in novel ways to reframe ethical practice in ways that may be perceived as either promising or dangerous. In Buenos Aires, as the contingently produced, yet potentially universalizing techniques of biomedical psychiatry encroached on new terrain, a philosophical question was posed to everyday practice: If there was no scientific basis for a given understanding of the human, on what grounds might experts defend a vision of the specificity of their object and the unique demands of their task?

# 1
# Diagnostic liquidity

"Information is, at the end of the day, the coin of the genomics realm."[1]

In June 1997, the French genomics firm Genset announced a collaboration with the psychopathology department of a public hospital in Buenos Aires to collect and map the DNA of patients suffering from bipolar disorder. The genes or markers linked to susceptibility to bipolar disorder, if found, were to be patented by Genset as part of its strategy to enter into partnerships with major pharmaceutical companies for the development of new diagnostic and therapeutic technologies. This gene hunt was significant in its institutional form, as well as in its potential implications for the reconfiguration of knowledge about mental illness. As an alliance between genomics and psychiatry across continents, and between public and private institutions, it represented a new type of assemblage oriented toward the understanding and regulation of human behavior. The central problem it raised – both practical and epistemological – concerned the potential universality of genomic knowledge about mental disorder.

The success of the company's gene-hunting effort hinged on the global validity of a standards regime designed to commensurate divergent illness experience into a common classificatory scheme. Such commensuration, it was hoped, would enable psychiatric illness to be coded as genomic information, and would thus make the illness experience of Argentine patients convertible with that of patients in other parts of the world. How such experience was rendered liquid – that is, able to circulate and to potentially attain value as information – is the focus of this chapter. I show that in the case of mental illness, the effort to generate a space in which information flows seamlessly between biomedicine and the market is challenged by the difficulty of knowing just what a psychiatric disorder is. As the setting in

Argentina demonstrates, the extraction of valuable knowledge from patients' DNA relies on the development of diagnostic standards whose validity and extendibility remain in question.

The process of gathering large amounts of data about the prevalence of illness in populations has historically been linked to public health initiatives: in order to gauge and improve the health of the population, national and transnational governmental agencies have, in collaboration with medical and scientific professionals, sought to accumulate epidemiological knowledge.[2] Recent genomics research in places like China, Iceland, Russia, and Argentina is distinctive in that it is often conducted by private database firms in collaboration with local clinics. The case I describe here – in which the actual collection of DNA was carried out by local clinicians working in public hospitals, under contract to a genomics database firm – is not atypical of such arrangements. This pattern of collaboration is conditioned upon recent economic and techno-scientific developments: on the one hand, the emergence of health as a significant global marketplace, and on the other hand, the rapid development of DNA-sequencing technology and bioinformatics in the wake of the Human Genome Project. For this reason, highly capitalized biotech firms have come to be interested in the possibility of attaining valuable genetic information through research on specific local populations. In this emergent space of exchange between industry and the life sciences, the role of government remains salient: the health marketplace as a target of techno-scientific innovation is structured by the legal forms that ensure that biological information can attain value – that is, intellectual property regimes.

It should be emphasized that this strand of genomics research targets health consumers in the advanced industrialized countries. The most valuable information in the health marketplace pertains to specific kinds of populations: North Americans and Europeans at risk of chronic illness, whose insurance will pay for the extended use of patented medications. Thus, the type of DNA collection and analysis in which Genset was engaged seeks to demarcate specific illness populations that are simultaneously potential market segments. As this case illustrates, in other parts of the world patients serve as potential sources of valuable information rather than target markets, and they are often easier to access due to relaxed regulatory controls.

The Genset bipolar study was one of a number of transnational projects in the late 1990s involving newly minted genomics database firms based in the United States or Western Europe and health clinics in other parts of the world that were contracted to provide supplies of DNA from sample populations.[3] Biotech industry strategists shared a sense that there were hidden riches buried in the genomes of these clinically diagnosed patient populations. Mining was one common metaphor for the search for these valuable resources.[4] Another was the frontier: as the Human Genome Project progressed, what legal theorist James Boyle called "an intellectual land grab" began as genomics database start-ups competed to find and patent genes or genetic markers linked to common, complex disorders.[5] While the eventual value of such genes was a matter of speculation, these genomics companies were confident that patented sequence information would prove a marketable resource in the burgeoning health marketplace. In Argentina, Genset sought to secure a supply of blood samples from an ethnically diverse patient population whose genetic background was similar to that of European and North American target markets, but without certain of the regulatory and legal complications that characterized such work in the North.

At stake in the process of gathering, analyzing, and developing proprietary knowledge from patients' DNA samples was the relation between truth and value in the global biomedical economy. At the scientific level, the translation from genetic material to significant information depended upon the validity of the diagnostic criteria used in gathering sample populations – criteria that in the case of psychiatric disorders, had emerged in local and contingent circumstances. The economic value of such information, meanwhile, hinged on an intellectual property regime that granted monopoly rights to genomic innovation and on a market that structured demand for such information. Transnational epidemiology, in turn, made it possible to locate that market and gauge its size.

A key question emerged in Genset's research that focused attention on the classificatory devices to be used in gathering the sample population: to what extent could these criteria be claimed to measure the same thing across different spaces? How to know, for instance, whether a case of bipolar disorder in the United States was the same "thing" as a case of bipolar disorder in Argentina? The apparently universal validity of biomedical knowledge must be materially and discursively forged through the standardization of practice across multiple domains.[6] In the case of the Genset study, what must be examined is the complex process of commensuration that was necessary for subjects with diverse histories to both recognize themselves as having bipolar disorder and to be so classified by doctors. At the same time, the difficulties faced in conducting the study in Argentina illustrate the epistemic and political challenges to such commensuration.

To analyze the process of forging consistent illness populations so that Argentine patients' DNA could enter into circulation, I borrow the term "liquidity" from the field of finance. Bruce Carruthers and Arthur Stinchcombe describe the production of liquidity in futures markets as the creation of generalized knowledge about value out of idiosyncratic personal knowledge.[7] Producing equivalence among disparate kinds of things involves both social regulation and political negotiation, they write. Standardization is a social and cognitive achievement: buyers, market makers, and sellers have to share the conviction that "equivalent" commodities are really the same. Turning an illiquid asset into a more liquid one is a process of reduction and standardization of complexity.

To be transferable – liquid – an asset must lose its specificity and locality. Classificatory technologies work to simplify, stratify, and standardize such assets. Thus, to use Carruthers and Stinchcombe's example, a distinctive house becomes a liquid asset only when there are agreed-upon conventions for evaluating it in comparison with other houses. Similarly, William Cronon has shown how wheat was made into a liquid commodity in nineteenth-century Chicago through the invention of a set of technical standards for classifying the characteristics of specific bushels of wheat in terms of general quality grades that made it unnecessary for buyers to inspect each bushel purchased.[8] Individualized evaluations of quality were thus shifted into collectively sanctioned criteria, enabling bushels of wheat to be abstracted and circulated as currency. In order to successfully implement such a system, these analysts have shown, the existence and legitimacy of a governing body that regulates the practice of measurement is crucial.

It is possible to consider the circulation of bipolar patients' DNA in terms of this process of abstraction through technical classification: the patients' illnesses assumed potential informational significance – and therefore, value – only insofar as their specific life trajectories could be brought into the same space of measurement. That is, their illnesses had to be made "liquid." From the vantage of genomics research, one should not need to know about the specific life trajectory of the person from whom DNA has been extracted in order to evaluate the significance of the information it bears. Diagnosis is the convention that produces such equivalence; in the case of bipolar disorder, what might seem like an implausible association then becomes natural: a young woman who has attempted suicide in Buenos Aires is brought into potential relationship with a middle-aged man in Chicago who goes bankrupt through risky business ventures. They are both members of a group of previously distinctive individuals now sharing a diagnosis. The emergent group is alternately an epidemiological population, a market segment, and a community of self-identity.

Thus, while "liquidity" is typically understood in terms of finance, here techniques of classification enable biomedical knowledge to be assimilated to the domain of market exchange. In biomedicine, forging such a space of liquidity requires consistent classificatory practice among doctors – a problem that remains fraught in psychiatry, especially in Argentina. In this chapter, I describe how doctors in Buenos Aires performed classificatory work with psychiatric patients in order to render their illnesses liquid – that is, abstract and therefore exchangeable. This process involved the temporary extension of both a technical and an ethical standards regime. The setting of the DNA collection in Argentina revealed not only the reliance of techno-scientific objects, such as bipolar genes, on such regimes, but also the limits to their extension.

## Circulatory networks

The bipolar study at Hospital Romero crystallized through a contingent set of associations and opportunities. In 1997 Daniel Mendelson, an unemployed Argentine molecular biologist, was making a living by supplying genetic material from human organ tissue to Genset, a French biotech company that was building a cDNA library – a compilation of expressed human genes for use in detecting significant genetic information. Mendelson's work was a bit grisly. He would call up contacts who worked in forensic pathology laboratories in Buenos Aires hospitals, and ask them to send over healthy tissue from newly dead cadavers. Genset wanted various organs for its collection: kidneys, hearts, even brains. Once the tissue was sent over to him, Mendelson would process it in a lab he had rented at the Campomar Institute, a well-known biological research center near the Parque Centenario in Buenos Aires. He had been trained there before going off to do post-doctoral work at the Pasteur Institute in Paris with his wife, Marta Blumenfeld, also a molecular biologist. Now she was vice president of genomics at Genset, and he was struggling to establish a beachhead back home in Buenos Aires.

Mendelson had a new idea: they could expand their business of providing genetic material by obtaining DNA samples from patients with mental disorders. Genset was looking for populations of patients who had been diagnosed with schizophrenia and bipolar disorder for its gene discovery program in complex diseases. An old friend of Mendelson and Blumenfeld's from school now worked as a psychiatrist at Hospital Romero, and offered to recruit patients there. After some back and forth negotiation, the details were worked out: Genset would give a hundred thousand dollars to Hospital Romero for structural improvements, and in exchange, doctors there would provide blood samples from two hundred patients diagnosed with bipolar disorder, types I and II.

Genset was in a hurry to get hold of such material. As a genomics database company, its strategy depended upon finding and patenting genes linked to susceptibility to common, complex diseases. With its emerging patent portfolio and proprietary genomic search technologies in hand, Genset sought partnerships with large pharmaceutical firms to develop new diagnostic and therapeutic applications. It had recently formed strategic alliances with Abbott Pharmaceuticals, a leader in the diagnostics market as well as the maker of the leading medication for bipolar disorder, and with Janssen pharmaceuticals, producers of the antipsychotic Risperdal. Pharmaceutical industry strategists expected the next series of significant discoveries of drugs for mental disorder to emerge from the Human Genome Project; closer on the horizon was the prospect of diagnostic tests linked either to disease-susceptibility or medication-response. In order to have commercial rights to such products, Genset had to beat a number of competitors, in both the academic realm and the private sphere, to the relevant genomic loci. The alliance with Abbott was an early signal that major players in the pharmaceutical industry saw genomics as an important strategic arena. Given the possibility of royalties on a range of products, it seemed in the late 1990s – a moment of intense speculation in the life sciences, both conceptual and financial – that genomic information had potentially exponential value. As one biotech analyst wrote of the collaboration, "the Genset-Abbott deal is clearly geared toward creating a resource that the pair can sell again and again."[9]

The value of such resources relied first of all on the prospect that something scientifically significant would be found – which was by no means a foregone conclusion. Despite decades of academic research and a string of false alarms, no genomic loci had yet been confirmed to be linked to any of the major psychiatric disorders. According to Mendelson, it had only recently become possible to hunt seriously for such genes. First, developments in molecular biology and information technology now allowed genome-wide searches for disorders with complex genetic and environmental interactions. Genset's proprietary SNP (single nucleotide polymorphism) map provided dense markers to guide its researchers through the immense human genome, giving it an edge over academic and private-sphere competitors. And secondly, it was now possible to forge coherent populations of clinically diagnosed patients: standardized criteria for diagnosing bipolar disorder had been spelled out in 1980 with the publication of the third edition of the diagnostic manual of the American Psychiatric Association (DSM-III) and had evolved in subsequent editions.

According to DSM-IV (1994), which guided Genset's protocol, bipolar disorder was characterized by fluctuations in mood, from states of manic excitement to periods of abject depression. The presence of affective disorders within the patient's family was also a diagnostic clue. There were at least two types of bipolar disorder: type I was "classic" manic depression, characterized by severe shifts in mood between florid mania and depression; type II included cases in which severe depression was punctuated not by full-blown mania, but by mild euphoria, "hypomania."[10] The condition had to be diagnosed longitudinally, since in its synchronic state it could be difficult to differentiate the manic phase of bipolar disorder from the delusional symptoms of schizophrenia, or at the other extreme, from the melancholia of major depression.

The kind of mapping in which Genset was engaged did not presume a causal relation between a given DNA sequence and onset of disease; rather, it hypothesized that certain markers of variation could be statistically correlated to greater susceptibility to that disease. Mendelson explained the process of looking for single nucleotide polymorphisms – natural variations in the genome – associated with bipolar disorder: if Genset could find a corresponding variation in multiple patients, it was likely that a genetic susceptibility locus would be near, or statistically associated with, that variation. It was not a new or original scientific idea, he admitted, but it was one that was, practically speaking, incredibly daunting. Five years earlier it would have been technically unimaginable.

Once Mendelson and Blumenfeld made arrangements with Genset on the one hand, and with the hospital on the other, there was some delay in getting the DNA collection going. First, the Buenos Aires city government blocked the project on the grounds that it violated the law against trafficking in blood. After the concerned parties convinced the city's legal office that DNA was distinct from blood, and therefore saleable, another problem emerged: according to city regulations, a public hospital could not be paid by a private company for its services. This regulation was eventually circumvented, with the help of contacts in the municipal government, by changing the wording of the contract from payment to voluntary donation.

By the time such regulatory hurdles had been taken care of, six months had passed.

And then when the study finally began, doctors at the hospital faced an unexpected problem: they could not find enough bipolar patients. It turned out that bipolar disorder was rarely diagnosed in Argentina. The North American diagnostic system in which it was recognized had not permeated the Argentine mental health world, nor had "bipolar identity" spread to raise awareness of the condition among potential patients.[11] Without such techniques of classification in place, the extraction and exchange of DNA could not begin. Doctors in the men's ward at Romero remained in need of donors even after recruiting at a nascent self-help group for patients with bipolar disorder, and were forced to make announcements in the newspapers asking for volunteers. In July 1998 a number of articles appeared in the city's major dailies describing the symptoms of bipolar disorder and promoting Romero's study.[12] These articles sought to inform the public about what bipolar disorder was, given the absence of general knowledge of the condition. The publicity campaign turned out to be quite successful in drawing volunteers to the hospital, and by late September, psychiatrists in the men's ward were almost two-thirds of the way through their assignment to compile two hundred samples. I was able to observe some of the collection process.

## Collection

On a Tuesday morning in September, a diverse group lingers around wooden benches in the entryway of Hospital Romero's psychopathology department, all waiting to be attended: patients and family members, pharmaceutical company representatives, known as *valijas* or "suitcases" because of the large satchels full of samples and promotional literature they carry around, and various cats who have wandered in from the hospital grounds. Through a swinging door on the left, I enter the men's wing, passing a dozen old cubicles, where a few patients lie on sagging cots, on the way to the examination rooms. Some of the other patients are playing cards, or listening to the radio. The floors are of once-white, broken tile; the smell of ammonia is in the air.

A woman in her fifties, led by her daughter, is shown into a small room, bare except for a few chairs. They have traveled to Romero from a town about an hour away, having seen an article in *La Nacion* on the study of bipolar disorder being conducted there. After a preliminary phone interview, they were invited for an examination at the hospital. The mother and daughter do not seem particularly interested in the details of the gene study. They have come not so much to give blood as to ask for help: a diagnosis, a drug, a competent doctor. Gustavo Rechtman, a staff psychiatrist in his thirties, interviews them for about five minutes. He is formal and to the point, asking first whether the woman has had any depressions. Yes, she answers, looking to her daughter for reassurance. Very serious ones, adds the daughter – with suicidal thoughts. And are these sometimes followed by euphorias? She nods. Has she used any medications? She has taken anti-depressants in the past, and lithium – though, Rechtman notes, perhaps at too small a dosage. Her weight indicates that there might be a thyroid condition. Rechtman gives his diagnosis: bipolar disorder, type II – with hypomania. He mentions FUBIPA (*Fundación Bipolares de Argentina*), the support group for bipolar patients and their families that helped publicize the study, but discourages the woman from seeking further treatment at Romero: it is very busy here, he says, and besides, this is a men's ward.[13] Instead, he will write a note to the doctor at her health clinic telling him of the diagnosis.

Rechtman then explains the scientific research to them: a French laboratory is doing a study to see if the genes of bipolar patients are different from normal genes in order to eventually create a treatment for the condition. The study will have no direct benefit for her. Is she willing to participate? A glance at her daughter. Sure. A form is filled out: age, gender, marital status, occupation, ethnicity, financial status, familial antecedents, medication history. Then she is brought to a larger room, where test-tubes sit on the table, some already filled with blood. A male nurse, after considerable difficulty, finds a vein. A notebook is annotated, a code number put on the test-tube. While the blood is drawn, the woman is handed a consent form, which she glances at briefly before signing. The blood will then travel the same route as the organ tissue before it – DNA will be extracted at Campomar and sent by special courier on to the Genset research campus at Evry, outside of Paris.

The transferability of genetic material depended not only on Genset's technical capacities to derive information from the patient's blood but also on the extension of an ethical-legal regime that sanctioned the technique: norms and regulations surrounding the circulation of genetic material between public institutions and private companies and across national boundaries. The consent form legally detached the DNA from the patient. Drawn up by psychiatrists at Romero, it did not mention the possibility that the extracted genetic material might be patented. In a context where biomedical research was relatively rare and doctors retained significant authority, the consent form was not a well-recognized device, and therefore was something of a hollow ritual designed to meet the demands of the North Atlantic ethical sphere – it would be a part of the protocol that the firm would include along with any scientific achievements in a patent application or publication. What the patient received at the hospital was not a payment, but a diagnosis and a referral.

In general, the circumstances of the study did not especially concern observers I spoke with in Buenos Aires. Only a foreign company, some commented – and certainly not the Argentine state – could possibly do such advanced scientific work here, many told me. As for the role of the private sector, given Argentina's recent history of state violence and political corruption there was little sense that the state was more trustworthy than private companies. And compared to some famously scandalous experiments conducted in Argentina by foreign institutions, this one seemed fairly innocuous, involving only the taking of blood, and might lead to scientific advance.[14] Meanwhile, there was little worry over the political implications of finding genes linked to mental illness, no discussion of the return of eugenics – although, especially from members of the city's large corps of psychoanalysts, there was considerable skepticism as to whether anything significant would be found. Nor was the question of whether genes should be patentable much broached, except insofar as transnational bioethics discourse was beginning to be imported via global humanitarian networks.[15] Both anxieties and promises around the Human Genome Project, so prevalent in the North, had not yet arrived in Argentina.[16]

For some Argentine scientists, publicity around the study provided an opportunity to encourage more local attention to such issues. Mariano Levin, a molecular biologist who had worked in France with Genset's scientific director, Daniel Cohen, suggested that Argentina was an appealing place for the study precisely because of its lack of regulations on genetic research and patenting, not to mention that it was a good bargain for Genset. Cohen is a "marchand de tapis," he remarked, a rug merchant. For what was pocket change in the field of genomics, Genset would receive samples of diagnosed patients from a population whose ethnic origins were similar to those of target drug and diagnostic markets in Europe and North America. As Blumenfeld said, the city's "out-bred population," predominantly of Italian, Spanish, and Jewish descent, was one reason, along with its large supply of well-trained psy-professionals, that Genset chose to work in Buenos Aires.

Of several articles that appeared in the Argentine media concerning the gene study, only one, in the short-lived progressive weekly *Siglo XXI*, was critical of it. This piece was accompanied by pictures of multiple Barbie and Ken dolls, and a table, translated from the American magazine *Mother Jones*, showing multinational pharmaceutical companies' claims to patented genes. The article began with a joking reference to an Argentine penchant for melancholia:

> In Canada they study the gene for obesity. In Chile and in Tristan da Cunha, that of asthma. In Iceland, that of alcoholism. In Gabon, that of HIV. In the international partitioning of the body by the Human Genome Initiative ... the French private company Genset chose Argentina to investigate the genetic roots of manic depression, as if this illness were an innate characteristic of the national being.[17]

The Genset study was used, in the article, as an opening for a discussion of the potential abuses of transnational genomics research. "It's a huge business straddling the frontier between medicine and biopiracy," said a geneticist who wished to remain anonymous. Why did Genset bother to go to Argentina to look for the genes? Mariano Levin was quoted in the article: "In this country there are no laws on genetic research and patenting, which diminishes the risks and costs if something goes badly, and increases the benefits if the research is successful." Levin's argument was not that such research should not be conducted in the country, but rather that Argentina needed to adopt and implement new forms of regulation – and ideally, to develop its own biotechnology research sector – in order to avoid being exploited by multinational firms seeking inexpensive genetic resources.

Alejandro Noailles, the director of Romero's psychopathology ward, suspected that the peripheral status of Argentine clinicians made the country an especially good place for Genset to do the study. This is a private company, he emphasized in our first meeting, with a purely cost-benefit logic, and it is relatively inexpensive for them to do the study in Argentina. But even more, they won't have to share patent rights with those who do the work of collecting the samples: if the company were to do the study in Europe or the United States, he surmised, they might have to split the proceeds with the clinicians.

The key legal device making illness susceptibility genes potentially valuable was the agreement that well-characterized genes could be registered as intellectual property, which had been supported, though not without controversy, by European and United States patent offices since a landmark 1980 Supreme Court decision allowing living organisms to be patented.[18] Patents guarantee an exclusive license to commercialize discoveries for a limited period of time – normally twenty years. The question of what kind of information was sufficient to grant patent rights was a matter of some contention. In 1998, the Director of Biotechnology Examination at the US Patent and Trademark Office gave a provisional answer: "For DNA to be patentable, it must be novel and non-obvious in light of structurally related DNA or RNA information taught in nonpatent literature or suggested by prior patents."[19] After an initial stage of broad acceptance of patent claims on new genetic information, the tendency by the late 1990s was toward a more narrow vision of patentability – an insistence that the function and potential uses of the information be well demonstrated. Patent or no, the eventual value of such information was uncertain, as genomics-based products remained far on the horizon.[20]

Genset's research strategy of opportunistically seeking genetically heterogeneous patient populations was distinct from that of some other genomics companies, such as deCode, which sought to take advantage of the ethnic homogeneity, detailed genealogical records, and comprehensive clinical data available on the Icelandic population for its potential informational value.[21] Genset's research also provoked a far more muted response from the public than deCode's work in Iceland: while deCode's project led to a national referendum and a spirited transnational debate on its ethical implications, research like Genset's remained mostly within the background noise of the 1990s biotech boom. An exception was a 2000 article in the *Guardian*, which noted that gene patenting was far from an exclusively North American phenomenon:

> European firms have become some of the most enthusiastic stakers of claims on human DNA. Patent applications on no fewer than 36,083 genes and DNA sequences – 28.5% of the total claimed so far – have been filed by a single French firm, Genset. Andre Pernet, Genset's chief executive officer, said: "It's going to be a race. The whole genome will have been patented two years from now, if it hasn't been done already."[22]

Genset had fashioned itself as a company specializing in disorders of the central nervous system – specifically bipolar disorder and schizophrenia. As its founder Pascal Brandys said, "I believe that the brain is the next frontier, not just in genomics but in biotechnology as a whole."[23] Given the increasing size of the central nervous system (CNS) market, genes linked to mental illness that might provide new targets for drug innovation or lead to diagnostic technologies were potentially quite lucrative. Worldwide drug sales for CNS disorders were $30 billion in 1999, and CNS was the fastest growing product sector in the United States pharmaceutical market; by 2000 CNS had overtaken gastroenterology as the second largest market segment, after cardiovascular.[24] A venture capitalist noted the increasing interest in the CNS market, invoking the land rush image: "Every doctor knows that the brain is the final frontier of medicine, but VCs are just now starting to sniff opportunity. There'll be a lot of opportunities to play this sector because there are just so many problems that fall under the heading CNS."[25] Such opportunities ranged from Alzheimer's disease to attention deficit disorder, anxiety, and schizophrenia.

## Risk and genomics

In considering the possible implications of the discovery of genes linked to mental illness, it is useful to consider in more detail the aims of contemporary genomics research into complex conditions like bipolar disorder. The goal of companies such as Genset in seeking genes linked to mental disorder should be distinguished from earlier attempts to link mental illness to genetic inheritance. Unlike the kind of state-based eugenics programs that resulted in mass sterilization campaigns in the United States, the interest of this form of genomics research was not in establishing stable population norms and excluding the abnormal, but in delineating variations within populations in order to help meet regulatory guidelines in drug research and to provide technologies for managing patient risk.[26]

Such risk management was to be performed at the level of the individual and family rather than by centralized authorities. In the late 1990s, finding genes linked to susceptibility to common disorders promised to provide marketable risk technologies for subjects to manage their own futures. According to an industry magazine, "an understanding of genomics, along with genetic testing, is expected to help individuals be informed about their risks for developing diseases. They and their doctors can use the information to manage their health and optimize or customize treatment."[27] The goal of this kind of research was to map correlation rather than causation – risk, not determination: it was not that genotype determined phenotype, but rather that gene identification provided a means for delineating the combination of inherited and environmental factors that conferred risk.[28]

Francis Collins, head of the National Human Genome Research Initiative, discussed the implications of genomics research into mental illness in terms of individualized risk management: "Some people with manic depressive illness commit suicide before they are ever diagnosed. Having a predictive test might prevent that."[29] In families prone to the disorder, screening for susceptibility genes might lead to various kinds of risk management: prophylactic medication use, career choice, prenatal screening. Knowledge of genetic risk for bipolar disorder could be used to help people with genes indicating potential vulnerability to make "prudent life decisions," wrote a group of experts:

> It might be helpful to know, for example, that a teenager presenting to a therapist with "adjustment" problems is at genetic risk for early-onset MDI [manic depressive illness]. In this case, prophylactic treatment with lithium or another mood stabilizer might prevent a severe manic or depressive episode at a critical stage of development.[30]

Here technologies of classification and modes of subjectivation combined in the discourse of prophylactic medication. This was not a retrospective investigation into the patient's past, but rather a form of future-orientation, which patients and families were to apply to themselves by monitoring their own mood and behavior. Nikolas Rose describes such an orientation as part of the "new prudentialism" characteristic of advanced liberalism, in which "individuals are increasingly held responsible for the management of their own fate and that of their families through a kind of calculation about the future consequences of present actions – a bringing of the future into the present and making it calculable and hence, in our dreams at least, manageable."[31]

In an essay written at the start of the Human Genome Initiative, Paul Rabinow provided some early guideposts for thinking about the way in which genomics might interact with changing forms of political rationality and modes of self-formation. Looking at the social formations that were emerging around genomics research, he predicted that the Human Genome Project would usher in an era of "biosociality" rather than a rehearsal of sociobiology. For sociobiology, nature was a metaphor for society: the social organism was to be protected through the exclusion of diseased bodies. In the genomics era, on the other hand, as new identities formed around disorder, and these interacted with medical authorities, scientific researchers, and legislative bodies, culture would work to remake nature along social lines. Rabinow identified groups whose affiliation was based on a common disorder or genetic risk, and who influenced health policy and scientific research, as emerging signs of biosociality. "Such groups," he wrote, "will have medical specialists, laboratories, narratives, and a heavy panoply of pastoral keepers to help them experience, share, intervene, and 'understand' their fate."[32]

In the case of psychiatric disorders, the question of how such groups were to be located, delineated, and made aware that they had a common condition or shared potentiality remained open. Moreover, as we saw in the Introduction, a person identified as having a given psychiatric disorder may not agree with the expert's characterization. Without agreed-upon physiological markers, the boundaries of disorder remained open to negotiation. One question that was critical to the eventual success of ventures such as Genset's was whether the phenotypic characteristics of illness populations as they had been constituted through the diagnostic standards of the American Psychiatric Association could be linked to variations at the genomic level.

## Diagnostic infrastructure

Noailles had recently returned from a visit to Genset's high-tech laboratory near Paris, stocked with millions of dollars worth of gene-sequencing machines and high-speed computers. There, a committee of European psychiatrists had gone over the research protocol for the study with Romero's staff to ensure consistent diagnostic practice. It was hoped that such standardized diagnostic protocols would mediate between the subjective interpretation of the clinician and the impersonal evidence of the gene. Genset's protocol presumed that for the purposes of gathering consistent populations, psychiatric disorders were not inherently different from other common illnesses with complex inheritance patterns, like osteoporosis or diabetes. If this were the case, the process of making illness liquid should have been relatively straightforward, at least at the level of diagnosis. However, as Genset's experience in Argentina proved, the ecology of expertise and the dynamics of patient identity in psychiatric disorders are considerably distinct.

Genset's collection process was based on a more general assumption, in cosmopolitan psychiatry, of the existence of an undifferentiated global epidemiological space. The World Health Organization estimated that 2.5 percent of the world's population between the ages of fifteen and forty-four suffered from bipolar disorder.[33] If this was the case, where were the Argentine bipolar patients? Why was it so difficult for Romero's doctors to come up with 200 samples? Like the WHO, Genset's research protocol presumed that bipolar disorder was a coherent and stable entity with universal properties – that it existed independently of context. But, as a number of analysts of the production of scientific knowledge have argued, the existence of a given techno-scientific object – here, bipolar disorder – is contingent upon its network of production and stabilization.[34] An individual experience of suffering becomes a case of a generalized psychiatric disorder only in an institutional setting in which the disorder can be recognized, through the use of concepts and techniques that format the complexities of individual experience into a generalized convention. In other words, global rates of illness do not precede measuring techniques such as DSM, but rather co-emerge with them.

## The emergence of bipolar disorder

Bipolar disorder is an especially intriguing category of illness because it seems to exist on both sides of certain key boundaries of mental disorder – in DSM, the boundary between affective and thought disorder, and in psychoanalytic epistemology, between neurosis and psychosis. Moreover, its increasing visibility over the past two decades relates to the rise of pharmaceutical treatment in psychiatry. From the early twentieth century until the introduction of psychopharmaceuticals in the 1950s and 1960s, psychiatrists considered the "functional psychoses," such as manic depression and schizophrenia, to be chronic conditions requiring life-long institutionalization. Following confirmation of the effectiveness of lithium in the 1960s, bipolar disorder became a rare success story within psychiatry, able to be managed if not cured.[35] Despite this relatively privileged place in the field, the boundaries of the disorder as well as its origins and its defining symptoms remained at issue up through the 1990s.

How did bipolar disorder – or its predecessor, manic depression – first emerge as an entity distinct from other forms of mental illness? The history of the disorder is part of the history of the disassembling of the notion of "madness" as a generalized form of ontological otherness in modern Europe. In this process, the broad social category of madness was taken up by medical experts and broken up into illnesses of varying degrees of severity and relative pathology.[36] Until the nineteenth century, "mania" was a term for madness in general, and "melancholia" – not yet understood as sad affect – was a subtype of mania. Pinel's disciple, Esquirol, introduced the concept of monomania, or "partial insanity," in the early nineteenth century, to distinguish a subtype of mania in which not all of the faculties were implicated. A dysfunction of affect or volition, rather than of intellect, might explain why someone who seemed rational when questioned nonetheless could not be held responsible for his actions.[37] The existence of such an entity implied that madness was not an all-or-nothing proposition. Soon after, Esquirol coined the term "lypemania," the precursor of depression, to describe delusional melancholia with sad affect. In 1854 the separate entities of mania and melancholia were brought together as poles of one illness, "circular madness," named in France by the alienists Falret and Baillarger.[38]

By the 1880s, this new illness-entity was generally accepted among European alienists. It became "manic-depressive insanity" in Emil Kraepelin's famous classification system of 1899. Kraepelin established the major categories of "functional psychosis," a term that referred to the forms of severe mental disorder that did not have a known physical cause: dementia praecox, manic-depressive insanity, and paranoia. Manic-depressive insanity was the most commonly diagnosed condition among Kraepelin's asylum patients: 19 percent of his patients were manic-depressive, whereas only 6 percent had dementia praecox, the forerunner of schizophrenia. Kraepelin differentiated among these illnesses according to their temporal course, rather than by specific symptoms: dementia praecox was marked by progressive mental deterioration, and had an especially poor prognosis, whereas manic-depressive insanity could leave the intelligence intact. For Kraepelin, abnormal affect was a symptom, but not the most salient characteristic of manic depression. Rather, manic depression was a disorder of the will:

> Under these circumstances, it will be permissible here to speak of an impediment of volition, in the sense that the transformation of the impulses of the will into action meets with obstacles which cannot be overcome without difficulty, and often not at all by the patient's own strength. This constraint is by far the most obvious clinical feature of the disease, and compared with this, the sad, oppressed mood has but little prominence.[39]

Not only has the clinical definition of manic depression varied considerably over the twentieth century, but so has its recognized prevalence. Whereas for Kraepelin there were three times as many manic-depressives as patients with dementia praecox, in the postwar United States schizophrenia was far more commonly diagnosed. This was because experts saw symptoms such as delusion or hallucination not as manic episodes, but as what Kurt Schneider called the "first rank" symptoms of schizophrenia. The predominance of psychodynamic models in US psychiatry in this period was an important factor in the high rate of schizophrenia diagnosis: given their interest in the expression of unresolved unconscious conflicts, psychodynamic psychiatrists focused on the content of delusional symptoms as the key to the illness, rather than temporal fluctuation of symptom presentation. This was not the case in European psychiatry, where psychodynamic models had not been widely taken up.

The disparity between diagnostic practices between the United States and Europe became apparent when a comparative study seeking to explain the much higher prevalence of schizophrenia in the United States was published in 1972.[40] In one part of the study, investigators showed a film of a patient interview to both American and British psychiatrists. One third of the Americans diagnosed schizophrenia and none of the British did. It turned out that many American psychiatrists regarded "schizophrenia" as the general term for serious mental illness. Meanwhile, the diagnostic rate of manic depression was as much as twenty times higher in British hospitals than in American hospitals. In the United States, clinicians simply did not "see" manic depression.

The authors of the study commented on this disparity as a reflection of the condition of the discipline: "Because of the lack of objective or quantifiable data, there is no doubt that of all branches of medicine, psychiatry is most prone to this hazard."[41] In conclusion, the study called for a standardization of disease definition in order to make disciplinary communication possible. Psychiatry desperately needed a common language, the authors argued: "This disastrous effect of differences in diagnostic concepts on communication overshadows all the other consequences – the creation of spurious disparities in prevalence and admission rates, misguided arguments about which illness the patient is 'really' suffering from, and so on."[42] Such standardization would only become possible through the series of events that led to the publication of DSM-III in 1980.

With the adoption of DSM-III, a diagnostic infrastructure came to underpin diverse phenomena in US psychiatry, ranging from drug development and regulation, to third-party reimbursement, clinical research, and patient self-identity. The new diagnostic standards made it possible to forge comparable populations for research and to measure the relative efficacy of specific intervention techniques. Once enacted, these conventions then proved useful across a number of arenas of administration and practice – for health management, transnational epidemiology, patient self-identification, and the re-biologization of psychiatry as a clinical research enterprise. Diagnostic standardization in psychiatry thus made mental illness transferable between the domains of industry, government, and biomedicine.

## Genotype and phenotype

While DSM-III apparently met the demand for consistent diagnostic practice across diverse sites, the question remained whether the forging of such populations was based on valid – rather than simply reliable – criteria of inclusion.[43] Standardized psychiatric measures are founded on contingent agreements on rating scales among experts rather than on pathophysiological measures. This is where psychiatric genomics research such as Genset's faced a conundrum. To go forward, this research required that codified diagnostic standards be in place. At the same time, it sought to eventually remake these standards by producing a new technology of measurement, the gene-based diagnostic tool.

The problem of how to definitively recognize a given illness phenotype remained critical to psychiatric genomics research, leading to professional reflection on the process of mutual adjustment between the surface and substrate of mental disorder. In a 2002 review of "psychiatry in the post-genomic era," two leading experts focused specifically on this challenge – as a conceptual as well as a practical problem:

> There will be critical conceptual difficulties and none are more important than readdressing the phenotypes of mental disorders. The ability of genomic tools to find the appropriate disease-related gene(s) is limited by the "quality" or homogeneity of the phenotypic sample ... There will be a somewhat circular process of understanding phenotype as we gain a better understanding of genotype; this, in turn, will affect our understanding of phenotype. All of this circularity may seem unsettling and unsatisfying to philosophical purists and it is difficult to see any way out of a process of constant adjustment. However, in the meantime, it is critical that we collect broad and thoughtful phenotypic information and not be handcuffed by diagnostic criterion sets that have reliability as their strong suit but were never meant to represent valid diagnostic entities.[44]

Thus experts were at the same time both using the agreed-upon definitions of illness phenotypes such as bipolar disorder and assuming that they were provisional and would necessarily be superseded by advances in genomics. Indeed, the psychiatrists who were gathering blood samples at Hospital Romero were skeptical that the diagnostic protocol given to them by Genset would be sufficient to find a gene: in our discussions they remarked that several different forms of the illness were being included in the study. A journalistic account of the study characterized this anxiety about the use of DSM-IV criteria:

> For the Argentine psychiatrists, this classification could be insufficient. As a matter of fact, they admit, other classificatory schemes point to the existence of up to six types of presentation of the illness, which for a long time was considered a psychosis and now is characterized as an affective disorder.[45]

Despite professional agreement on descriptive criteria, it was uncertain whether bipolar disorder was clearly distinguishable from schizophrenia or depression, as the ambiguous status of "schizoaffective disorder" suggested. Genetic and neurological studies continued to confound researchers trying to establish consistent means of differentiation. Estimates of its prevalence in the population ranged from 0.5 percent to 5 percent, depending on the criteria of inclusion used.[46] Some psychiatrists argued that there was a "psychotic continuum" from bipolar disorder to schizophrenia, from predominately affective traits to thought disorder.[47] Meanwhile, expert advocates of the diagnosis claimed that many actual bipolar patients had been incorrectly diagnosed with unipolar depression and given anti-depressants, which could set off a manic episode.[48] Such proposals would radically expand the bipolar population. Geneticists struggled to define the disorder's boundaries in order to gather consistent populations for research:

> There is growing agreement that in addition to BPI [bipolar illness], MDI [manic-depressive illness] encompasses several mood disorders related phenomenologically and genetically to BPI. These include bipolar disorder type II ... some cases of major depressive disorder without manic symptoms ... and some cases of schizoaffective disorder (in which symptoms of psychosis persist in the apparent absence of the mood disorder). The MDI phenotype may include other, milder manic-depressive spectrum disorders such as minor depression, hypomania without major depression, dysthymia, and cyclothymia, but this is less certain.[49]

Would finding susceptibility genes once and for all pin down the *thingness* of the disorder? In academic studies of the genetics of bipolar disorder, the late 1990s were a time of frustration. While twin and family studies had indicated heritable susceptibility since the 1930s, hopes that the advent of techniques for gene identification in molecular biology would quickly make it possible to find the biological mechanisms involved were disappointed. After a period of excitement in the 1980s as various reports of loci for linked genes appeared, a decade later the glow had receded after repeated failures to replicate such studies.[50] Experts gave dour assessments of the state of the field: "In no field has the difficulty [of finding genes linked to complex disease] been more frustrating than in the field of psychiatric genetics. Manic depression (bipolar illness) provides a typical case in point," wrote two Stanford geneticists in 1996.[51] By 2001, newly reported findings of a susceptibility locus on chromosome 10 were greeted warily by researchers.[52]

There were a number of possible suspects for the mixed results: "the failure to identify BPI loci definitively, by standard loci approaches, probably reflects uncertainty regarding mode of inheritance, high phenocopy rates, difficulty in demarcation of distinct phenotypes, and presumed genetic heterogeneity," wrote a team at UCSF.[53] These researchers thought that conceptual difficulties around defining the phenotype for diagnostic purposes posed an insuperable technical challenge. The Stanford team, in contrast, argued that no dominant gene had been found because of the biological complexity of the inheritance mechanism.[54] Surveying the state of the field, some geneticists posed a worrisome question about the diagnostic entity they were looking at: "The question remains: do our modern definitions of clinical syndromes (presently considered as phenotypes) accurately reflect underlying genetic substrates (genotypes)?"[55] In other words, for the purposes of genetic studies, was there really such a thing as bipolar disorder?

The phenotype question created a paradox for these studies: on the one hand, genetic research promised to resolve such problems by making clear the underlying biological processes: "Currently the major problem is the unknown biological validity of current psychiatric classifications and it is worth bearing in mind that advances in molecular genetics are likely to be instrumental in providing the first robust validation of our diagnostic schemata."[56] In order for such validation to occur, however, researchers had to know what they were working with. Yet they lacked objective tools to do so: "In the absence of a clear understanding of the biology of psychiatric illnesses the most appropriate boundaries between bipolar disorder and other mood and psychotic disorders remain unclear."[57] Genetic studies might even turn out to undermine the notion of a clear distinction between these disorders:

> One of the exciting developments has been the emergence of overlapping linkage regions for schizophrenia and affective disorder, derived from studies on independently ascertained pedigrees. These results raise the possibility of the existence of shared genes for schizophrenia and affective disorder, and the possibility that these genes contribute to the molecular basis of functional psychoses.[58]

The unfulfilled promise of genetics led psychiatry back to its old curse, the problem of how to stabilize its objects – that is, how to ensure that its illnesses were "real" things, whose contours could be recognized and agreed upon by diverse experts. Despite the discipline's adoption of neuroscientific models, and ongoing genetic and neuroimaging research into mental disorders, the question of the relation of psychiatry to biomedicine remained: to what extent could psychiatric conditions be considered equivalent to "somatic" illnesses? The effort to achieve such equivalence was one rationale for the re-biologization of US psychiatry beginning in the 1980s.[59] Difficulties in confirming genetic linkage challenged the legitimacy of psychiatric knowledge, and the very existence of its objects.

A leading researcher expressed frustration at the epistemological status of psychiatry relative to other fields of genetic research:

> [Psychiatric geneticists] continue to face an obstacle that does not hinder their colleagues who investigate non-psychiatric diseases; psychiatric phenotypes, as currently defined, are based entirely on clinical history and often on subjective reports rather than directly observed behaviors ... In no other branch of medicine have investigators (and practitioners) been called on to demonstrate time and again that the diseases they study really are diseases.[60]

This problem was especially palpable in Buenos Aires, as doctors struggled to locate patients who had been diagnosed with bipolar disorder. The dearth of bipolar subjects in Argentina was due not to a cultural difference in the expression of pathology or to the country's genetic heritage but to a different set of conceptions and practices, within its professional milieu, of the salient forms of disorder and the tasks of expertise.[61] The nosological revolution in North American psychiatry – the shift to DSM-III and its successors beginning in 1980 – had not extended to the Southern Cone. In Argentina, DSM faced professional resistance on both epistemological and political grounds. The pervasive presence of psychodynamic models among psy-professionals led to an emphasis on the unique clinical encounter between doctor and patient, and a suspicion of diagnostic categories that purported to generalize across cases. Meanwhile, there was political opposition to the incursion of such standards on the grounds that they were being imposed in the interest of managed care and pharmaceutical industry interests. Many Argentine psychiatrists associated the use of DSM with neoliberalism, the privatization of national industries, and the dismantling of the welfare state.[62]

A number of absences also posed obstacles to standardization: in contrast to the North American situation, the Argentine psychiatric profession was not structured by a demand to forge populations for epidemiological or neuroscientific research. Disciplinary prestige did not come from producing scientific articles in transnational journals, and professional training did not include an emphasis on standardized diagnostic classifications. Further, insurance reimbursement systems did not require the use of "evidence-based" protocols in diagnostic and intervention decisions. Thus while the Argentine population had been made available for genomics research in ethico-legal terms by Genset's contract with Hospital Romero and the consent form, it had not been rendered equivalent in epistemological terms.

Across the hallway from where the genetic study was being conducted, the women's ward of Romero's psychopathology service achieved the surprising feat of practicing Lacanian psychoanalysis within a public hospital that served a predominantly poor and socially marginal population. A number of times women who had received a bipolar diagnosis and then given blood samples for the bipolar study in the men's ward were later hospitalized across the way during psychotic episodes. Such patients' claims to have bipolar disorder were mostly disregarded by the physician-analysts there, who understood such self-diagnosis as a form of resistance to subjective exploration in psychoanalytic terms, and considered "bipolar disorder" to be a condition that owed much of its existence to the promotional efforts of the pharmaceutical industry. As they saw it, their task was to penetrate beneath these generalizing categories to understand the distinctive life history and process of subject-formation of the patient.[63]

Meanwhile, there remained the question of how the patients themselves understood their condition. The problem for Genset was at one level a technical one: how to find a pool of patients that would prove amenable to genomic research. But insofar as psychiatric diagnosis also names a subjective mode the question involved self-identity as well. Bipolar identity – which emerged in the United States as part of a burgeoning self-help apparatus in the 1980s and 1990s – was not widespread in Argentina. And given the prevalence of psychoanalysis in Argentina, along with the absence of the kind of patient advocacy movements that have transformed the North American milieu, it was not necessarily a receptive site for the inculcation of such identity. Despite the efforts of some biomedical psychiatrists to publicize the disorder, potential subjects for the study had not yet come to see their own life trajectories in terms of an illness characterized by extreme mood swings that had a biological underpinning.

## Local conditions

As historian Ken Alder writes, "understanding the process by which artifacts come to transcend the local conditions in which they are conceived and produced should be one of the central tasks facing any satisfactory approach to technology."[64] DSM emerged from a specific conjuncture within North American psychiatry in the 1970s, and spread to other sites – both administrative and scientific – because of its ability to make behavioral pathology transferable across domains. DSM was not just an isolated set of technical innovations within psychiatry: its eventual widespread use in professional milieus (and resulting controversies from such use) had to do with its ability to serve a diverse set of needs: for drug development given regulatory guidelines; for insurance protocols based on "evidence-based medicine"; for the re-professionalization of psychiatry as a biomedical science.

As I have argued, technical protocols such as diagnostic standards structure the production of a space of liquidity: they mediate between the domains of science, industry, and health administration. These devices are part of an infrastructure, both material and conceptual, that enables goods, knowledge, and capital to flow across administrative and epistemic boundaries. They link social needs such as health to profit-seeking ventures and to scientific communities. The use of such devices in practices such as professional training and DNA collection undergirds the abstraction of a global biomedical information economy.

Popular discussions of globalization processes typically describe an increasingly rapid flow of information, capital, and human bodies across national borders in the wake of technological innovation and political-economic transformation. As a number of analysts have noted, however, such global circulation operates in relation to regulatory techniques and governmental strategies – at local, national, and transnational levels – that both encourage and constrain these flows.[65] The negotiation of institutionalized regimes of coordination or harmonization – the linking of places through the creation of commensurable standards – is often necessary to make such circulation possible.

The challenges to performing the study point to the limits of such transcendence of the local. The setting in Argentina indicates that the extension of a diagnostic infrastructure does not occur uniformly across space but rather through networks, and must be supported or imposed by institutional and regulatory demands. The lack of bipolar patients there pointed to a larger disparity in forms of rationality around health. The shift in North American and Western European psychiatry from "clinical" to "administrative" norms had not taken hold in Argentina by the late 1990s, despite initial efforts to privatize parts of health management along North American lines.[66] The advance of DSM was an element in a health apparatus oriented toward bureaucratic management that had not suffused the Argentine milieu. Nor was there a significant patient-activist movement shaping collective action around the recognition and legitimacy of specific disorders. And a professional culture whose epistemological forms were incommensurable with DSM was entrenched. For these reasons, individual clinicians retained considerable autonomy in terms of diagnostic and therapeutic practices.

The difficulty of finding bipolar patients in Buenos Aires pointed to the halting extension not only of diagnostic standards, but also of modes of self-identification around illness labels such as bipolar disorder. In order to be a viable diagnostic entity, the disorder needed an epistemic niche in which it could take root and thrive. Bipolarity came into being temporarily in the men's ward of Hospital Romero, but only through the imperative to find a sufficient sample of patients for the Genset study. In turn, it disappeared when patients traveled to the women's ward. Patients' illnesses were rendered liquid without permanently transforming patient-identity, since a diagnostic infrastructure for managing health in terms of specific sub-populations was not in place. Thus, while information may be "the coin of the genomics realm," the extraction and circulation of such information is not a simple matter.[67] In the case of mental illness, the value of genomic information depends upon the stabilization of the very thing it claims to represent – the disorder itself. As we will see, the fraught history and impassioned politics of knowledge in the Buenos Aires *mundo-psi* made it unlikely that DSM-IV Bipolar Disorder would assume its projected prevalence there any time soon.

# 2

# Medicating the symptom

"There is an old joke," says Juan Carlos Stagnaro, "about how the Mexicans descended from the Aztecs, the Peruvians from the Incas, and the Argentines from the boats, because we are a country of immigrants." Stagnaro, a psychiatrist in his fifties, graying with a thin mustache, leans forward with enthusiasm. It is already late evening in his office, but we will spend two more hours talking. He is speaking of his publishing ventures: Stagnaro is editor of *Vertex*, the most widely read psychiatry journal in Argentina, and head of a publishing house that prints classical works in psychiatry, both European and Argentine. He was exiled during the dictatorship because of active involvement in the labor movement, and went to France, where he studied with the psychiatric theorist and historian Georges Lanteri-Laura. Stagnaro returned to Buenos Aires with a strong vision of the political and epistemological importance of sustaining a European tradition in Argentine psychiatry.

Our discussion of the expansion of the "North American" paradigm in global psychiatry, based on DSM and neuroscience, provokes Stagnaro to reflect on Argentina's complicity in processes of "cultural colonialism": "We have always felt, above all in Buenos Aires, that we were something like the Europe of Latin America. But this has brought us both light and shadow: on the one hand, we strive to emulate the thinking of more central countries and, on the other hand, we have a mania for the copy. I think it can be understood very well if one understands the concept of cultural colonialism as having two elements: it is the intention of those who colonize, and it is also the passivity of those that let themselves be colonized." Explaining one of his publishing projects, to trace the national history of psychiatry, he says: "As an historian, I prefer to speak of psychiatry in Argentina and not of Argentine psychiatry."

Even if there is not an "Argentine psychiatry," psychiatry in Argentina takes on a distinctive form, one structured by the configuration of a widespread psychoanalytic culture, a recent history of political violence, and an unrealized project of social modernity. In this chapter, I look at the ethos and practice of a diverse group of psychiatrists and psychoanalysts who share an orientation toward "the social" as both source of explanation and target of intervention. The experts whose practice I describe are mostly either veterans of, or identify themselves with, the *salud mental* [mental health] movement of the 1960s and 1970s. Their work takes place along two axes: a theoretical conception of mental disorder that implies an understanding of the human subject as a social being; and a political program of institutional reform designed to create structures of treatment based on prevention and social reintegration.

Many of these experts understand their practice to be engaged with a project of progressive social transformation. Relatedly, they are inclined to see mental disorder as the result of factors in the social environment: certain kinds of illnesses are prevalent under given social conditions. Thus current "epidemics" of addiction and familial violence may be attributed to the dismantling of social welfare through neoliberal structural reform. Politics and epistemology come together in a theory of the human subject that coheres with a particular vision of the state's responsibility to its citizens. A fundamental contrast between depth and surface makes possible this doubling between psychiatric knowledge and sociopolitical structure: the symptom, at both the individual and social level, points towards an underlying pathology that must be treated at its depths.

## Salud mental

The mental health movement originated in the United States after the Second World War as an institutional reform movement, in response both to a critique from within psychiatry of the ineffectiveness of the psychiatric hospital as a therapeutic instrument and to broader political criticism of the inhumanity of the asylum.[1] The movement's principles were based on the mid-century model of the social individual, "whose character was shaped by social influences, who found his or her satisfaction within the social relations of the group," as Nikolas Rose puts it.[2] This socially oriented mental health reform implied a redefinition of both the objects of psychiatric knowledge and the aims of its interventions. Severe mental illnesses were now seen as potentially transformable, given an appropriate social environment, and the logic of therapeutic intervention shifted from isolation in the hospital to reintegration into the community. Meanwhile, mental health reformers sought to expand the terrain of psychiatry outside of the hospital, developing office-based practices that focused on less severe conditions and promoting a program of preventive mental health care in the general population.

The movement was institutionalized in Argentina, with the assistance of the World Health Organization, with the founding of the *Instituto Nacional de Salud Mental* (INSM) in 1957. While *salud mental* was part of a transnational "social" movement, its trajectory in Argentina was marked by its political context – developmentalist modernization (*desarollismo*) in the wake of the first Perón regime. Perón had articulated a popular-nationalist vision of a state-directed "mass democracy" that would guarantee social welfare to neglected sectors of the population.[3] Like other early and mid-century "social" projects, Peronism challenged the legitimacy of a notion of democracy that was limited to formal political rights.[4] It sought to integrate the economic and social realms into the political through the figure of the "worker" as a social citizen, the subject of rights.[5] These rights included not only civil liberties, but also social rights – education, good wages, and health. It is important to underscore that this "social" imagination was distinct from the North American variant, in its explicit anti-liberalism.

The period following Perón's first government – the mid-1950s through the 1960s – was the era of the developmentalist state, which was oriented toward modernization through social planning. While many *desarollista* thinkers were adamantly opposed to the anti-intellectualism and cultural traditionalism of Peronism, they shared with it a substantive notion of democracy that included a right to social welfare.[6] These thinkers articulated a vision of society that included the new political subject of the worker but that, unlike Peronism, would be amenable to elements of cultural modernization such as psychoanalysis and the new social sciences. In the late 1950s a number of new institutions and disciplines were founded in order to develop and apply social and psychological knowledge to the general population.[7] The goal was to transform the social field through the application of these new forms of expertise. As the maverick psychoanalyst Enrique Pichon-Rivière put it, "social psychology is the science of planned social change."[8]

In their effort to modernize the treatment of mental illness in accordance with the aim of social reintegration, *salud mental* thinkers were closely engaged with these emerging forms of social knowledge. The social was not only an object of thought, but was also a mode of governing. More generally, the project of *salud mental* was bound up with the ideals of social citizenship: for *salud mental* thinkers, the achievement of social welfare would require attending to the collectivity's psychic well-being. As the 1969 Mental Health Plan for the city of Buenos Aires put it: "Mental health is not only the absence of disease but a state of complete physical, mental and social welfare."[9] The task of expertise in *salud mental*, then, would include the overall welfare of the population.

*Salud mental* implied a transformation not only in the institutional forms and therapeutic techniques for approaching mental illness, but also in the epistemology of expertise. The classical psychiatry of the asylum era understood mental disorders as relatively static and distinguishable entities, and focused on cataloguing their multiple forms. The category of the "psychoses" indicated conditions that were severe and untreatable, and which typically led to life-long confinement in psychiatric hospitals. Classical thinkers contrasted the psychoses with the neuroses, such as hysteria, which were potentially treatable. This sharp distinction between neurosis and psychosis functioned as a kind of self–other polarity, defining the boundary between pathology that was treatable and illness so dire that it could only be isolated and managed in asylums.

In contrast, *salud mental*'s goal of social reintegration implied an epistemological commitment to the mutability of psychic structure. *Salud mental* thinkers argued that the basic structures of psychopathology – neurosis and psychosis – were continuous with one another. Mental disorders were shifting, malleable forms rather than discrete and stable entities. Symptoms did not point to specific disease entities located in the body but were a response to a lack of fit between the self and the social environment. In 1957, in the pages of the influential *Acta Neuropsiquiatria Argentina*, Guillermo Vidal attacked the idea that abnormal behavior and thought could be understood in terms of "disease." He contrasted the disease model with a dynamic, interactive understanding of psychic distress:

> Probably schizophrenia is nothing other than an anomalous style of life . . . one is not talking of a disease, of a morbid entity, but of a reaction or form of personal transaction, before lived situations that are intolerable to the self . . . in other words: the symptoms of neurosis and psychosis are nothing but defenses that the self establishes against disturbing stimulations in an attempt to maintain the homeostasis of the psychic apparatus.[10]

Enrique Pichon-Rivière theorized a unitary mental illness process in which both neurosis and psychosis were defenses against basic anxieties.[11] To argue that mental illness was unitary and malleable made it possible to recuperate the severely ill into the domain of the treatable, the potentially normal. Thus Pichon-Rivière criticized organicism for its therapeutic pessimism: "To consider the form endogamous implicitly negates the possibility of modifying it." Psychic structures were mobile and complex, instrumental and situational. This meant that it should be possible to treat even the most severely ill patients with psychoanalysis. Pichon-Rivière was a pioneer in applying psychoanalytic techniques to psychosis in the hospital.

While the new medications developed in the 1950s made possible such experimental social therapies with psychotic patients, these drugs did not play a significant role in the self-understanding of *salud mental*. Pharmacological treatment was placed in the background, as a tacit practice, while a variety of dynamic therapies were the focus of knowledge production and clinical experiment. For *salud mental* experts, drugs facilitated social treatment, but were not in themselves the means of social reintegration. Thus, in 1960 Vidal criticized the idea that the world-wide decline in the number of interned mental patients could be attributed to pharmacological innovation: "The new psychopharmacology, inheritor in a certain way of the magic of the alchemists, is now capitalizing on a great part of the successes obtained by social psychology."[12]

In his proposal for the development of the "therapeutic community," the psychoanalyst Emilio Rodrigue was inspired by transnational social psychiatry.[13] For social psychiatry, mental illness was caused by pathological human relationships and so its treatment would demand restoring healthy social ties to the patient's life.[14] Its founder, the Viennese *émigré* analyst Joshua Bierer, articulated its program: "Treatment must include the whole social environment of the patient and all his social relationships. He must be treated not only as a person but as a part of the community."[15] Specific techniques and institutions included group therapy, family-oriented community care, and outpatient clinics in general hospitals. Rodrigue's vision for the therapeutic community involved the superimposition of a therapeutic system and a socio-political system. He called for the democratization of management in psychiatric institutions, the decentralization of authority, and patient participation in governance. The internee was to be both a patient in treatment and a citizen of the community. Such communities would also serve as models for generating democratic structures in other institutions.[16]

## The *Plan Goldenberg*

In 1958, psychiatrist Mauricio Goldenberg, president of the INSM, proposed a plan to modernize the aging Argentine mental health system, which was centered around overcrowded and deteriorating psychiatric hospitals that had been built at the turn of the century. The *Plan Goldenberg* sought to transform the institutional structure of psychiatric intervention from one based on hospital confinement to a network of community-based treatment centers. According to Goldenberg, the old *manicomios* were symptoms of psychiatry's distance from modern medicine. Locating psychiatry in the general hospital, he argued, would bring the discipline into contact with general medicine and thus encourage the use of more scientific criteria.

For Goldenberg, the primary aim of *salud mental* expertise was social reintegration, and its means was work on the social tie: "All the therapeutic measures that are applied should be directed to reestablish or create ties that permit him to reintegrate himself in society."[17] Such reintegration was to be accomplished institutionally through the decentralization of treatment. Goldenberg proposed the creation of acute care services in public hospitals as part of a network of community-based clinics. These services would focus on prevention and short-term treatment, and so make it possible to move patients quickly back to their homes rather than isolating them for long periods in psychiatric wards. The new centers of care would also function as healing communities, providing a milieu of sociality that would itself be therapeutic.[18]

When Goldenberg was appointed Director of the Psychopathology department at the "Evita" Hospital in Lanús, one of the public hospitals built under Perón to serve the poor, he began an experiment in putting the ideals of *salud mental* into practice. At Lanús, Goldenberg encouraged the use of multiple techniques in order to achieve the overall goal of reintegration, ranging from electroshock therapy to group therapy and job training. The Lanús service incorporated a variety of specialists: it included not only psychiatrists, but also psychologists, nurses, occupational therapists, and social workers. The service produced many of the current leaders in *salud mental* in Argentina, and as we will see, its legacy remains central to the identity of contemporary mental health practitioners. As psychoanalyst Dicky Grimson reflected in 1999, in a column in the weekly "Psychology" section of *Página 12*: "The training experience that many professionals of my generation had in Lanús under Mauricio Goldenberg's direction had certain characteristics in common: training according to a dynamic view, preoccupation with the social, and the certainty that the response to problems must come from institutions."[19]

Beginning with the Ongania dictatorship and the right-wing takeover of the university in 1966, the field of *salud mental* became increasingly radicalized. Along with universities and factories, public hospitals were sites of militancy and insurgency. Mental health *trabajadores* (workers), now located in general hospitals like Lanús and in smaller clinics, were entangled in the intense political confrontations of the period. *Salud mental* activists linked their techniques of treatment, especially psychodynamically oriented group therapy, to broader social and political movements. Among these activists, deinstitutionalization and the public provision of psychoanalysis were just one aspect of a larger political struggle on behalf of marginalized sectors of the population. For many, the progressive vision of the social was best articulated through militant engagement, whether aligned with left-Peronist groups or the Communist party.

The process of institutional, therapeutic, and political transformation that leaders of *salud mental* advocated was violently interrupted by the military coup in 1976. The right-wing generals that led the coup saw socially oriented psychiatry and psychoanalysis as subversive to traditional Christian values and stable hierarchies. Many *salud mental* activists were victims of the dictatorship's program of "cleansing" the nation through kidnapping, torture, and murder.[20] The military government shut down centers of care that had been set up in general hospitals and neighborhood clinics. The Lanús service was closed, and the successor there to Goldenberg as director, Valentin Barenblit, was sequestered and then forced into exile. From 1976 to 1983 the institutional practice of psychiatry was mostly sheltered in the traditional asylums, where an organicist understanding of mental illness rooted in classical psychopathology remained in place. This legacy explains, in part, why contemporary *salud mental* thinkers typically consider the practice of psychoanalysis in public hospitals to be progressive and democratic, whereas they associate biological psychiatry with right-wing authoritarianism.

Following the fall of the military government and the return to democracy in 1983, many of the leaders of *salud mental* returned to the Buenos Aires psychiatric community and assumed prominent roles at the professional or governmental level. Serious institutional reform of the mental health system nonetheless foundered in the following years. Attempts to renew the effort were hampered by bureaucratic inertia, lack of sufficient replacement mechanisms, and financial crises. In the democratic transition, alternative public institutions for acute treatment multiplied, training residencies in *salud mental* were founded, and the psychology degree program was reinstituted in the university, but the old *manicomios* remained full of chronic patients, and became markers of unachieved reform.

In the late 1990s, despite a deepening economic crisis and neoliberal reform policies aimed at decreasing the role of the state in providing for social welfare, *salud mental* leaders using a discourse of "the social" called for a renewal of Goldenberg's plan for decentralization of care and widespread networks of assistance. The lingering presence of the old psychiatric hospitals at the center of public mental health care meant that *salud mental* continued to have a ready target in its calls for reform. At the same time, the progressive wing of psychiatry was in power in many of the city's mental health institutions, including one of the old psychiatric hospitals of Buenos Aires, Hospital Borda. What was the practice of *salud mental* like, I wondered, within a site that itself stood for failed reform?

## The asylum today

Fernando, a psychiatry resident in his late twenties, welcomes me in the entryway to Hospital Borda. After excusing himself to negotiate with a burly representative from Eli Lilly, he comes back smiling triumphantly, cradling a carton of Zyprexa capsules, worth several hundred dollars, which he has acquired for an indigent patient as a "promotional gift." The hospital is part of a huge *manicomio* complex dating from the late nineteenth century, located in the south of the city, in Barrio Barracas. Borda has recently been renamed by its reformist director, who was trained in *salud mental*: it is no longer a Neuropsychiatric Hospital but is rather a "Center for Interdisciplinary Psycho-Social Care." Across the street, Hospital Moyano, the women's asylum, is still "neuropsychiatric" and is considered the last refuge for the Argentine school of biologically oriented psychiatrists, classically trained in the European tradition of psychopathology.

A steep incline on the north side of Borda leads to a forty-foot drop down to the street; the main entrance is on the south side. Of the one thousand or so patients housed at Borda, many are there for what Fernando terms "social" reasons: old age, poverty, drug and alcohol addiction. The new "open door" policy means that patients wander freely throughout the hospital grounds; the men I see walking aimlessly through the halls are mostly in their forties or older.

Through a courtyard, in back, into the old pavilion, Fernando leads me to the unit headed by Humberto Garcia. Garcia is a cheerful if maniacal figure, leaning over his desk and gesturing expressively with prominent eyebrows. He is in his late thirties, with a shock of thinning dark hair and a goatee, and wears a T-shirt and jeans underneath his white coat. He enjoys being the center of attention in the crowded, small office where he presides. Garcia is young to be the director of a unit, though this one, in an old section of the chronic ward, is not very prestigious. He is surrounded in the office by assistants, mostly volunteers and students, who huddle with clipboards and packages of the various combinations of medications that will be administered to patients. Besides being a central repository of the chronically mentally ill, Borda is an important site for training students and residents in psychiatry and psychology. The young woman nearest to me, volunteering here as part of her post-graduate training in psychology, leafs through a copy of Lacan's *Seminar 11*.

One challenge for Garcia is to sustain an ethos of progressivism in this unlikely setting. Garcia has read a lot of Foucault, he says, and so he runs his meetings in an anti-hierarchical manner – sometimes the residents complain that he is not authoritarian enough. Now he is telling everyone about a clinical trial they are going to conduct concerning the effects of an atypical anti-psychotic on patients with long histories of using typical anti-psychotics. The trial is sponsored by Gador, an Argentine company that makes an unlicensed copy of Lilly's olanzapine (brand name Zyprexa). Julio, a smoothly dressed young psychiatrist in the office, will coordinate it. A neuro-psychologist will go over the protocol with them on Thursday: they will use the PANSS [Positive And Negative Symptoms of Schizophrenia] scale to measure cognitive improvements in twelve to fifteen "paradigmatic" cases.

Outside in the hallway, a nurse shaves an elderly patient who sits complacently on a stool. A chart on the wall indicates staff meeting and group therapy schedules. A patient nicknamed "Moyano" – after the women's hospital – comes up and tries to kiss me. Garcia explains that his unit is in the oldest, most deteriorated part of the hospital, built in the last century. The unit's forty patients are divided between two long rooms with rows of beds separated by dividers. Some have been here over thirty years. Garcia speaks about the patients in front of them, as though they are not there. Many of the beds are in poor condition and furniture is missing or broken. One room is in worse shape, as are the patients in it. Several lie awake on their beds, immobile.

Garcia offers to show me around, and tells me about Borda's history. We walk towards the steep south wall, past the huge old factory kitchen. A lot of changes have been taking place over the past decade under the new reformist director: he wants to reduce the number of beds to 700 and put them all in the new pavilion, while moving the accounting and administrative headquarters to the old building and renovating it. And there is again the idea of constituting a network between Borda and the other municipal hospitals, Garcia continues, but it is not working. The reforms seem doomed to failure. The other hospitals send only their most intractable cases to Borda, the ones no one else wants to deal with. Outpatient care does not work in the general hospitals because the hospital directors refuse to buy psychiatric medication, so the patients have to come to Borda, where the less expensive drugs are given out for free.

Garcia, a student of the philosophy of science, is especially interested in the historical relation of paradigms in psychiatry to broader political contexts. The founding of the hospital, he says, was linked to the emergence of the modern state around 1880 under President Roca, who applied positivist doctrines to education, the military, and medicine. Garcia describes the work of Domingo Cabred, the father of Argentine psychiatric institutions, who started the original patient colonies in the provinces and the neuroanatomy laboratory at Borda, modeling these innovations after the European institutions he had toured. "We always copy European models here, for better or for worse – and now, American," says Garcia. "We are strongly colonized."

The next week I arrive at Borda with some of the residents who are in rotation in Garcia's ward. An interned patient wanders around asking for money. Another sleeps on the bench. Garcia unlocks the door after we knock and identify ourselves. We forget to lock the door behind us, and shortly Carlito bursts in violently, with *yerba maté* all over his hands and clothes, demanding a cigarette. Fernando ushers him out, and the door is locked again. "Open doors" means that the doctors must lock themselves in. Garcia and Lisa, a post-graduate trainee, are organizing medication for the nurses. Halpidol, Rivotril, Trapax: little plastic bags filled with pills and powders. The more expensive olanzapine is kept separate. "You don't keep it locked up?" asks Lisa, surprised. "No, we've got plenty," says Garcia: Gador has donated supplies for the study.

Beatriz, the group therapist, is eager to educate the visiting North American. In their team they do not use the "American" style, she tells me: "Here we are more European." She launches into a critique of

American ego-psychology that echoes Lacan's Rome Discourse: in America, Freud was transformed by Hartmann into ego-psychology, whereas in Argentina, Melanie Klein rather than Anna Freud was influential, and so the defense mechanisms of the ego were less emphasized. "Here it is more in the Freudian style," she says, "working to sustain the tradition of the unconscious – there are less of the behaviorist schools. We try here to get rid of the guilt of the family, the shame, the pain – and to work with the unconscious dimension of the mother and father."

Beatriz recounts the history of psychiatric institutions in Argentina: it is a story of the struggle of psychoanalysis against authoritarianism. Pichon-Rivière first brought psychoanalysis to the hospital, she begins, but all of the analysts at Borda were fired under the dictatorship. Psychoanalysis asks the subject to think: because of this, under the dictatorship Goldenberg, Stagnaro, and others had to leave the country. Centers of primary care were shut down, psychopathology services in general hospitals were reduced to one doctor. Now, she continues, a network may be possible. But Borda remains a space of marginality, made up of *locos, adictos, HIV positivos*: those left outside of society.

*Salud mental* discourse exists within the asylum itself, criticizing the outdated institution yet sustained by its continued operation – that is, by the ongoing need for reform. They are moving away from the word "chronic" to describe their patients, which is a means of social marginalization, Beatriz continues. The hospital is still in a stage of transition here, following its recent municipalization, the entrance into a network. They used to get the most hopeless patients from all over the country. But the reform is only a charade, she says: this is not a true process of deinstitutionalization – the new mental health law is just an excuse to cut funding further at the hospital. Outside there are shouts, banging – it is Carlito, yelling "my father is immortal." Garcia is taking care of it. Beatriz looks to make sure that the door is locked.

The following week, when Garcia arrives at the staff meeting, Beatriz wants to know the title of the clinical trial they are conducting – she is meeting with a representative from a pharmaceutical company to ask for a "fellowship" to the Hamburg conference. It is called "Olanzapine in long-term chronic schizophrenic patients." Garcia is rifling through his papers to see what each member of the research team is going to do. There is the ECG, the lab tests, the psycho-diagnostic – yesterday they gave neurological tests to seven of the ten patients. The PANSS scales will be given every fifteen days. It is apparently an excellent measure of psychiatric evolution, says Garcia.

On the fifteenth of the month they will begin with the olanzapine treatment in order to have completed twelve weeks in time to work on the conclusions before the conference in early August. Garcia turns to Susana, a psychology intern, and gives her quick instructions on how to do the trail-marking and three-letter tests. These are tests of cognitive ability, thought to measure the less visible "negative symptoms" of schizophrenia. Susana goes off to give the two tests to one of the patients, a small man named Hugo, and I come along. We find Hugo outside, and Susana calls him in, tells him she is going to do some tests and seats him in a room down the hall. Hugo is passive and indifferent. He gives a monosyllabic response to each letter offered, then refuses to come up with any more. Susana does not expect much, vaguely urging him to try to think of another word. We move on to the trail-marking test: number-letter; number-letter. Again Hugo is hopeless. "You see what kind of condition these patients are in," she says apologetically after he amiably shuffles out behind our thanks. There is no expectation that the medication will improve things.

The next week, Julio is filling out the PANSS scale for two or three patients in absencia. He finds the delusions of one of the patients "interesting" – they have to do with being controlled by the military. Julio checks "moderately severe or severe" for positive symptoms on the chart. A forensic psychiatrist comes in and tells him that one must follow an interview procedure in order to fill out these scales. Julio shakes this off. Later, I ask the student-interns about the study. They look at each other, at first subdued, then break out: It's garbage, a joke; they'll say whatever they want; the whole thing was rushed. "They don't care about the science," says one, "there's not even a control group. They're doing it so they can go to Hamburg."

The students understand that this type of clinical trial is not meant to contribute to knowledge about the effects of the drug on hospitalized patients. Rather, like the gift of Zyprexa samples to Fernando, the trial is a form of exchange between doctors and pharmaceutical companies.[21] From the perspective of the company, sponsoring the trial is part of developing and maintaining a relationship with the doctors, as well as promoting their drug. And for the doctors, it provides an opportunity to travel internationally in order to present their "poster," as well as receive free supplies of expensive medication. In addition to being a place for the reproduction of the social discourse of *salud mental*, then, the psychiatric hospital serves as a site for fostering relations between doctors and pharmaceutical companies.

In a critical commentary on the institutional situation in the late 1990s, Hugo Vezzetti argued that given the country's severe fiscal crisis and the implementation of structural adjustment policies, *salud mental*'s goal of building a widespread preventative network was no longer feasible.[22] All that remained for public assistance in mental health, he wrote, was to provide primary care for the most direct consequences of social exclusion. He predicted a future of growing inequality in access and a public scene dominated by mental pathologies associated with marginalization and abandonment. The residual function of the public hospital would be as a space of emergency treatment, reduced to the most invalid and needy. That this had not yet occurred, he mused, was due to the peculiar organization of public mental health services, sustained by the voluntary work of interns who by their presence made it possible to attract and maintain a sector of users that belonged to the same social sector – the "impoverished middle class."

## Underdevelopment

In the late 1980s and early 1990s, after more than a decade of fitful attempts to shift away from the planning state, the Peronist government of Carlos Menem began a radical experiment in market liberalism, through rapid privatization of state-owned entities such as electric utilities, railroads, and the oil company, and the de-regulation of protected markets. Like other neoliberal policies, the goal of these reforms was to limit the role of the state in overseeing human welfare, and to extend market rationality to areas that had been in the public sector, such as energy and transportation.[23] The premise of such efforts was that market competition rather than state planning was the most efficient and effective way to provide such goods: given a space of ideal competition entrepreneurs would quickly step in to offer the best service at the best price, whereas states were hampered by bureaucratic inertia, corruption, inflexibility – the inability to deal with rapid change. In the context of a discussion of health, it should be noted that despite structural adjustment policies, the Argentine welfare state had by no means been stripped away in this period. In fact, per capita spending on health, 40 percent of which was in the public sector, increased by 50 percent from 1990 to 1999.[24]

Argentine critics on the left were increasingly impatient with the liberalization policies embraced by the Menem government. Unemployment rates were between 15 and 20 percent, and economic growth was slowing to a halt in the wake of the Russian fiscal crisis. Monetary policy in which the peso was pegged to the dollar made it impossible to stimulate growth through devaluation. The "hyper-recession" would lead to a financial crisis culminating in an historic default on the national debt and the fall of two presidents in 2001. "*Basta globalización*!" declared an enraged announcer on a tango radio station. "Who can live on three hundred pesos a month?"

Opposition to globalizing regulatory regimes and neoliberal structural reforms – such as the introduction of managed care – took form in the Argentine left in an interpretation of globalization as imperialism in new guise, and in an appeal to defend "the social" against the incursions of neoliberalism. According to the analysis of dependency theorists, globalization was a myth that legitimated the imposition of neoliberal policies to the advantage of centralized capitalist interests. As sociologist Atilio Borón wrote, globalization was a "neoliberal hermeneutic" that cloaked domination as a "natural secretion" of uncontrollable forces. Meanwhile, there continued to be "classes, structures, economic interests, and power asymmetries that crystallized in relations of dependency."[25] For these critics, the overarching agenda of structural adjustment was the dismantling of the state, which would leave the poor without recourse to public remedies of social health insurance or guaranteed employment.

In an interview that appeared in the widely circulated newspaper *Clarín* in 1999, political economist Aldo Ferrer provided an analysis of the place of Argentina in transnational political and economic relations. For Ferrer, what was called globalization was simply a continuation and intensification of the core–periphery relations of inequality that had been dissected by world systems theorists in the 1960s and 1970s:

> There are central countries, which are those that have reached advanced capitalism, and there are peripheral countries, which insert themselves in the world primarily as providers of food and primary materials, and as importers of capital and of industrial products. History reveals that this conforms to a type of capitalism without much possibility for development, strongly dependent on the decisions that others make in the international system.[26]

Ferrer argued that the reduction of state spending and the encouragement of competition through the privatization of state-held enterprises, enforced by lending institutions such as the International Monetary Fund, sustained this relation of inequality. "Argentina, in this moment, must be the most 'foreignized' country in the world; all of the infrastructure of former public businesses that were privatized passed, in great part, to outside title-holders," he said. This imposition of outside norms was then mistakenly attributed to an impersonal globalization: "What we call globalization processes, as though they were apparently unmanageable forces of reality, are in great part regulatory frames imposed by the central countries, in commercial material, in the financial sector, in intellectual property." Argentina lacked agency in the process: "The advanced capitalist countries are those that insert themselves fully into globalization, maintaining control of their own project. And we countries that wind up as underdeveloped are those that insert ourselves passively and those that are caught up in a process over which we don't exercise control." Ferrer's reference to passivity was a resonant one given the Menem government's term *relaciones carnales* to describe its close economic partnership with the United States, and the left's ironic use of the phrase as a critique of Argentina's submissive position in these relations.[27]

Juan Carlos Stagnaro explained the spread of a "neuroscientific" paradigm in global psychiatry in similar terms: "In globalization, not all the points of the global sphere are of equivalent power: there are points that are much more potent than others. So the process of transnational domination continues, repeating itself today in another manner." Normally courtly and diplomatic, Stagnaro bristled at the subject of the influence of the United States. "North American culture tends toward a world expansion in all its manifestations, and the economic power of the United States tends naturally to expand itself toward an imperialist hegemony. What we are seeing in Yugoslavia," he continued, referring to the NATO intervention in Kosovo, "is a demonstration of the force in play. But this force is expressed in every sense, including culturally. In this sense you don't have to do more than count the translations into other languages of DSM-III, DSM-IV, to DSM-V, and the ever-shortening amount of time between translations. It also has to do with the expansion of the American culture industry, the spread of English as lingua franca." In Argentina, he said, neoliberal policies facilitated this "because, in the same way that they open the market to foreign products and liquidate the state, they liquidate the forms of hospital care, the training criteria, training institutions, and the public university as the center of knowledge dissemination."

## Thinking in English

While North American diagnostic standards had not, for the most part, been adopted in Argentine clinical practice, the prospect of their use as a means of regulating expert practice nonetheless generated a visceral response among many members of the *mundo-psi*. Some doctors suggested that the DSM system presented an opportunity for psychiatry to become more medically responsible, but more commonly, it was seen as a sign of US hegemony and the abandonment of a social welfare project. In such debates, the term "paradigm" was often invoked as a means of distinguishing among possible positions – not only scientific, but also ethical and political – with respect to the new biomedical psychiatry. The use of this term signals the importance of historical consciousness to this milieu. There is no need for the social analyst to teach these actors the lesson that social context structures psychiatric knowledge. What is more appropriate for the analyst is to trace the *uses* of various historical understandings of the relation of knowledge to politics. These experts are historically reflexive, attuned to ongoing links between knowledge and power in the psy-sciences.

Let me illustrate some of these dynamics with a case. Each month, psychiatrist Lía Ricón hosts a clinical case presentation at the headquarters of the *Asociación Psicoanalítica Argentina* (APA), a grand old building in Barrio Norte, which a number of older professionals as well as students attend. At these events, cases are read, but the patients are not present. The APA, founded in 1942, is the oldest and most established analytic institute in Argentina.[28] In one session I attended there, the question of the relation of medication to diagnosis was the focus of debate among the assembled clinicians. The case at the center of debate concerned a man in his early twenties whose father had recently died of lung cancer. After his father's death, the young man began to have delusions that his father was still alive: he heard the voice of his father calling to him at night.

The presenter, a therapist in his fifties, explains that he gave the patient a preliminary diagnosis of schizophrenia, and began treatment with a powerful older generation anti-psychotic to stem the delusions so that the patient could engage in group therapy. The therapeutic team then began work with the family, including the patient in discussions with the mother and brother. The patient's delusions receded, but the family – disturbed by the side-effects of the medication – gradually became convinced that the psychiatrist was poisoning the patient with it. The presenter interpreted this as a case of collective paranoia, but the family found another psychiatrist who agreed with them and changed the medication.

The discussion at the APA concerned first, whether the diagnosis should have been schizophrenia, an affective disorder, or post-traumatic stress disorder, and secondly, whether the treatment strategy had been appropriate. The issue was framed as a question of paradigm: did the presence of delusion point to schizophrenia – and therefore indicate the use of antipsychotic medication? Or instead, could mood-stabilizing drugs be used to make a differential diagnosis, and thereby shift the disorder into the affective realm, away from the structural dichotomy of neurosis and psychosis? In other words, could a "therapeutic trial" be used in order to make a diagnosis?

Lía Ricón begins the discussion by suggesting that it might be a case of post-traumatic stress disorder, because of the very graphic scene of the father's death in the family living room. A physician-analyst, noting this "Oedipal scene," then wonders if the delusions might be part of a psychodynamic mania – a break between the ego and its ideal. He uses the patient's response to medication as evidence against the presenter's diagnosis: "If a sedating neuroleptic put the delusion in remission, it is not a schizophrenia" – in other words, the drug alone cannot stem a schizophrenic delusion. Ricón agrees: "There is no permeability of speech in schizophrenia." Perhaps it is a case of borderline personality, she says.

"There is a problem of paradigm in play here," says Gustavo Lipovetsky, a bearded, red-headed physician-analyst in his forties. "One can do a psychodynamic history, but the DSM-IV diagnosis, from another paradigm, would be bipolar or schizoaffective disorder. This has implications for the psychopharmacology. From the DSM-IV perspective one would try mood stabilizers and atypical neuroleptics." He complains that the presenter's material is crossed through by a mixture of two paradigms, psychoanalysis and DSM.

"The diagnosis comes later," the presenter responds. "You have to begin by medicating the symptom." Thus he started with the neuroleptics. He is indicating a specific use of the pharmaceutical, one that distinguishes between surface symptom and underlying structure: medication works only on the symptom of an underlying disorder. The question of "paradigm" here is not whether or not to use medication, but rather what the medication actually does. For the presenter, medicating the symptom is necessary only insofar as it makes it possible to do group therapy, his favored technique. Lipovetsky speaks from a different vantage, in which the issue of medication poses the question of the illness itself – that is, of diagnosis.

Lipovetsky counters using the terms of biomedical psychiatry: "But the familial antecedents indicate a bipolar spectrum. The paranoid crisis of the father – was it a depressive crisis? An acute delirium followed by depression? Depending on where one is speaking from, it could be depression before, and mania after. In DSM-IV, criteria A, the prodromic phase is three months. With the bipolar spectrum, we can include the delusion, the hallucinations. Psychodynamically, there's no doubt something strange here ... But if we take Akiskal," referring to a North American bipolar disorder expert, "who says that 'borderlines do not exist,' who medicates and sees them as bipolar, that despite being borderline, they do well with mood stabilizers, you treat them with the bipolar paradigm, and they do well." His argument is that even though one could do a psychoanalytic reading of the case, it is also comprehensible in terms of the DSM category of bipolar disorder – which would direct the clinician to mood-stabilizing medication.

Ricón is not interested in the name of the condition: "The 'illness' [*enfermedad*] does not exist: it is a theoretical construct. We can call it whatever we want. DSM-IV is Esquirolian, not Kraepelinian." She is scornful here in her dismissal of the DSM system as "Esquirolian," indicating a mere catalogue or nomenclature rather than a philosophically grounded nosology, one that reverts in spirit back to the early nineteenth century. But she also has little patience for a purely psychoanalytic interpretation of the case. An analyst in the audience proposes an interpretation of the delusion: the son and the father were one person – he could not live as himself; the father continued to live within him, and he was rebelling against this family structure through his illness. Ricón criticizes this approach as antiquated and potentially harmful: "With this idea that the hallucination is a way of departing from mourning," she pronounces, "we are still in anti-psychiatry here, leaving him delusional."

"If he were a manic," insists the presenter, defending his initial presumption of schizophrenia, "he wouldn't have slept. He had never been exposed to psychopharmaceuticals and was very thin." This is why the low dose of antipsychotic medication stemmed the delusion. More possible diagnoses are then bandied about: PTSD, schizoaffective disorder, borderline personality.

"There is an ethical problem here," a man at the back finally declares. "It concerns the problem of the pharmaceutical companies, and our collaboration in terms of diagnosis and health insurance. DSM-IV is annulling clinical diagnosis. Just as we are speaking in English, we are thinking in English." In fact they are still speaking in Spanish; what he means is that the terms being used, such as "bipolar disorder," come from an English-language diagnostic system. His objection is to the use of such terms in place of the psychoanalytic terms neurosis and psychosis.

Such objections to DSM were part of a more general resistance to a new vision of the role of psychiatric expertise, and to a changing understanding of its subject matter. Indeed, it is worth noting that the attack on DSM is itself a globalizing form. In a 1993 book, *salud mental* veteran Emiliano

Galende approvingly cited the French psychoanalyst Marc Leclerc, who denounced the use of DSM as an example of American cultural imperialism:

> DSM-III is not a challenge, it is an undeclared war on Europe, and on the extraordinary invention that was made by way of the voice, the pen and the flesh of the representative of one of its highest civilizations, the Austro-Hungarian empire, dismantled in Freud's lifetime. This invention, psychoanalysis, respectful to the highest degree of man, of his quality, of his specificity, has always been thrown out by America, of which it is good to remember that Freud expected nothing.[29]

Leclerc's claim that psychoanalysis protected human specificity is exemplary of a more general anxiety provoked by the extension of DSM as a rationalizing technique. As Wendy Espelund and Mitchell Stevens argue, processes of commensuration – "the transformation of different qualities into a common metric" – threaten forms of life that are based on the uniqueness of the individual, such as psychoanalysis, and thereby inspire conflicts that are often cast as ethical: "the incommensurability of individuals that is basic to so much ethics confronts the radical commensuration of formal rationality. Conflicts generated by such confrontations are irreconcilable."[30]

Among psychoanalysts in Argentina, the DSM system was epistemologically disreputable because it did not include the structural categories of neurosis and psychosis. Moreover, it was politically suspect because of its ties to the marketplace: to the privatization of health in the form of managed care; and to the promotional endeavors of the pharmaceutical industry, which sponsored and distributed the Spanish translation of DSM-IV. Some critics argued that DSM was not a psychiatric nosology, but rather a catalogue for marketing psychopharmaceuticals. For them, the growing strength of DSM was linked to broader transformations: globalization, structural adjustment, a lost common project of social modernity. Thus, in Argentina, the reaction against DSM took form not as a tribute to old European civilization but as part of an anti-imperialist politics of knowledge and a defense of social democracy.

Argentine mental health experts are cosmopolitan intellectuals, but locate themselves at the periphery of the global system. For Lía Ricón, this position provided them with the possibility of an alternate conception of the human, one that was perhaps not possible in the center:

> This discourse of subjectivity, only possible in our practice and also in the forgotten aspects of the doctor–patient relation, cannot be forced to adequate

> itself to the strictures of a savage capitalism that makes demands according to time, that hypostatizes a symptomatic effect to the detriment of a more stable and profound change. This is what makes the development of psychoanalysis difficult in first-world societies.[31]

For Ricón, psychoanalysis not only defended the human against the encroachment of technicity, but also struggled against the forces of global capitalism. In the Argentine left, this identification was not a new one. As psychologist Eduardo Keegan pointed out, referring to one of the founders of Argentine social psychology: "from Bleger on, psychoanalysis has been identified with anti-capitalism."

## Epistemic resistance

Juan Carlos Stagnaro is not fatalistic about the power of the North American paradigm. Indeed, he is engaged in an effort to prove its scientific insufficiency. Having an agreed-upon paradigm, he argues – a common language – is not equivalent to having scientific status. The neuroscientific paradigm is characterized by three premises, he explains: first, the objective, atheoretical identification of disorder; then, localization of each disorder to a specific part of the brain; and finally, correction of the disorder via pharmaceutical treatment or therapy based on learning theory. If one can find its logical flaws, he thinks, one can help to dismantle it. He is optimistic that in the coming years these problems will become clear:

> I am dedicating myself to studying the three pillars and to knocking them down one by one, and I've realized that they have very strong internal inconsistencies. This paradigmatic proposal, in the present moment, for those who seriously study the situation, far from tending toward unifying itself and reigning as the new paradigm, tends to disaggregate . . . I have serious doubts that there is going to be a DSM-V. Serious doubts.

It is through his study of the history of psychiatry that Stagnaro's sense of DSM's ephemerality is grounded. "I think that the merging of an epistemological gaze with an historical gaze permits one to analyze the contemporary crisis of paradigm in psychiatry with serenity. Not to charge behind the latest thing out there." The notion of a "crisis of paradigm" serves as a reference point for critics like Stagnaro, helping them to situate themselves in a normative field: their historicism provides a position from which to analyze and perhaps undermine developments emanating from the North. An ironic observer of Stagnaro's editorial project – to republish classic works by Argentine psychiatrists – noting its nationalist and anti-imperialist resonances, remarked on his unwillingness to read American journals: "A good Peronist can never learn English."

At the annual APsA (*Asociación de Psiquiatras Argentinos*) Conference in Mar del Plata in April, Humberto Garcia and four philosophers present a "Phenomenology" panel, which about fifty people attend. Garcia, after completing his psychiatry training, began studying for a graduate degree in philosophy, specializing in epistemology. He begins his talk with a discussion of Heidegger's 1938 declaration on the "Age of the World Picture," describing Heidegger's distinction between modern science and premodern knowledge. These are different ways of seeing nature: modern science has a mathematical approach based on visualization, quantification – on "technique." For Heidegger, Garcia says, science is not merely a cultural activity, but actually re-shapes contemporary reality.

He describes recent epochs in psychiatric knowledge, linking each to its social context. The paradigm of the "great structures" – the idea of the psychic apparatus, and the differentiation between neurosis and psychosis – first emerged around 1910, he says. It was the result of the crisis of European science, war experiences, the critique of scientific rationality, and the development of psychoanalysis and phenomenology. During this period, techniques of psychotherapy – individual, familial, and social – were emphasized while the biological was marginal. This paradigm entered into crisis around 1970 due to a number of external developments: the economic crisis and its impact on health budgets, the emergence of neoliberalism, the impulse to privatization, and increased social exclusion. This transformation in the representation of the social implied a shift in emphasis from the psychological and collective to the biological and the individual, coinciding with the development of the field of neuroscience.

Garcia then turns to the present: proposals emanating from the Anglo-Saxon countries, especially the United States, through the power of the US cultural apparatus and the American Psychiatric Association, have now achieved diffusion throughout the world. The aspiration of this movement is to be the new paradigm for global psychiatry. The paradigm is based on a metaphor of the person as a computer, in which the psyche is its software. This can be interpreted in Heideggerian terms as a view of man as an object, whose use is based on efficiency and efficacy as determined by the market. It is impossible to put the suffering of the person into this scheme, Garcia says. "What space is left for phenomenology?" he asks, to conclude: "It must deal with the anguish and suffering that are not treatable by pharmaceutical prescription."

"Is there a crisis of paradigm in psychiatry here in Argentina?" I ask Garcia in his private consultation office, where a framed portrait of Eugen Bleuler looks down upon the couch. "There is a world-wide crisis," he replies. He tells the story of his visit to the 1996 World Psychiatry Association Conference in Madrid, which was called "One World, One Language" – referring to the global adoption of a standardized diagnostic system. The conference was held in Spain, and many Argentine psychiatrists attended. But the conference proceedings were entirely in English, excluding most from participation. Garcia wrote an invective about the conference for Stagnaro's journal, called "*En la tierra de Cervantes*, English-Only."

The American line is trying to turn itself into the new paradigm, according to Garcia. There is an internal and external logic to it. The internal part involves drawing a connection between illness phenomenology, neurobiology, and pharmacological indications. But the external elements are what give it strength: globalization, money, publications, graduate training, the power of the American Psychiatric Association, the prestige of the *American Journal of Psychiatry* – all these push the American line. What's wrong with the new paradigm? I ask. In his view, there is an impoverishment, a loss of "the clinic." The North American model erases 150 years of very rich history of psychiatry, of structural guides, of detail. DSM is nothing more than a catalogue, he says, it has neither psychiatry nor the clinic. "DSM was a witch-hunt against the category of neurosis." New psychiatrists have poor training – they don't read Bleuler or Jaspers. They are mechanistic – they think there is a computer inside the head. One needs to think about the patient's history, his needs, to ask: what caused this illness? As for the drug companies, says Garcia, after arms and narcotics they are the leading industry in the world. They have conferences, invite 250 people, and if you sit though the whole thing you get a free trip to the APsA conference.

Four decades after beginning his stint as editor of *Acta Neuropsiquiatria Argentina*, the inimitable Guillermo Vidal, now in his eighties, promotes a social-humanist conception of the work of psychiatry from his office in the *Fundación Acta* center in Old Palermo. He describes the process of reform somewhat differently now than he did in 1960, when he scolded psychopharmacologists for taking credit for the achievements of social psychology. "The mad were furiously mad before neuroleptics, and tranquilizers just put them to sleep," he now says. Neuroleptics made it possible to talk to the patient, transforming the relation between doctor and patient into a personal one, rather than treating the mad like animals. It was at this moment that "medicine was humanized." For Vidal, medication is a potentially humanizing technique – but only by making it possible to bring patients back into a social field.

Vidal focuses on "specificity" as the flaw of the contemporary paradigm: "This specificity of psychopharmaceuticals is a clumsy invention." The medical model is mechanistic, "insufficient in all lights to be able to understand madness ... To think, for example, that sadness or melancholy is a problem of neurotransmitters is ridiculous. One gets sad because of things that happen in relation with others, with human beings." Walking over to a bookshelf, he pulls down a heavy copy of DSM-IV, translated into Spanish, and opens it disdainfully. With this, he says, psychiatry is trying to become completely medical, to the advantage both of the doctor, who makes more money with shorter sessions, and the patient, who gets to look at a specific disorder – he points at the open section of the manual – and hear, "you have *this*." Vidal pounds his fist on the book. "The patient doesn't want to have to think about how his problem might have to do with his own life, a wrong decision in the past. We live in an ever more medicalized society," he pronounces regretfully.

For Juan Carlos Ferrali, the crisis of *salud mental* is part of a larger crisis in the social order, in which one finds a generalized search for rapid solutions based on norms of efficiency rather than concern for the whole human being. Ferrali is president of the Argentine Psychiatric Association (APsA), which was founded as a *progresista* professional organization following the return to democracy in 1983. In his office in Villa Freud, he scrambles between phone calls, patients, pharmaceutical company reps, and the ever-buzzing door. A graduate of the Lanús residency in the late sixties, he describes himself as a former pupil of "maestro Goldenberg." Ferrali is pessimistic about the contemporary moment, and nostalgic about the early years of his career. There is a lack of confidence now, he muses, a sense that each person does what he can in his own life, whereas before, one practiced therapy in the belief that in helping people to live one was making the world a better place. Perhaps there was an excessive sense of the social determination of all things then, he says, but at least there was a belief in social justice.

In his practice, Ferrali says, he sees a general loss of interest in deep self-exploration. The growing use of medication and patients' desire for pills has to do with an idealization of technology – the desire for a "click" to make everything easy. He too attacks the premise of targeted pharmaceuticals: "this model plays on an old ideal of medicine, that for any given syndrome there is one specific treatment to cure it," he says. There are two ideals of what it means to be a doctor in play: first, as a "social" activity, and secondly, as scientist. The latter, in the market society, stands for efficiency: managed care inspires the growth of the medical-engineer model at the expense of humanist medicine.

*Salud mental* thinkers understand the contemporary crisis of paradigm in terms of a general emphasis on surface at the expense of depth. As Ricón puts it, "the crisis of the end of the century without doubt attacks all that aims toward a deep and radical understanding, or that seeks solutions that lack this surgical mode of effectivity." Meanwhile, "psychoanalysis, with its respectful search for conflicts in the totality of the psyche, has to compete with brief therapies that solve symptoms, with psychopharmaceuticals that do not imply self-seeking, self-investigation, but that move toward a solution that comes directly from outside."[32] Medication, which comes from outside and does not demand deep work on the self, is an inauthentic mode of self-transformation.

Hugo Vezzetti also links pharmaceuticals to the crisis of *salud mental*. "The uncontrolled expansion in the use of medication is a direct expression of the crisis of the role of psychoanalysis and the modern social sciences in the *salud mental* movement," he writes. He sees the rise of the new biological psychiatry in terms of reaction and retreat: "From this crisis, one already sees the return of neuropsychiatric models, of biological therapies and the use of medication alone." Drugs treat only the symptom, not the underlying structure of disorder: "It is clear that the purely pharmacological approach is concordant with forms of treatment that aim to control the already established symptom." Vezzetti is not optimistic about the future, which will be "characterized by the expanded use of drugs, as much legal as illegal. Evermore, bodily functions (eating, sleeping, sexual potency) and the necessities of relational life will require a chemical accompaniment as a more or less permanent auxiliary."[33] Chemical prostheses will be used to make up for the attenuation of the social imagination.

## Historical consciousness

Sergio Visacovsky, an anthropologist who has studied the *salud mental* community, describes the ongoing symbolic importance of Goldenberg as a reformer and of Lanús as a model historical experiment to the contemporary milieu. Visacovsky analyzes a recent conference organized in honor of Goldenberg as a "rite of commemoration." In the event, what he calls the "Lanús myth" functions as an exemplar and Goldenberg as a culture hero. Speakers call for pluralism, freedom of thought, and social inclusion. "We must battle against individualism," several declare; the patient must be treated as a person, not as an object. The memorial links Goldenberg and Lanús to values of humanism, engagement, and militancy, and to a politics of democracy and pluralism. These ideals are to be put into practice through politically engaged psychoanalysis.[34] An affiliation with historical Lanús is a sign connoting a certain authority and legitimacy earned through activism and martyrdom. The Lanús service, Visacovsky concludes, is an "historical expression of progressivism in the *campo-psi* [psy-field]."

Visacovsky notes that in their emphasis on *militancia*, contemporary *salud mental* thinkers typically overlook the role of the North American community mental health movement in shaping Goldenberg's plans for the new institutions of *salud mental*. He also points out the continuities between *salud mental* and earlier Argentine reform programs, such as *hygiene mental*. As Hugo Vezzetti puts it, "the heroic myth of Lanús obscures its conditions of possibility."[35] In his revisionism, Visacovsky seeks to demystify the *progresista* idiom of "the political" as a taken for granted indicator of the good in the contemporary *mundo-psi*. For Goldenberg, he argues, the Lanús service was not about political militancy but about primary care and prevention. The radical politics now associated with the service came from elsewhere, and may even have been what drove Goldenberg out of Lanús in 1972, when he went to work at a private clinic.

## Psychic citizenship

In April, Valentin Barenblit, the former director of Lanús, returns to Argentina for a visit from his current base in Barcelona for the APsA conference in Mar del Plata. In a magazine interview, he describes the premises underlying a politics of *salud mental*: it requires "democracy in full force," which implies "the responsibility of the state for health, culture and education, and a system of equity based on need. In other words, the fulfillment of the Declaration of the Rights of Man."[36] When *salud mental* leaders speak of "democratic rights" they are referring to a right to well-being (*bienestar*) in addition to formal political rights, reflecting the inherited legacy of a notion of social citizenship. As Lía Ricón writes, "democracy implies access to minimal socioeconomic conditions for the effective exercise of citizenship – education, health, employment. Democracy without citizens is a political project for social exclusion."[37] The democratic subject of *salud mental* is not the liberal subject of North American dynamic therapies, but is rather one whose mental health is bound up in collective well-being.

Social democratic rights can, in this context, extend to a kind of "psychic right," one that is protected by psychoanalysts. Ricón argues, "We psychoanalysts continue to believe in and practice a theory that points toward self-knowledge, toward subjectivity, to the respect of the individual in all his rights." Similarly, at a public round table on the formulation of a new Mental Health Law, a psychoanalyst in his fifties argues that the "social engineering" techniques of globalization, manipulated through the debt, are working to destroy social welfare. He links this process to the rise of the neurosciences in transnational psychiatry. One can see the "Decade of the Brain" in two ways, he says: either as a scientific advance, or as a movement toward social exclusion. "The pharmaceutical companies have a great interest in reductionism." Psychoanalysis, in contrast, protects social rights: "We psychoanalysts privilege speech [*la palabra*], social politics, primary care, social inclusion. We are defending the rights of patients in the face of globalization."

What was at stake in such claims was not the practice of psychoanalysis *per se*, but its place in public health. The link between psychoanalysis and social democracy was a response both to epistemic transformation and political reform. Psychoanalysts working in the public sector felt embattled given neoliberal attacks on the inefficiency of state-based social welfare provision, and their potential to lead to a changing regime of mental health practice.

In the first week of May the city's psychiatry and psychology residents are required to attend a day-and-a-half conference on training in *salud mental*. Earlier in the week, the Menem government announced a sudden and extreme cut in the university budget – which was retracted after a series of strikes shut down the city – and there is a general sense of militancy around the *Facultad de Medicina* where the conference is being held. Several speakers compare President Menem's program of public sector budget cuts and the privatization of national industries, impelled by the IMF, to the authoritarian measures of past military dictatorships – specifically, to the infamous day in 1966 when the Ongania dictatorship shut down the universities.

One of the featured panelists, an official from the *Facultad de Psicología*, delivers a presentation that reflects the historical consciousness of members of the *salud mental* field. She summarizes the history of Argentine psychology, linking the strength of given paradigms to corresponding political situations in the country's history. It is a story in which biological understandings of behavior are linked to authoritarianism and psychodynamic ones to democracy, beginning with positivism in the late nineteenth century, continuing through biotypology and eugenics in the 1930s, *salud mental* in the 1950s and its repression under the dictatorship, and then the rise of psychoanalysis with democratization in the 1980s.

"Today," she warns, alluding simultaneously to structural adjustment and to neuroscience, "a biological fundamentalism is again working to tranquilize the subject, to reduce psychopathology to genetic foundations, or to treat it only through psychopharmacology." She concludes with a call to action: "Our work, then, is to defend the breach in the subject, the special place of psychoanalysis. What is the place of subjectivity in the public sphere? Democracy consists of subjects who have the right to be heard. It is participatory. This is not a biologizing subjectivity."

There was a shared sense that the crisis of *salud mental* was linked to the dismantling of social welfare and a concomitant idealization of the market. Vicente Galli, a leader of *salud mental* and Minister of Mental Health under the Radical government of Raúl Alfonsín in the 1980s, argued that the current boom of brief therapies was impelled by two factors: "the perspective of the market, and a paradigm of cultural urgency that pacifies everything that disconcerts and generates suffering [*malestar*] through the illusion that everything can be resolved rapidly. It is a kind of instant-service." He contrasted this emphasis on efficiency with the more subtle interpretive capacity of psychoanalysis: "The proposal of analysis is the inverse, to try to understand suffering ... It can take more time than giving medication, but for many it is worth it."

Hernan Kesselman, a founding member of the Lanús service, also saw encroaching global capitalism as the source of the decline of *salud mental*. In an opinion piece in the weekly psychology section of *Página 12*, he complained of the effect of "the ethical perversion of individualism and efficiency-ism, the dominant ethos of the market," on the practice of group therapy.[38] Neoliberal capitalism, "the competition of all against all," is "a social infection" that wounds both patients and therapists, he wrote. In his practice, Kesselman was witnessing the emergence of an "ethic of anti-solidarity, of individualist survival. Therapists and patients, therapists amongst one another, patients amongst one another, all get accustomed to mutual mistrust and the connection is as ephemeral as the temporary contracts of the labor market." As a result, "patients are resistant to psychoanalysis or any type of processual (prolonged) therapy." He linked psychopharmacology to plastic surgery, one of President Menem's vain indulgences, writing that patients are "in search of a psychological 'lifting' that will put them back in the circuit of success." Lack of social solidarity, the end of guaranteed employment, and the crisis of psychoanalysis were part of one movement: the emergence of neoliberal subjectivity.

In *Vertex*, the psychoanalyst Victor Giorgi provided a cogent articulation of the social analysis of neoliberal subjectivity. The ideology of neoliberalism, he wrote, encourages the naturalization of competition and individualism; these are seen as "natural laws." Meanwhile exclusion, poverty, and unemployment, formerly thought of as social injustice, are now looked at as signs of the lack of competitiveness of those who suffer. Values of equity and justice do not have a place in the dynamic of the market; there is a "readjustment" of our sensibilities.

Structural adjustment implied a new form of the human. "Neoliberalism considers the human being as a 'subject of the market,' confusing quality of life with consumption, and identifying self-realization with economic success."[39] It substitutes "consumer" for "citizen"; universal rights are regulated through supply and demand. Privatization is part of the cultural offensive. The health market as well is to be regulated through market mechanisms. The user is no longer a subject using his right to health according to his needs, but rather a service-buyer, according to the function of acquisitive power.

According to Giorgi, this "neoliberal imprint on subjectivity" includes skepticism, individualism, an absence of future goals, the negation of cultural roots, and a perception of the other as a potential competitor. Its terrain was prepared by the military dictatorship's work against the social tissue. We are participating in a "*desarollo reflejo*" he concluded, a pseudo-development based on imitation, the renouncement of our own proposals and of our creativity. It is a pathetic form of dependency, characterized by the tendency to develop pseudo-identities, false selves. His words evoked the calls of *desarollismo* and third-worldism for an alternate mode of development, not only in the sphere of political economy, but correlatively in terms of subjectivity. But now, it was a melancholic reflection on the lost optimism of the developmentalist era as a time of forging distinctive models of the social collectivity and of the individual human subject.

What can we make of the identification of psychoanalysis with the protection of social welfare and human rights? During the height of *salud mental*, attention to the patient's essential humanity as inhering in social relations was part of an impulse toward the modernization of the mental health sector. But by the late 1990s, Goldenberg's technical interest in employing multiple forms of therapy as part of the broader goal of social reintegration had become an ethical imperative to sustain the practice of psychoanalysis in the public sphere. The social human was invoked in reaction to epistemic and institutional change, in recollection of an era of *militancia* and engagement.

While this vision of the human incorporated transnational knowledge-forms, its political valence was tied to the specific position of Argentina in the global system. Resistant experts saw attempts at the regulation of practice based on professional norms, such as the importation of DSM-based treatment protocols, as an instance of cultural imperialism. They countered these incursions not with a localized discourse of indigenous authenticity, but with an alternative cosmopolitanism grounded in an understanding of the human as that which exceeded pragmatic, scientific reason – and which was fundamentally structured in and through social attachments. These critics argued that psychiatry, because it deals with the disorders of the human as the subject of social ties, could not be assimilated to the rationality of biomedicine. As Vidal put it: "Psychiatry can't just be another branch of medicine. If we do not listen to our fellow man, if we do not dialogue with our fellow man, we are merely druggists. Our field and our specialty have neither the limits nor the precision nor the objective characteristics of the modern *techne*."

In his discussion of rationalization and the modern "disenchantment of the world," Weber pointed not toward a decline of religion but to its gradual displacement outside of the sphere of rationality. "Every increase of rationalism in empirical science increasingly pushes religion from the rational into the irrational realm." Tensions between religious and scientific knowledge came to the fore whenever rational, empirical knowledge had achieved such disenchantment. In the face of rationalization processes, the claim of incommensurability between different life orders was made in order to defend the place of religion. Science opposed a meaningful, ethically oriented cosmos, and religion defended itself "by raising the claim that religious knowledge moves in a different sphere and that the nature and meaning of religious knowledge is entirely different from the accomplishments of the intellect."

In Buenos Aires, were *salud mental* experts, in their claim that psychiatry operated according to a different rationality than biomedicine, occupying the position of religion in this scheme? The question was whether the treatment of mental illness required a scientific system or an ethico-religious one. The anxiety that something "human" was being lost in the spread of neuroscience, diagnostic standards, and psychopharmaceuticals can be seen as a response to the rationalization of new spheres of life. In Buenos Aires, psychoanalysis – initially brought into *salud mental* as a novel medical technique – now functioned in the service of a secular counter-modernity.

We may empathize with the criticisms of the abstracting qualities of DSM, and of pharmaceutical treatment as an element of an encroaching and sinister technicity. But the case I described earlier in the chapter – in which a doctor used powerful antipsychotics in order to make his patient amenable to group therapy – shows that we should be wary of the potential pitfalls of this desire to be human in a *social* way. It is worth noting in this regard that Lipovetsky's defense of the use of DSM criteria was also made on ethical grounds; but it was based on an ethics of professional practice rather than one of humanistic values. DSM was not capable of providing meaning to the world it ushered into existence. But if it entered into a practice of knowledgeable care, this latter position seemed to suggest, neither did it necessarily imply the dissolution of the subject, or the technologization of the soul.

# 3
# The Lacan ward

Soon after I arrived in Buenos Aires in 1998, the physicist and science warrior Alan Sokal came to the city to promote his new book, *Intellectual Imposters*, and delivered a lecture to a large audience at the University of Buenos Aires. As expected, Sokal decried the influence of postmodern cultural relativism and anti-scientific thinking on progressive political thought. Moreover, he said, while this was merely an academic debate in the United States, in Buenos Aires, where Lacanian psychoanalysis dominated the mental health sector, it was a problem of public health. There were loud cheers from the audience.

Sokal's accusation was echoed by several of the doctors in the men's ward at Hospital Romero. Patients were often misdiagnosed and given the wrong medications, these doctors complained. More generally, they argued, an anti-scientific ethos presided among analytically oriented mental health professionals, such that it was impossible to adequately measure and efficiently approach the city's mental health needs. The problem was especially acute given the effects of structural adjustment policies and economic crisis on the public sector. They pointed across the entry corridor to the women's ward – the "Lacan ward" – as an exemplary site for such malpractice. Such criticism suggested a possible disjuncture between the resolutely pragmatic needs of the public hospital and the ethereal realm in which Buenos Aires *lacanismo* traveled. While following the collection of bipolar samples for the genetic study in the men's ward, I became curious about this institutionalized practice of Lacanianism across the entryway. I began to spend time in the women's ward, posing the question: how could this hermetic knowledge system be put to work in the context of the public hospital, whose infrastructure was deteriorating and which took in patients from the most marginalized social classes?

## Psychoanalysis in the hospital

Hospital Romero's psychopathology service is an outgrowth of postwar psychiatric reform in Argentina, whose aim was to shift patients from overcrowded asylums back into the community by replacing life-long institutionalization with brief hospital stays and a decentralized network of care.[1] From a North American vantage, the practice of Lacanian psychoanalysis in a public hospital psychopathology ward was surprising. In Buenos Aires, this was not a particularly unusual situation – in fact such sites were privileged spaces for the reproduction of psychoanalytic knowledge and practice. There were a number of explanations for the phenomenon. Some observers suggested that *lacanismo* was simply the latest fad in a long-running Argentine fascination with psychoanalysis. Others argued that the turn in the mental health community toward Lacan's hermetic philosophical system had been complicit with the military dictatorship's efforts to depoliticize the mental health field – that this form of thought's detachment from social problems allowed it to survive the dirty war period, while more engaged movements were brutally repressed by the dictatorship following the 1976 coup. Historians, meanwhile, pointed to the structure of the city's mental health system and the organization of the professions over the previous half-century as an explanation for the rise of Lacan in Buenos Aires.[2]

For the first two decades after its founding in the 1940s, the practice of psychoanalysis in Argentina was located far away from hospital psychopathology wards, as a private treatment for the neuroses of the educated classes. In the wave of intellectual renewal following the fall of the Perón regime in 1955, the Argentine urban milieu nourished a thriving psychoanalytic culture.[3] In this period, the growing middle class combined progressive politics with a passion for cosmopolitan cultural forms. They were ardent consumers of psychoanalysis: to be analyzed came to be seen as a necessary part of maturation, a sign of health rather than illness.[4] By the end of the 1960s, Buenos Aires was the second most psychoanalyzed community in the world.[5]

Through this period, the Argentine Psychoanalytic Association (APA) oversaw the orthodox practice of psychoanalysis: in an office, with a couch, under the assumption of a contract between analyst and analysand. Psychoanalysts' professional identity developed in opposition to classical somatic psychiatry, which was based in the large neuropsychiatric hospitals built at the turn of the century. In the wake of the Perón regime, mental health reform and a changing political landscape provided the conditions for the entry of psychoanalysis into the hospital. *Salud mental*, a progressive movement for reform of the treatment of mental illness, was the venue for this integration of psychoanalysis into the space of public health.

For mental health reformers, psychoanalysis was one of a number of experimental approaches used in the effort to modernize the treatment of mental illness. The main focus of reform efforts was the development of alternative institutional spaces. Psychoanalysis made inroads into the public hospital mainly through the new institution of the acute psychiatric care ward. The work of analysts in public hospital wards required a break from orthodox models of psychoanalysis: therapy was provided for free, there was no couch, and transference was potentially hampered by the difference in social class between therapist and patient. As Mariano Plotkin has noted, the setting of psychoanalysis in public hospitals raised new questions for these practitioners.[6] The role of social and political conditions in the development of illness became central to their reflection; and even more, some analysts began to envision psychoanalysis as a possible tool for social change.[7]

Following a workers' revolt in Cordoba in 1969 known as the *Cordobazo*, political mobilization gripped the left intelligentsia, spreading quickly through the *mundo-psi*.[8] Younger analysts and trainees reacted against the conservatism of the Argentine Psychoanalytic Association. After a struggle over whether to officially support the student and worker uprisings, a group of rebellious analysts challenged the APA's hierarchical structure, leading to a splintering into multiple psychoanalytic societies. The rebellious analysts defined themselves both as psychoanalysts and as *salud mental* "workers." They sought to bring psychoanalysis into public hospitals where poorer patients could receive treatment. One of the most distinctive features of the contemporary Buenos Aires *mundo-psi* emerged at this intersection: psychoanalysis became "public" as both a technique to be used in public institutions and a form of knowledge concerned with broader social transformation.[9]

## The study group

The institutional form of the "study group" played a critical role in the widespread adoption of Lacanian thought in Argentina. Silvia Sigal has analyzed the importance of the study group as a distinctive Argentine cultural institution, whose origins were in the Peronist era of the banishment of progressive thinkers from the university.[10] From the 1950s to the 1980s, progressive intellectuals in the university were repeatedly persecuted by authoritarian regimes: whole departments were shut down; faculty were fired and replaced with ideological supporters of the regimes. The fragility of their institutional positions led intellectuals to form networks outside of the university based on shared interests. In the study group, students would pay an expert on a given topic to lead an ongoing seminar. These study groups functioned autonomously, sustaining the activity of thought until the political situation changed so that intellectuals could reenter the university. Sigal estimates that by 1966 there were about 2,000 study groups in Buenos Aires, with eight to ten members each.

Since it was a means for under-employed intellectuals to sustain themselves, the feasibility of a given study group was at least in part a question of market demand. For this reason, fashion and personality played a central role in the dynamics of the study group. The combination of a famous name and a popular theme, such as psychoanalysis, was especially valuable in the marketplace of ideas. With the help of the study-group phenonemon, the charismatic philosopher Oscar Masotta was able to spearhead the impressive dissemination of Lacanian thought into the Buenos Aires intellectual milieu.[11] Lacan's support of May '68 made him a hero among the Buenos Aires left intelligentsia, and by the end of the decade, Masotta's weekly seminars were drawing an audience of three hundred.

Lacan's critique of orthodox psychoanalytic practice was enthusiastically received among idealistic young psychiatrists who sought to extend their techniques from the *consultorios* of Barrio Norte to public clinics in poor neighborhoods. The psychiatrist Jacinto Armando was part of Masotta's first study group, and is credited by many as the first to bring Lacan's thought into Buenos Aires public hospitals. He is a gruff, friendly man in his fifties, with effusive gestures and a scraggly beard, who enjoys reflecting on his part in this history. What was important was the idea of a return to reading Freud, he begins: Masotta's background was in philosophy and he argued that one did not have to be a medical doctor to do psychoanalysis – that it was the "reading" and not the title that was important. The dominant group at this time, the APA, was a product of the diaspora of European analysts, he says, and had a vaguely Kleinian orientation, but it was not very "rigorous" in its training: "for them reading Freud was secondary."

This was in the late sixties, continues Armando, during a time of great hope for a confrontation with imperialism. He emphasizes that the field was *salud mental*, not psychiatry. When members of the APA broke off into radical splinter groups, their efforts turned toward bringing psychoanalysis into the local treatment centers "where theoretical, clinical, and ideological positions encountered one another." From 1967 on, Masotta encouraged his students to go into hospitals and discuss what they found there. Armando rejects some contemporary critics' claims that Lacanian thought was apolitical: Lacan's thought was so influential in Argentina because it gave an authentic and renovating interpretation of "social" discourse. "Anti-psychiatry entered our thought through reading Cooper and Laing, and although Lacan was opposed to anti-psychiatry, the two were merged here in Argentina."

In 1969, Armando went to work in the *Centro de Salud Mental #1*, whose director was the *salud mental* pioneer Hugo Rosario. "The psychoanalysts gave space to Lacan among the residents. At this point, there was room for all kinds of treatment positions: the point was to listen." Armando finished his residency in 1972 and entered the men's ward of Hospital Pirobano as a volunteer intern. In describing the period, he does not place much emphasis on Lacanian theory – he is more interested in talking about the politics of the movement. This was under the Ongania dictatorship, he says, which was much less harsh than the later one, and so they staged many little protests in the hospital. The patients painted a sign saying "Revolutionary Army of Pirobano" on one wall. There were confrontations with "traditional psychiatry" in the internment ward – protests against electroshock, for example. They were trying psychoanalysis on psychotic patients and producing many books and articles on the experiment.

During this period, he continues, many people worked at Pirobano for free – the point was to train people, not to have a hospital career. After a few of his colleagues left, he took charge of the ward and eventually of the whole service. It was a heady time: "we were Lacanian and anti-psychiatric, in our late twenties, and in charge." I ask Armando what was distinctive about a Lacanian approach to psychosis. "We didn't medicate," he says. "It isn't that we listened first, then medicated. Listening was the priority. And we thought there could be a restitution of psychosis assisted by the hospital. Medication erases the delusion, but Freud said that the delusion was the restitution."

The military coup of 1976 had a devastating effect on the *salud mental* movement, including such experiments in the public hospital. The right-wing junta considered psychoanalysis to be a subversive practice, and sequestered many politically active analysts and mental health workers. Most public hospital acute psychiatric care wards were shut down.

Analysts were forced to retreat from public space. During the dictatorship period, which lasted until 1983, a number of Lacanians led private study groups and were able to maintain their communities outside of established institutions.

When the Faculty of Psychology at the University of Buenos Aires reopened in 1983 after the fall of the dictatorship, Lacanian analysts were well placed to lead the institution. In the rapid growth of interest in psychoanalysis that accompanied the democratic transition, these instructors trained literally thousands of psychology students. Since the orthodox APA limited the authorized practice of psychoanalysis to medical doctors, many clinical psychology graduates embraced Lacanian theory as a way to rebel against the strictures of the APA and to authorize themselves as analysts without medical training.[12] Meanwhile, Lacanians attained prominent positions in the city's public hospital psychopathology wards, which became important sites for postgraduate clinical training and for the production of psychoanalytic knowledge. Hospital Romero was exemplary of this process.

The Director of the Psychopathology Ward at Hospital Romero, Alejandro Noailles, was a well-known Lacanian theorist of psychosis in the 1980s, before becoming disillusioned with the approach. His office in an upper-middle-class neighborhood of Belgrano is a serene white, decorated with Van Gogh and Cezanne, with an oriental tapestry laid over the couch. I ask about his training in the 1970s. When he began the residency at Hospital Pirobano, he says, it was the only possible choice if one wanted to work in a general hospital and was interested in a dynamic orientation. It was difficult to get into Pirobano as a resident, and the position was quite prestigious. For residents at Pirobano many opportunities were available afterwards.

Noailles had studied psychoanalysis for two years, he says, but given his Marxist background he was prejudiced against Lacan. At the time he was working with Rafael Paz, a Communist Party militant and founder of a leftist association of psychiatrists. Paz said that you had "missed the train" if you did not study Lacan. They broke with the APA, which they saw as the establishment. Noailles recalls the role of Jacinto Armando in the Pirobano residency: although he was actually just an unpaid intern, he was functioning as chief of the ward, and meeting with thirty people at a café on the corner to do supervisions and case presentations.

Lacanian thought developed on the margins of psychoanalysis in Buenos Aires, outside of the APA, observes Liliana Hirsch, a physician-analyst at Romero, in an interview in her office. The *consultorio* in her airy

Palermo Viejo loft has an antique wooden desk, a sleek divan, and bookshelves full of worn paperbacks. As she tells me about the role of Lacan in the hospital, she goes through her books, showing me various texts describing early psychoanalytic experimentation with the psychoses. Oscar Masotta was the supervisor of Jacinto Armando, who brought Lacan into the public hospital. "The institutional presence of Lacan first surged in Pirobano," she says. When Hirsch graduated from medical school in 1977, Pirobano was the only place in Buenos Aires with a psychoanalytic orientation, and it was Lacanian, led by Armando. A year or so after she arrived, the dictatorship closed thc in-patient ward and ended the residency at Pirobano "with an odd mixture of authoritarian caprice and bureaucratic rationality": since the residents still had contracts, they were told to choose somewhere else to go. After the director at Pirobano was promoted and moved to Romero, all of the residents at Pirobano followed her there.

The director didn't know much about psychiatry, Noailles recounts, but she was a powerful political figure, and managed to get forty new posts at Romero by 1982. With an additional fourteen residents and seventy volunteers, it was a "mini-city." They treated patients anywhere there was space, even in the hallway. Noailles explains his embrace of Lacan's thought during this period as an expression of revolt against authority: "Around 1980 we began to be Lacanian," he says. "It was a way of talking: the old standards seemed ridiculous to us. In this repressive time, the orthodoxies of the APA seemed authoritarian, hypocritical. Lacanian thought "presented itself as a very attractive line for young people who wanted to change things, and for whom the only thing they could do was to change the place of the chair – because at this moment to change the place of anything else would end your life." Everyone wanted to see what was going on at Romero, says Noailles. There was enthusiasm, a desire to work together – "the miserable practice you see today of supervising to make money did not yet exist."

They began to forcefully push Lacan, recalls Hirsch, mainly in order to be oppositional. They were fighting for "a space of thought" – it was a way of resisting official discourse. Waving the flag of *lacanismo* was combative, an institutional politics. "We judged people according to how Lacanian they were. This is the juvenile part, but there was a real part too," says Hirsch. They were treating psychotic patients, they were with "*los locos*." And the work of Lacan was the only one with a consistent logic for reading psychosis – which is not nothing, she adds. "Noailles, before he stopped being a psychoanalyst, used to say that he was trained as an analyst in the hospital. And this was because psychosis was in the hospital, not in private offices. Lacanians taught there: Romero was the place to go for psychoanalytic training in the hospital." When well-known foreign analysts, such as Jacques-Alain Miller and Colette Soler, came to Buenos Aires, they visited Romero. "They didn't know what we were doing, but they wanted to come," says Hirsch. She had been in Chile in the early seventies under Allende when they would show foreigners around as observers of the process of socialism. "It was like this in Romero."

At this point, recounts Noailles – the mid-eighties – they also began to teach at the Faculty of Psychology at the University, in the "Department of the French school" – Masotta's department. This was university-based psychoanalysis, he says – "a new species was born." Their students from the Faculty of Psychology also came to Hospital Romero – as many as a hundred at a time. "All of this turned us into celebrities," he says, "we entered the structure of power."

In 1986 Noailles won the post of chief of the women's ward at Romero, and physician-analysts there began giving post-graduate courses at the hospital, which were attended by large crowds of students. "With all these students around, you become a megalomaniac," says Noailles. "It was like Bioy Casares' novel *The Diary of the War of the Pig* – killing off everyone who was not Lacanian. We were like Stalinists." Noailles recalls this period as "the acme of my Lacanian delusion" and the beginning of his disillusionment, mentioning the name of one famous analyst who said that you had to know about Borges and the tango to do psychoanalysis. They thought that psychosis could be explained outside of any organic foundations, says Noailles. The base of the whole thing was the idea that the foreclosure of the Name-of-the-Father could explain everything. Now this is the most difficult thing to maintain. "We created an entire frame of reference around a theory that was only relevant for around 5 percent of the patients."

Noailles' shift in thought coincided with his accession to power in the hospital – he became Director of the ward in 1990. "Something began to happen to me that had never happened before, which is that it is very easy to criticize power but when one has it – this crappy little bit of power ... and one begins to say, 'let's see if the patients get better or not.' My personal impression is that this began to change when I began to get bored of psychotics. They stopped being a marvelous world of madness, poetry and who knows what and began to seem a squalid world of the loss of things, of extreme pain, of poverty ... The impression I had was this: that schizophrenia is a terrible illness, that it screws people up, that it begins to screw people up at a very early age, that many patients do better with drugs and that the explanation of foreclosure seems totally insufficient."

"It worked at first, and then it didn't work any longer," says Hirsch. Why not? "Well, there were *desencuentros* with reality. For one, our techniques weren't as effective as we had hoped. And it subverted the institutional order – we would do things you just cannot do." There were the "exits," for example: teams would go out of the hospital on excursions with patients – "we did all kinds of things." Hirsch remains a passionate advocate of hospital psychoanalysis, but she also seems to sense a battle lost, the end of a golden age. "We psychoanalysts occupied a respected position at Romero, where people were trained. Given Noailles's objectives after his rupture the situation is more difficult now. We are 'bothersome' characters. Romero used to be full of people who wanted to be taught; it no longer is."

## The medical order

The official function of the in-patient ward at Romero was one of risk-prevention: in making decisions as to whether to intern or to release patients, doctors had to balance the threat of suicide or violence – which was the justification for hospitalization – against the institutional logic of limited hospitalization times. While doctors were instructed to move patients in and out of the ward – in Lorna Rhodes' phrase, to produce "empty beds" – and there were attempts by the municipal government to audit the length of patient stays, these remained considerably longer than in comparable institutions in the United States.[13] In the women's ward, patients were sometimes hospitalized for as long as four or five months at public expense. If a case seemed to be intractable, the patient might then be transferred to the city's main psychiatric hospital for women, Moyano, labeled a *manicomio* (asylum) by the analysts at Romero.

Such requirements formed part of what physician-analysts there called "the medical order" – the set of bureaucratic demands governing institutional action.[14] As Alicia Fiorentino, one of the physician-analysts at Romero, put it: "In the hospital, we have to operate within a specific juridical discourse in which we diagnose and medicate the crisis, and then control it." Doctors in the ward saw their real work as analysts to be in tension with this administrative imperative. They occupied an ambiguous position: on the one hand, they were authorized to direct the institution because of their official certification as medical doctors within the order of a public hospital. But their formal status as physicians often came into tension with their professional identity and self-formation as psychoanalysts: the filling out of forms, medication decisions, and patients' somatic complaints interfered with what seemed to be more crucial work on patient subjectivities.

Public hospitals in Argentina provided both steady (if very modest) incomes and a source of prestige for doctors since they remained central sites of medical training and knowledge production. But employment in a psychopathology ward carried the danger of being associated with "psychiatry." While membership in the analytic community connoted cosmopolitan sophistication and political progressivism, analysts associated psychiatry with the medical-penal order, with violent techniques such as shock treatment and lobotomy, and with the authoritarian space of the asylum. For this reason, physician-analysts resisted any ties to biomedical psychiatry. If one was both employed in a psychopathology ward and politically progressive, to insist on being an analyst – and *not* a psychiatrist – was one way to avoid the stigma associated with the asylum. In Hospital Romero the distinction was publicly visible: the urbane, professorial habitus of the analysts contrasted with the harried disrepair of the self-consciously biomedical psychiatrists of the men's ward.

There were twenty beds in the women's ward, and patients slept in parallel rows of wooden cubicles that led toward a meeting room in the back. The open-door policy of the ward meant that patients could move about the hospital grounds during the day but had to have permission to go beyond, into the city. Doctors came in only during the morning, while nurses, residents, and voluntary interns managed the patients the rest of the time. In the afternoon, the doctors typically returned to offices in more prosperous Barrio Norte or Palermo where they saw private clients, often working twelve to fourteen hours per day. The staff gathered at least once a week to discuss the progress of the patients. A computer was used, sometimes to track patients, but also to look up references from a complete index to Lacan's seminars.

Meetings, workshops, classes, and patient presentations provided some solace from the din of the ward itself. One psychology resident called it "the trenches," a term that called attention to the difficulties of defending a sheltered space of thought from the disorder of the ward. In these gatherings, however, the medical order would often impinge from outside: insistent banging on the door by patients, babies' cries, visits from hospital administrators or pharmaceutical company representatives. And it was also within: the patients under discussion had typically been hospitalized either by judicial order, because of suicide risk, or due to questions about the source of somatic syndromes. On particularly chaotic mornings, the head of the ward, Jorge Gitel, would do his best Robin Williams imitation, calling out "Good Morning, Vietnam!" in English. Dark humor was one way to deal with the ironies of the situation: "Another success for psychoanalysis!" he would exclaim when patients failed to improve.

In this context, with neither contract nor couch, there was no question of treating patients with orthodox psychoanalysis. Nonetheless the hospital was a space for generating analytic thought and practice. This was a challenge given that patients in the hospital were far from ideal analysands. The practice of analysis was accomplished through a strict differentiation between the work of the doctor and that of the analyst, which mapped onto a separation between the body and the subjectivity of the patient. Medication played a crucial but unspoken part in maintaining this distinction, as the means for managing symptoms so that subjectivity could be investigated.

## Structuralist dualism

"What I can't explain is how you could have a theoretical construct like *lacanismo* and medicate heavily without having your head explode." Alejandro Noailles was musing about the seemingly contradictory practices of his colleagues in the women's ward. The issue in the ward was not whether or not to use medication. Patients who are hospitalized in a psychiatric ward are not those who raise the question of "cosmetic psychopharmacology," because their suffering is quite obvious and severe.[15] But the everyday use of medication was not much discussed in staff meetings, perhaps because it was not especially interesting: transformations effected by medication did not provide material for analytic conversation.

In the biomedical model, psychotropic medication is understood to restore reason and agency to the subject by directly treating the chemical pathology that has disrupted normal mood or thought. But this is not the only way for experts to understand – indeed, to use – such medication. For physician-analysts in the women's ward, medication did not act directly on the site of disorder. Rather, it worked in an indirect way to help sustain what was simultaneously the object of psychoanalytic knowledge and the source of its authority – patient subjectivity. In this setting, the production of subjectivity practically depended on, but remained conceptually autonomous from, the effects of medication. Physician-analysts considered psychopharmacology to be part of "psychiatric" discourse, an element of the normalizing medical order. This did not mean that they were averse to using medication, but rather that psychoanalysis and pharmacology could not be in dialogue. They might coexist, each in its proper sphere. "Medication works on the symptom, but not on the subject," explained Gabriel, a young psychologist who worked with the patients to develop their narratives. "The neuron is the medium of subjectivity, but they are not the same." It was not that he was against psychiatry, said Norberto Gomez, one of the staff doctors: he was interested in psychiatry and psychopharmacology, he just did not agree with the erasure of subjectivity. "They are different realms," he said: "to medicate a symptom does not require one to stop investigating subjectivity."

Medication took form in the ward as an element of a disciplinary technology: it worked on the body, in order to help produce the subject as a speaking being. As Alicia Fiorentino told me, whereas "neuroscientists give medication so that patients don't speak, I give it to help them speak." Liliana Hirsch echoed this: medication "helps when it accompanies speech." Patients were medicated in order to be calm and manageable enough to engage in some form of talk therapy. "When a psychosis is unraveling," a psychology resident told me, "medication is a necessary intervention – in order to be able to work by using speech."

Gitel explained the division of labor between pharmacology and words in the following way: "I think that psychopharmaceuticals operate to lower the threshold of sensitivity of the stimulus response, but do not operate on the reader. So I can medicate and change the hormonal or neural equilibrium of the apparatus, but the reader, who is the producer of the delusion, is an effect that I don't think is regulated by the neurochemical but is this subject. The delusion comes from here" – from the subject. For Gitel, medication treated only the symptoms, not the structure of the illness. To do work on the structure it was necessary to distinguish problems of the organism from questions of subjectivity.

Gitel described the relation between the organism and the subject as "a dualism, not idealist but structuralist, in which there is no suture between the apparatus of the central nervous system and the reader." The physician treated the brain with molecules, while the analyst dealt with the patient's psyche. I asked Gitel, who is a jazz musician, if it was difficult to reconcile the two roles of physician and analyst. "It is like listening to a concert in two or three planes: on the one hand you listen to the harmony, and on the other you listen to the melody, and on the other, you also listen to the texture. But yes, you have to be a good musician to hear so many planes."

"Psychoanalysis listens for the particularities of the patient," said Cecilia, a psychology resident, "while the pill is for everything. In this point the two discourses are incompatible: in how to understand the subject. Psychiatry thinks it knows and the patient doesn't, whereas psychoanalysis says the patient is the one who knows." But what if the patient claims to have a certain disorder? I asked. This was a knowledge that was difficult to access, she said: "unconscious knowledge is a knowledge that is unrecognized [*desconocido*] by the patient." Patients could not act as experts about their own condition, since unconscious structure could emerge only in the therapeutic encounter. Patients who claimed such authority were often considered "contaminated" either by analytic categories or by biological ones. I was especially interested in moments when the models of the patients came into conflict with those of the analysts.

In one case, a woman had to perform a long sequence of rituals in order to avoid contamination. She washed her hands repeatedly, for hours at a time, including at the hospital. Fiorentino thought that it was a very grave case: "there is no subjective commitment," and so no possibility of transference. While the attending therapist, Cecilia, tried to work on the rituals, the doctors were more interested in the problem of contamination, in the idea underlying these symptoms. What kinds of objects were contaminated? What was the significance of the number of stages of contamination? "Putting oneself in the symptoms won't do anything," advised Gomez. In doing so, "one is sustaining the pleasure of the symptoms." The psychologist should work instead on questions of subjectivity: "what is the structure?" he asked.

"We could arm the rituals," someone suggested. That is, if it was a psychosis, the intervention might involve using the rituals to reinforce the patient's delicate defenses.

"The rituals take five or six hours," Cecilia pointed out. "Maybe we can 'arm' something else?"

"The only observation, in the psychoanalytic sense, would be not the rituals but the obsessions," said Gitel: one should focus not on specific behaviors but on the question of contamination.

But the woman seemed to be more interested in talking with the psychologist about her current symptoms than about her past. "She doesn't talk about her history," Cecilia said. "For her what's going on is genetic, organic." The patient was, it seemed, something of an expert in psychiatric semiology. She claimed to have obsessive-compulsive disorder, and said that it was an organic condition. "She speaks of Henri Ey and manic-depression, about the genetic sources of her illness."

Lacan was explicit that the analyst should not take seriously the patient's self-description. Understanding was not the point of the analytic relation: "If I understand I continue, I don't dwell on it, since I've already understood," he wrote in his seminar on the psychoses. "This brings out what it is to enter the patient's game – it is to collaborate in his resistance. The patient's resistance is always your own, and when a resistance succeeds it is because you are in it up to your neck, because you understand. You understand, you are wrong."[16]

"If we go that way," warned Gitel, "we won't get anywhere. We need to look at the life of the signifier. She cannot reside in speech if she thinks it's genetic. She is not going to talk to you if she doesn't know that it is overdetermined by speech."

"She says that it's a chronic illness, that it needs to be medicated," said Cecilia. "This is a match," Gitel responded. "She is a calculating subject: she is the genetic, and you are the psychologist. Unless she is neurotic the match is equal – genetics versus speech."

## Human specificity

For the analysts, the human was defined by language and subjectivity, as opposed to the animal-like body. Their objection to biomedical psychiatry was to its refusal to admit that humans are distinctive, and therefore require a special kind of technique for knowing. As Fiorentino explained: "The subject of desire is what is left out of psychiatry, and is what psychoanalysis concerns itself with." Whereas psychiatry's emphasis on the biological threatened to erase subjectivity, psychoanalysis was concerned precisely with bringing it out.

Analysts argued that their site of investigation was beyond what "objective" science could approach. Gitel defined the epistemological status of psychoanalysis as a "conjectural science" based on the premise that "man is an incarnate being, differentiated from animals by his use of speech." Language placed human psychic phenomena outside of the realm of the natural sciences.[17] "In medicine they look at the sign, and are not interested in hearing the patient speak," said Fiorentino. "Psychoanalytic symptoms," on the other hand, "are read through words."

The human transcended the organism, and subjectivity was what was universal within the human individual. "Psychoanalysis points at something irreducible in human being which is subjectivity," said Gomez. "Subjectivity is of each one, it is the most personal of each one. What one tries to read in the discourse of the patient is not the history of the patient, but the impressions of subjectivity in the history of the patient – these points of rupture in the story. The posture of each one in front of his own story."

The specificity of its object – human subjectivity – lent psychoanalysis its characteristic of being a science of the individual, whose logic was distinct from the biomedical. As Fiorentino told me, "Psychoanalysis differs from psychiatry because it is interested in the individual case as its clinical object, not in generalized diagnostic categories. Each madness has its own logic."

How does one come to know this object, characterized by its singularity? In asking whether or not psychoanalysis should be considered a science, philosopher John Forrester argues that psychoanalysis is an example of "thinking in cases."[18] In its practice, a set of paradigmatic cases form exemplars that serve as models for analysts' encounters with their patients. These cases come from Freud's founding texts: Dora, Schreber, Little Hans. According to Forrester, this way of thinking forms a distinctive "style of reasoning" within the sciences, as opposed to deductive logic or probabilistic analysis. Importantly, sciences of the case not only study individuals, but also participate in their production. In hospital psychiatry, for example, the patient's file is not just a source for understanding the patient's past, but in fact produces that past in concrete form, in the written traces left by consecutive doctors and therapists.[19]

In the women's ward, individual cases were produced around practices of writing and metaphors of reading. The thick folders of repeatedly admitted patients contained psychiatrists' changing diagnoses, the notes of various analysts, medication histories. And the process of coming up with an understanding of the patient's psychic structure was spoken of as a "reading." But in the hospital one did not encounter texts but patients, and they were generally in bad shape, not immediately willing to provide adequate narratives. They were often silent, or crying, sometimes heavily sedated. In order to do psychoanalytic work with such patients, they had to be assimilated to discursive needs. This meant finding analyzable stories in the patients' utterances, stories that pointed toward an identifiable structure such as hysteria, phobia, or melancholia. "Interesting" patients were those whose stories were available, and who made an analytic reading possible.

The complex labor of shaping interpretable narratives was performed by psychology residents and student-interns, trained in what to look for by academic study of the classic works, and finding in the hospital an opportunity to bring these texts to life in the clinic. The psychologists' theoretical background from the university was usually psychoanalytic; study groups and courses in the hospital continued this training in the light of experiences they were having with patients. Most psychology residents told me that they chose to come to Romero because of its reputation: it was known in psychoanalytic circles for its Lacanian orientation. Given the lack of employment opportunities for psychology graduates, entrance to the residency was highly competitive. Of twelve hundred applicants, only twenty-five received posts. More generally in Buenos Aires, a major reason that it was possible to do psychoanalytic work in the hospital setting was the oversupply of psychologists in the labor market. In many public hospitals, psychologists worked for free, to gain experience and in the hope of attaining a rare paid post.

Let me give an example of how patients' stories were elicited in order to generate clues about psychic structure. A 53-year-old woman was interned in the ward after attempting suicide with a pair of scissors. She suffered from both hallucinations and depression. Carla, a psychology resident in her late twenties, described the situation to the staff in the women's ward: the woman claimed to hear the voices of birds telling her to kill herself, but Carla was skeptical about the "reality" of the hallucinations. Because they were inconsistent, Carla suspected that the patient was simulating, feigning delusion in order to convince her daughter to move back into the apartment with her grandchild.

Gomez disagreed, suggesting that the hallucinations tranquilized her fear – that the delusion was a "restitution." It was crucial to know whether the delusion was real or simulated because the psychic structure would determine Carla's approach. The immediate problem, for Carla, was that the patient refused any psychotherapeutic interventions: she would not even speak to Carla. Sebastian, a psychiatry resident who was working with the same patient, had an explanation for the patient's frustrating silence, but one that was not taken up by the analysts: that the side effects of the powerful anti-psychotic medications she was taking had made it physically difficult for her to speak – that she was "neurolepticized."

Several weeks after the patient's admittance, there had been little progress. In the hospital they were at a standstill. I accompanied Carla to her supervision with an analyst in Barrio Once, Mariano Cavelli, who worked with many of the psychology residents at Romero. Cavelli is tall and thin, in his early forties, with the requisite analytic goatee and a poker face. A front room in his upper floor apartment, with high ceilings, oriental rugs, and a single bed as divan, functioned as his office. Cavelli listened to the story that Carla had reconstructed from the patient's file, which included the notes of a long series of physicians and psychologists. There were several key incidents from the woman's past to recount. When she was a child she had fled political repression in the provinces with her family. There was the story of a rape attempt, her troubled early marriage, her son's departure for the Malvinas War. Carla then told Cavelli about the voices of birds telling the woman to commit suicide. She complained that she had yet to get anything to work with: she didn't know what to do – the patient would not speak, she would only make gestures, balling up her fists. Carla said that she was embarrassed about not having done anything – the patient tired her, she seemed impenetrable.

After listening to the case, Cavelli focused on the early incident – the family's flight from political repression – and began to construct a narrative. "I'm going to make a hypothesis, to invent a meaning," he began. "Hypotheses are images made in order to intervene." His hypothesis was that there had been some kind of catastrophe, perhaps a bomb that fell, leaving a hole – an *agujero*: There was an event, he mused, a moment: the three days of the 1955 "Revolution of Liberty," in which people had to flee.[20] In this period there was a saying, "the birds are coming," which referred to the navy's planes, coming with bombs.

"You could call this a coincidence, but I don't believe in coincidence," said Cavelli. "She has lived through a situation – a trauma, not in the classical psychoanalytic sense, with the father and genitalia, but a catastrophe, something concrete that happened in the Real. What we call trauma is the hole that the bomb leaves." Cavelli's analysis was "divinatory" in the sense that Carlo Ginzburg indicates: a form of detective work that involves gathering traces and symptoms into a singular and meaningful case.[21] "Where do we take this, transferentially?" asked Cavelli. The patient was not associating; the case was not yet showing itself as a catastrophic hole. "But the gestures – the fists, the hair – these are signs, hieroglyphics." Carla listened intently. "She is sitting like a baby with these gestures. I will make another hypothesis," he continued. This one was a warning. "A sign is not nothing. Killing herself would be the highest expression of staying put, in the place with the *agujero*," the hole. "In psychoanalysis," he said, "one tries to bring the subject near the catastrophe, to the Real, whereas she is trying to flee the catastrophe."

How, then, to bring her out of this? Cavelli suggested that Carla construct a text with the patient: "The position is to accompany her toward the construction of a history. The analyst takes notes, is the one who writes this catastrophic bond with her. What can we do in order to join with her in making an *historia* – a letter to the city? Why don't you try to write something with her?" When Carla asked if it was possible to make a diagnosis, Cavelli said: "what matters is the making of an *historia*."

## Authorship

Scholars of scientific knowledge production have recently turned to Michel Foucault's classic lecture, "What is an Author?" to frame questions about the historical and contemporary role of authorship in both validating and rewarding scientific creation.[22] In the lecture, Foucault argued that, during the early modern period, there was a reversal in the respective role of the author between science and literature: scientific discourses no longer had to be linked to their author's name in order to carry authority, whereas literature now required an author in order to circulate. In the lecture, Foucault noted the recent invention of a different type of discourse – one that fit the model neither of literature nor science. These were evolving forms of knowledge that nonetheless remained linked to their founders' names. The founders of such discourses continued to be present in subsequent transformations of the field of knowledge, even as new authors came into the fold. Psychoanalysis and Marxism were exemplary of these author-centered discourses.[23] In the lecture, Foucault outlined a possible research program that would follow the trajectories of such discursive formations "according to their modes of existence" – how they "vary with each culture and are modified within each."[24] The discourse of Lacanian psychoanalysis in the women's ward provided an optimal site for such an inquiry.

I spoke with members of the staff about the role of these founding texts, of key cases like Schreber or Dora, when patients in the hospital were so unlike these classical figures. Their responses complicated Forrester's analysis somewhat: for them the exemplary case, the "paradigm," was both the condition of possibility and a potential hindrance to psychoanalytic understanding. Freud as the founding author was present, but instructed *against* the automatic reproduction of his texts. The exemplary case was a convention, but one that had to be overcome.

AL: When your patients are not the typical psychoanalytic patients of Freud's couch, and yet the founding texts speak of such patients, how can one improvise a method? In the encounter with patients, what is your relationship to these texts?

Jorge Gitel: One has a tendency to make references to "the cases" all the time. For instance, in psychosis one is always referring oneself to two or three or to one above all, which was the Schreber case which, okay, it is a written text, we know that he never met with an analyst, he was never analyzed. One always tends to refer oneself to these typical cases. But it seems to me that the movement would be to be able to leave this permanent reference. If not, you cannot listen, you have completely stopped listening as a result of having taken a reference. This, it seems to me, is a daily clinical challenge for us. I think it is a question of daily practice.

Liliana Hirsch: In general, the cases that Freud published – four or five of them in all of his work – have been converted into paradigms. This makes it easier to think the clinic, and is also an obstacle to thinking the clinic. It gives us the chance to know how Freud thought about a clinical case, and gives us the stereotype that … all the hysterics are like Dora or that all the phobics are Little Hans and all the psychotics are Schreber. This is a prejudice that training gives rise to when one has just begun. It seems to me that to break with this is part of the work of those who participate in the training of the analyst, and is part of the work of the analyst himself, to make his own clinical course. I would say: to make of his case one in itself, something that for the patient results in a *writing*. If ever a paradigm for psychoanalysis arrived it would be welcome. The truth is that there are few cases like this, so typical. The cases continue to be singular. And this is what Freud taught, beyond whether or not hysterics are like Dora. That one has to be able to read the singularity of a case.

## Authorization

In the women's ward, the role of the founding psychoanalytic authors was not only to provide exemplary cases that might help in the interpretation of patient narratives. Their ongoing importance in the hospital was signaled by the decoration of the staff meeting room, where doctors, residents, and nurses met to discuss the progress of their cases: along with a chart listing the histories of the interned patients there were two framed black and white photographs, one of Sigmund Freud and the other of Jacques Lacan. What were these authorities doing on the wall, and how did their lingering presence relate to what was being said before their eyes? The question concerned the kind of discourse that was being practiced in the ward: was it scientific, aesthetic, or something else?

For Freud the invention of psychoanalysis heralded a scientific revolution that hinged on the discovery of the unconscious – a discovery he had made through a rigorous practice of analyzing his own dreams. He announced this discovery as a third blow – following Copernicus' restructuring of the cosmos and Darwin's reordering of the animal world – to human narcissism, to the notion of man as an autonomous, divine being at the center of the universe. The discovery was of the inevitable inscrutability of the self, that the ego "is not even master in its own house, but must content itself with scanty information of what is going on unconsciously in its mind."[25]

If knowledge of the unconscious was not directly accessible to the self, the question then became: how could one access and work on that which is hidden from view? Was there an instrument or device that could make it appear? And how could one guarantee the veracity of such knowledge? Philosopher Isabelle Stengers compares psychoanalysis – at least in its origin – to the experimental sciences, which are based on techniques of verification and purification. For Freud, the disappointment of hypnosis had been that it produced false witnesses, created artifacts. In his invention of the analytic scene, Freud sought to purge the artifact of influence through the technique of transference, which would transform the neurosis into an artificial illness so that it could be worked on in the "laboratory" of the analytic relation. The relationship between analyst and analysand was the crucial site of work, the laboratory in which the unconscious became manifest.[26]

Freud and his followers gave detailed instructions as to how the analytic scene should unfold – such as the position of the couch with respect to the analyst, the length of the session, and so on. The effort to standardize this process has been a subject of considerable discord within and among psychoanalytic institutions.

While Freud's discovery of the unconscious was the result of an individualized process of self-analysis, the fecundity of psychoanalysis then depended on the capacity to reproduce this process in others. Here the analytic institution has played the role of guarantor, through the standardization of procedures and an ongoing "genealogical" link to the founder.

My question for the analysts at Romero was whether the hospital could function as a site for the reproduction of psychoanalytic knowledge. Was the women's ward performing the role of an analytic institute? Although they acknowledged that Romero had once been a site for training, the analysts emphasized that authorization involved an experience of self-transformation that was distinct from the work I was following in the ward. This experience occurred in the intimacy of the relation between analyst and analysand. The key term, in their response, was "transference."

Alicia Fiorentino: Transference is a concept and it is also a practice. The transmission of psychoanalysis includes the question of transference. That is, one listens to one's masters in a particular manner ... I don't know how to explain this because it is understood ... It is not only to go to read and learn, but also to be taken by the experience. Because of this, to be an analyst first one has to analyze oneself.

Only their own experience of the analytic scene could lead to authorization as an analyst – that is, to the validated capacity to access the subjective structures of others:

Liliana Hirsch: The personal analysis, I would say, is what most differentiates the practice of analysis from any other practice ... This experience is what puts one in the position, in the condition of saying of oneself that one is an analyst ... And it does not have to do with what she has read or with what another tells her or with what a title authorizes her to do, but with her own experience of analysis, of having located in her analysis the routes of her own subjectivity. This brings her to position herself as an analyst for another. In this sense, it is totally different from any other practice where the subjectivity of the analyst is not included in the practice. In ours, it is included in order to be able to exclude it.

The centrality of this subjective experience to the capacity to access truth distinguished psychoanalysis from other sciences. As Norberto put it, "Without any doubt, methodologically, science necessarily tries to exclude subjectivity. In the scientific method subjectivity cannot be brought in, which doesn't mean that science is not useful. But in the field of psychoanalysis, this logic doesn't have any space."

Unlike the natural sciences, psychoanalysis does not have a "nonascetic subject of knowledge."[27] The capacity to access truth remains dependent upon the self-work of the knower. Only in going through the self-analysis, in discovering one's own "routes of subjectivity," does one become qualified to become an analyst. And one cannot speak authoritatively about psychoanalysis until and unless one has had this experience. Psychoanalytic authorization thus has characteristics of both *askesis* and revelation: it requires the discovery within one's self, through work on oneself in the analytic scene, of the truth of Freud's discovery of the unconscious.

According to Stengers, by making access to knowledge dependent on the experience of the analytic scene, psychoanalysis claims the privilege of not needing to give an explanation. "At the heart of the analytic scene there appears to function a very curious 'black box': the analytic scene itself."[28] As opposed to the black boxes of "hard" science, which are devices that confer meaning on certain facts, "the analytic scene appears to create those who will have the right to speak about it, and therefore operates in itself as the foundation of right."[29] As Alicia said to me, somewhat pointedly: "You have to be included in this experience to think about the question of transference and the relation with the masters."

Thus, although Lacan proclaimed, "the psychoanalyst is authorized only by himself," this work can be accomplished only in relation to a master, and the passage has a pregiven structure.[30] The technique of transference – institutionalized through the reproduction of the analytic scene – connects one to the founding experience of the initial "author," making it possible both to know one's own subjective trajectory and also to create an *historia* for others.

## Psychic structure

In order to decide what sort of intervention to make, analysts had to know what they had before them. The psychic structure indicated the position of the subject, which in turn directed the strategy of the analyst. The initial task, then, was to locate the patient according to one of the basic structures outlined by Freud. This was quite different, analysts emphasized, from making a "psychiatric" diagnosis, which was done only for bureaucratic purposes.

The most important structural distinction to be made was between neurosis and psychosis. This distinction structured the analyst's approach to the patient. Whereas with neurotic patients one could work with the tool of transference, there was no possibility of achieving transference in psychosis. Freud explained the difference between the two structures in terms of the site of psychic conflict: "Neurosis is the result of a conflict between the ego and the id" – that is, an internal psychic conflict – whereas "psychosis is the outcome of a disturbance in the relations between the ego and the external world."[31] The split between the ego and the outside world accounted for the separation from reality that marked psychosis. The resulting delusion, wrote Freud, "is the patch that covers this breach in the relation between the ego and the external world." At a basic level, then, the presence of delusion was an indication of a psychotic structure. Moreover, the implication of the theory was that such delusion performed an important role in allowing the psychotic patient to function despite his or her "loss of reality." This made it a delicate problem to work with psychotic patients: one did not want to strip patients of their defenses.

For Lacan, translating Freud's spatial scheme into linguistic terms, psychosis was characterized by a failure to enter the symbolic order. He described a process of "foreclosure" in which an unwanted thought or image was expelled rather than repressed, a refusal of symbolization that had catastrophic effects. Lacan located the emergence of the psychotic delusion in this inability to internalize the superego, or "Name-of-the-Father" function through repression: "It is the lack of the Name-of-the-Father in that place which, by the hole that it opens up in the signified, sets off the cascade of reshapings of the signifier from which the increasing disaster of the imaginary proceeds, until the level is reached at which signifier and signified are stabilized in the delusional metaphor."[32] Cast outside of the symbolic order, the psychotic remained in a condition of ontological otherness, unable to enter into inter-subjective relations.

In a lecture to a group of medical students, Gitel outlined his approach to psychosis. Psychosis is not an illness, he said, but is, rather, the patient's position in front of reality: "hallucination is the lived language of the subject." The patient's delusion is an attempt to restore lost ties with reality – a "restitution." And since there is no transference in psychosis, one cannot work with the tools of traditional psychoanalysis. In fact, Gitel warned strongly against treating psychotic patients as one might treat neurotics, by trying to use the technique of transference: in doing this one might unleash the psychosis further, destabilize it. It was thus important to identify the structure early on. Neither medication nor psychoanalytic treatment could cure the psychotic. "Delusion is not medicable," said Gitel, "because, fortunately, there is no idea that can be changed by a pharmaceutical. What lowers is the level of anxiety, of anguish, and the productivity that this generates."

Gitel described the temporality of psychosis, based on a moment of rupture. He drew a schema of the history of a psychosis, in which there is a before and after the unraveling: "this episode represents a break with reality." It could take several months for the patient to take on this history, a process that included notes on therapy sessions, weekly staff meetings, perhaps a workshop, and the therapists' external supervisions with senior analysts.

How did this theoretical understanding of psychosis relate to the pragmatic task of dealing with psychotic patients in the hospital? What did a psychoanalytic approach look like in a situation in which the technology of psychoanalytic cure – the transference relation – was explicitly inoperative?

"Psychosis is a limitation of psychoanalysis," admitted Liliana Hirsch. Psychoanalysis "is a tool that helps me to think the subjective position of the psychotic. You cannot apply the same thing to a neurosis as to a psychosis. One does a 'deconstruction' with psychoanalysis. People criticize the use of psychoanalysis in psychosis with the idea of using a couch – this is not done, it would be an outrage [*una barbaridad*]."

"In psychosis a cure through therapy is not possible," said Gabriel, "but one can stabilize it." As opposed to neurosis, the treatment is not based in interpretation. The object is not to expand the delusion further by talking about it, but to deflate it. In fact, the act of therapeutic intervention can have a dangerous effect on the patient. "Speech can perform an unraveling," explained Gabriel. "One has to be careful with psychotics," said Rosana, a staff psychologist. "It doesn't help to listen to them."

Since transference was impossible, the idea of "arming" – or reinforcing – the patient's delusion was an alternative technique for treating psychotics in the hospital. Analysts tried to help such patients "construct a fiction" that would enable them to manage in the outside world.

A psychiatrist in the men's ward, Gustavo Rechtman, argued that the rigid distinction between neurotic and psychotic structure produced a group of marginalized others. "This question of the psychic structure," he said, "is fatalistic, conservative. In this culture if you call someone psychotic they are marginalized as a completely outside group: 'We are the neurotics, and they are the psychotics.'" Rechtman cited the results of mood-stabilizing medication to illustrate the problem of this way of classifying patients: "If you just give a bipolar patient sixty milligrams of lithium, one who might seem really crazy, he will be normal, like you or me." One may *seem* crazy but not *be* crazy, and it is the effect of the drug that provides the evidence. For Rechtman, this was an ethical question: in the act of diagnosis, the psychiatrist had the power to decide whether to include or exclude this person from the collective of the "normal."

The status of bipolar disorder was a source of controversy among doctors with differing theoretical orientations at Hospital Romero. In the men's ward, the condition was widely diagnosed and was the subject of the transnational genetic study that I described in Chapter 1. Within a biomedical framework, bipolar disorder is an organic problem of mood regulation, in which the patient alternates between states of intense agitation and heightened sensibility and periods of serious depression and withdrawal. Unlike schizophrenia, the disorder does not necessarily have a dire prognosis; it is potentially treatable – though not curable – with mood stabilizers such as lithium. There is even speculation that the disorder is linked to particularly creative personalities, to well-known artists and writers like Van Gogh and Edgar Allan Poe.[33] But the disorder is threatening to psychoanalytic epistemology since it has the potential to disrupt the strict differentiation between neurotic and psychotic structure. This is because in the manic phase of bipolar disorder, the patient may suffer delusions and hallucinations, but then, when stabilized with medication, these recede.

While Freud wrote of mania and melancholia, these cannot easily be assimilated to the biomedical concept of bipolar disorder. Freud explained mania in terms of the life history of the subject and a dynamic theory of psychic energy:

> In mania, the ego must have got over the loss of the object (or its mourning over the loss, or perhaps the object itself), and thereupon the whole quota of anticathexis which the painful suffering of melancholia had drawn to itself from the ego and "bound" will have become available. Moreover, the manic subject plainly demonstrates his liberation from the object which was the cause of his suffering, by seeking like a ravenously hungry man for new object-cathexes.[34]

DSM-based psychiatry, in contrast, emphasizes general descriptions that can be answered by a brief questionnaire. From the biomedical vantage, the content of delusion is not important to the diagnosis or treatment of bipolar disorder – since it is a question of mood, rather than thought, it is the patient's bodily chemistry rather than the subject and its history that is the source of pathology. Moreover, the use of the presence of delusion to distinguish between neurotic and psychotic structure no longer makes sense when the presence of delusion in the patient is unstable – that is, dependent on alterable neurochemistry.

Bipolar disorder was thus a dubious category for the analysts in the women's ward. Liliana Hirsch implied that the diagnosis had been invented to help sell psychopharmaceuticals. "The fashion of bipolarity is winning because it is something so objectifiable," she said. "The politics of psychiatry is correlated to the consumption of psychopharmaceuticals: 'bipolarity' justifies an exaggerated quantity of pharmaceutical consumption." Gitel had a more complex view. He accepted the existence of bipolar disorder but did not see it as commensurable with the analysis of patients in terms of their subjective structures. He considered bipolar disorder to be a physical condition that could exist parallel to either of the Freudian structures of neurosis and psychosis. He could thus speak of mania in the psychoanalytic sense and bipolar disorder as two distinct aspects of a patient. For instance, Gitel and Rosana, a staff psychologist, discussed a patient who had stopped eating, who became obsessed with death following a car accident. "She doesn't think she's ill," explained Rosana. The patient was an insomniac, disturbing other patients at night. "It is a mania, in the more Lacanian sense," explained Gitel, "the accident produced a question in the Real. And she's also bipolar."

Noailles attacked the notion that one could distinguish medication issues from structural questions. Each contaminated the other, he said: structural analysis was often used to make medication decisions. Physician-analysts diagnosed psychosis in structural terms, then prescribed anti-psychotic medication to alleviate the symptoms. This meant that delusional symptoms in bipolar disorder led inexorably to the use of anti-psychotics – and in Argentina, this usually meant the cheaper, older generation drugs whose side effects, such as parkinsonism, could be devastating – and could mimic the symptoms of schizophrenia. Noailles thought there was a public health disaster in Argentina, in which large numbers of patients were kept sedated and unnecessarily institutionalized through misdiagnosis and the wrong medication. This, for Noailles, was the scandal of treating hospitalized patients psychoanalytically: "If you're Lacanian you always diagnose psychosis," he said. "There's no choice, because the texture of the theory brings you to it. It is inevitable: 'the elemental phenomenon, non-dialectizable,' and then you go and you give halpidol or olanzapine."

According to Noailles, the effect of mood stabilizers on his patients had forced him to rethink his theory of the human subject. He found that a number of the patients that he had diagnosed as psychotic could be given mood stabilizers and function well, could even achieve transference in analysis. If apparently psychotic patients could be brought back to normality through lithium treatment, the otherness of delusional structure was called into question. As he told me:

> If foreclosure didn't function for me anymore, and if there was an entity that more than 1 percent of the population had, and I gave drugs that worked, how could I think that this was purely the oedipal constellation? It is like having an enormous abscess in your thorax and supposing that it is because of a conflict, and taking antibiotics and the abscess goes away and supposing this is because of the analytic interpretation. It began to seem very obtuse to me.

What happened when these different positions encountered one another? It is illustrative to look at the case of a member of the Argentine bipolar patient support group (FUBIPA) who was hospitalized in the women's ward in a manic state. The young woman, Marta, initially tried to educate her doctors about bipolar disorder, giving them literature from the support group and asking for lithium treatment. She was a particularly difficult patient, with many outbursts requiring attendance by the residents and tranquilizing medication. And although she was given mood stabilizers and other drugs, her condition seemed to worsen during her stay the hospital.

Marta's disturbances could be read in various ways. Sebastian, the psychiatry resident who was treating her, saw her as a "resistant bipolar," that is, a bipolar patient for whom the standard medication indications did not work. For him this implied that one should experiment with other drug combinations – perhaps an atypical anti-psychotic combined with a mood stabilizer. "Nothing can be accomplished here through chemicals," responded Fiorentino. "One can medicate for bipolarity," she said early on, "but not for hysteria." For her, to call the patient a "resistant bipolar" was to ignore the singularity of the case. "This is the thing about human beings," she told me, "they talk. And they thus become unique – you cannot place them in clear categories."

Marta's symptoms had different possible meanings: if she spent too much money, this might be a characteristic of bipolar disorder, or else she was "performing" its symptoms, since she knew the disorder's characteristics so well. Alcohol abuse? Again, it could be part of the bipolar symptomatology or else an identification with her father, who was an alcoholic. The questions that were posed among the staff had to do not with medication, but with her personal life: Why did she identify with men? What had happened in her love relations? Why did she think the hospital staff were uninterested in her? Because she reported hearing her dead father's voice, the possibility was raised of a psychosis. The psychologist noted that the first episode of her illness had come not long after her father's death, and so the problem of unfinished mourning became an axis of reflection in the case.

Gitel distinguished Marta's bipolar disorder from the "structural" issues involved in the case: there was perhaps a problem with her central nervous system, but the real question had to do with the subject. "It is a problem with love," he said. "She is bipolar, but what is the structure here?" he asked. "There is something more than being bipolar, it is a Freudian mania." As for medication, he wanted to be "empirical." "Let's go with a classic," he proposed – an anxiolytic and an anti-psychotic.

Like her father, Marta was a poet, and the analysts saw her writings as a possible place for "building a sustainable fiction" in order to construct a workable subjectivity and come to terms with her ambiguous sexuality. But the case became less hopeful as time passed and her actions grew more extreme: she attempted suicide twice within the hospital grounds, once by cutting her wrists with sharp rocks, and later with an overdose of medication. She routinely created scenes in the ward by throwing herself against the walls and furniture, and the staff physician-analysts instructed residents not to speak with her, but to directly inject tranquilizing medication.

"She doesn't have anguish in a Lacanian sense, something one could work with," Fiorentino worried. "this delusion, this mania, what can we do with it?" Eventually the staff agreed to describe her as having a "borderline personality" – a structure between neurosis and psychosis.[35] A psychology resident told me: "the bipolar disorder is child's play compared to the personality disorder she has."

Eventually a bureaucratic problem arose: Marta had been interned more than sixty-nine days, and special paperwork was required to keep her longer. In the space of the clinic, such demands came from the administrative rationality of the medical order, oriented toward reintegrating patients into society. As Fiorentino told me, "they think that by limiting internment times they can make psychotics into normal people," but it was impossible: "there is no social space for the psychotic."

"Maybe she needs a change," someone suggested. As the crises continued, the staff prepared to give up, and began the process of transferring her to the infamous woman's asylum, Hospital Moyano. "But what can they do for her in Moyano?" someone asked. There was no answer. "There just are patients like this," said Fiorentino to console Marta's psychologist.

Then, quite suddenly, Marta improved, and was released by the end of the month. Sebastian attributed the change to the correct medication formulation – valproate and clozapine – while the psychologist thought it had to do with a change in the therapeutic strategy, which had enabled her to face the problem of mourning in a new way. Marta left as she had arrived, without a definitive diagnosis or course of treatment. It was not clear whether her improvement was due to the medication, to the psychologist's approach, or to the threat of a transfer to Moyano.

In the women's ward, the distinction between neurosis and psychosis worked to differentiate normal from pathological, as Gitel noted in his lecture: "Eighty to ninety percent of us have neurotic structures. The rest are psychotic or perverse." Bipolar disorder and its treatment raised the question of whether a patient could move, via pharmaceutical intervention, from one state to the other, from psychotic to neurotic. Whether or not medication – in this case, a mood stabilizer – transformed the person, or rather what kind of transformation it effected, depended upon what stance the expert held *vis-à-vis* the configuration of the human person.

Given structuralist dualism, the pharmaceutical altered neither the delusion of the patient nor the knowledge system of the doctor. As Gitel said, "there is no idea that can be changed by a pharmaceutical." Bipolarity and psychosis could exist, side by side, in the organism and the subject respectively. The pharmaceutical worked on the organism so that humanness, as language – that which is impervious to chemical intervention – could emerge. It enabled the subject to speak. But then when the patient spoke, it was often in the language of neuroscience and genetics. The "match" between genetics and speech was a contest not only over how to name disorder, but also over who would be in charge of applying the medication, and to what end.

The question of the task of the healer and the role of the drug hinged on where to locate disorder. Was it in the organism or in language? If it was in language, treatment demanded an art that could never be encompassed by neuroscience. The attempt to make psychiatry a science was doomed, for Lacanians in Romero, because humans are a particular kind of being, "differentiated from animals by their use of speech," as Gitel put it. Or as Fiorentino said, "a mouse can have heart disease but it cannot be hysteric."

Structuralist dualism was a solution to the difficulty, in the public hospital, of being both a physician and an analyst. It allowed the realm of subjectivity to be bracketed off from the medical order, and medication mediated this function. The danger, as Noailles warned, was that in devoting themselves to the task of being analysts rather than physicians, they might produce more harm than good.

Referring to the Sokal debate, Rechtman told me: "We shouldn't be worrying about postmodernism here in Argentina – we need to meet basic health needs." He was pointing to the country's ambiguous status between developed and underdeveloped, and arguing that certain kinds of questions were not relevant in the space of the Buenos Aires public hospital, given the very palpable differences between health infrastructures in Argentina and in the North. This issue was clear when the doctors in the women's ward shut the door to the clinic and began to talk – not only about Freud and Lacan, but also about Spinoza, Hegel, Derrida: you could almost forget that you were in a crumbling hospital in a marginal sector of the city, with patients that were often illiterate and outcast. In this context, the analysts' distinctive use of medication – to sustain subjectivity rather than to transform pathology – made the hospital a place where one could remain an analyst, despite the exigencies of the medical order.

# 4

# Living with neuroscience

"This is for your fieldwork," remarks Pablo Velicovsky as he hands me a copy of the municipal hospital bulletin, which features a story entitled "The Psychoanalysis of Hunger." For Pablo, the bulletin is a typical example of the assumption, within the Buenos Aires *mundo-psi*, that psychoanalysis is a panacea for all social problems. I am sitting at the Hospital Romero cafeteria with Pablo and his colleague, Gustavo Rechtman, two psychiatrists in the men's ward. The turns of the conversation reflect the different priorities of these two colleagues. Gustavo describes the institutional structure of Romero: the hospital takes in many patients from the *villas miserias* (shanties) surrounding Buenos Aires, and from the provinces, since rural health care is quite poor and the hospital is located at the edge of the city. Meanwhile Pablo grabs a napkin and my pen to sketch a description of a behavioral genetics experiment involving chickens that he has just read about: scientists in the United States have transplanted genes from one chick to another and then studied its behavior profile, as mapped by three cameras in a closed dark box in which the chick's beak was painted fluorescent. Pablo is an enthusiast of all things "neuroscientific." He is editor of a new journal that tries to bring the latest news from North American neuroscience to Argentina. Gustavo is more skeptical about the immediate benefits of such scientific developments, and prefers to talk about problems of poverty and underdevelopment in Argentina.

As we get up and head toward the psychopathology service, I ask Gustavo what he means by the word "underdevelopment." "You're about to see it," he says, pointing ahead. A few moments later, as we walk through the men's ward, past rows of cubicles, Gustavo gestures around at the dilapidated surroundings: "See what I mean?" The head of the service, Alejandro Noailles, has been meeting with contractors to arrange the renovation that will be done with funds from the genetic study of bipolar disorder being conducted in the ward. Gustavo is interested in adolescence, unemployment, and suicide as subjects for research. He mentions a recent study of health indicators in Latin America: despite respectable per capita spending on health, Argentina has a high infant mortality rate due to easily preventable infections.[1]

He and Pablo are *bichos raros*, he says, "strange creatures": socially concerned psychiatrists who lend credence to biological research. No one thinks about these things here, he complains. If you propose that there may be something "natural" about behavior you are immediately associated with the right wing. Mention genetics and people think of eugenics and Nazism. It is considered reactionary in many circles to speak of a biological basis for schizophrenia. What is really reactionary, he thinks, is to ignore progress in medication and treatment because of a long-dead ideology.

In this chapter, I describe the practice of a group of young psychiatrists in Buenos Aires who see themselves as rebels against the orthodoxies of psychoanalysis. They seek to reassert their medical identity, which implies membership in a transnational scientific community. Their authorization of knowledge-claims in research and in the clinic refers to recent developments in cosmopolitan science rather than to founders of a discourse. This practice generates a distinctive subject of illness as well: rather than illuminating a hidden psychic structure whose contours are the result of a unique personal history, they treat a disordered neurochemistry whose irruptions into the self can be managed either through chemical or behavioral intervention.

The politics involved in these psychiatrists' adoption of cosmopolitan biomedicine are distinctive to their milieu. The reasons why a psychiatrist in Buenos Aires might advocate a neuroscientific perspective in the late 1990s were different from those of a psychiatrist in Boston. In the United States such an orientation was neither oppositional nor avowedly political. Rather, it was becoming technocratic, and for an ambitious young psychiatrist it was almost *de rigueur*. In Argentina, in contrast, these doctors sought to develop a politically engaged biomedical psychiatry whose aims would be congruent with the specific needs of the mental health situation in the country. Improving the care of the mentally ill, they argued, required a rationally managed mental health sector that was attuned to recent developments in cosmopolitan science. These psychiatrists advocated the adoption of the DSM system and other rationalizing techniques as an element of what French psychiatrist Pierre Pichot has called the "remedicalization of psychiatry."[2]

Adopting the new biomedical psychiatry would also imply a change in the structure of authority between doctors and patients: from the paternalistic attitude of traditional medicine, to a "service-provider" model, in which the patient would take an active role in determining treatment and even in guiding research. These doctors opposed both an old guard, asylum-based organicist psychiatry that they considered politically reactionary, and a psychodynamically oriented "social" psychiatry that they saw as anti-scientific and as a posture that served to replicate professional power rather than improve the health of patients. Mostly male and in their thirties, they were especially scornful of the prevalence of Lacanian psychoanalysis in Argentine public hospital settings.

## Illness and the person

Several times, members of this group brought up a 1998 article by the American neuroscientist Eric Kandel in order to characterize the current situation in the Argentine mental health field. In the article, Kandel describes what it was like to be trained as a psychiatrist at Harvard in the early 1960s, when a psychoanalytic approach was pervasive in leading American teaching hospitals.[3] He writes that teaching was dogmatic, that little reading other than Freud was done, and that there was no interest in thinking about any physical basis for mental illness. Psychiatry was a discipline in intellectual decline, he recalls. Biomedical reformers in Buenos Aires thought that Kandel's characterization of the 1960s American scene described their situation well, and the article gave them hope that a similar transformation could take place there.

In the article, Kandel articulates a neural basis for the treatment of behavioral disorder. He proposes a set of principles for linking psychiatric practice to the brain sciences – for subsuming the psychotherapeutic within a neuroscientific model. Kandel argues that since all human behavior has an organic basis, it makes sense to treat behavior problems as brain disorders. He locates human specificity in the complexity of the brain, rather than in the mystery of the psyche:

> The actions of the brain underlie not only relatively simple motor behaviors, such as walking and eating, but all of the complex cognitive actions, conscious and unconscious, that we associate with specifically human behavior, such as thinking, speaking, and creating works of literature, music, and art. As a corollary, behavior disorders that characterize psychiatric illness are disturbances of brain function, even in those cases where the causes of the disturbances are clearly environmental in origin.[4]

In US psychiatry by the 1990s, this position was the prevailing viewpoint. Critics of this transformation have argued that something "human" is lost in the turn toward organic models of disorder. Thus anthropologist Tanya Luhrmann sees a moral danger in the new biomedical psychiatry.[5] She worries about a decreasing ability to meaningfully encounter psychic suffering with the ascendancy of the biomedical model. Central to her critique is the premise that mental illness is inherently different from other kinds of illness. Here she cites Martin Luther's distinction between essential and inessential suffering: inessential suffering is what cannot be prevented, and what we must simply try to survive. It is not part of the person. In contrast, essential suffering is neither external to the person nor arbitrary, but is fundamentally human, and something for which we must take responsibility. For Luhrmann, the pain of psychiatric illness is essential to the person: "The illness is not out of his control but something over which he is potentially a master."[6] While medicine handles inessential suffering, religion treats essential suffering: the church is where we learn to accept our struggles as a necessary part of ourselves. In their approach to psychic suffering, psychoanalysts, for whom "self-knowledge is essentially good," are the clerics of a secular age.

Luhrmann argues that because the mentally ill in some sense choose to be mad, to destroy themselves and those around them, we cannot understand their illness the same way that we view a disease like cancer, because "the illness is a part of who they are."[7] The biomedical model seeks to rescue the person from the stigma of mental illness by treating it as something external to the self. But if thoughts are seen as diseased, the person becomes diseased as well and cannot take responsibility for his actions. If personhood is understood as independent from mental illness, but the illness inheres in everything the person does, he will never be seen as fully human since "what it is to be human" is diseased. Biomedical psychiatry thus threatens to refuse to recognize the mentally ill as fully human, a dangerous exclusion.

Perhaps what Luhrmann describes, and mourns, is the prospect of the decline of the psychiatrist as a distinctive kind of "medical personage," two hundred years after the invention of moral treatment. The roles of doctor and priest have been confused in the strange figure of the psychiatrist since the founding of the discipline, as Foucault pointed out: Pinel heralded the figure of the expert that takes charge of mental illness in a medical setting not by invoking science but rather through an assertion of the patient's moral responsibility, a role that reached its apogee with Freud.[8]

Luhrmann's psychodynamic humanism can be contrasted with a form of inquiry that does not begin with a conception of what the human is.

Rather than critique biomedicine as dehumanizing, this approach seeks to describe the new forms of human agency and responsibility that are emerging with developments in the life sciences. Thus, Nikolas Rose notes that unlike earlier organicisms, emergent forms of biological knowledge about human conduct are characterized neither by determinism nor by therapeutic pessimism. In its assumption that mental disorders are diseases of the brain, he argues, the new biological psychiatry does not thereby condemn sufferers to their fate or rationalize programs of exclusion or sterilization. Rather, current claims about the biological substrates of psychiatric conditions lead to optimism about new therapeutic interventions. Indeed, Rose suggests, the identification of such biological substrates now seems more likely than the ascription of suffering to biography, experience, or the unconscious to offer the possibility of effective therapies.

Whereas for Luhrmann an organic conception of mental disorder attenuates personal responsibility by separating disorder from self, Rose argues that new biomedical techniques of intervention in fact generate new possibilities for action: "At the very moment when our normality is revealed to be biological, put on the side of nature in what used to be termed the nature–nurture debate, it becomes open not to fatalism but to choice."[9] He calls these emerging practices "techniques of the molecular self." In the new organicism, there is an explicit interpenetration between the experiential and the biological: neuroscience at its best is not reductionist, but is interested in the complex interplay between organic structure and environmental experience. Given these looping and interactive relations of nature and artifice, the two sides are no longer separable. When the problem is framed as one of self-care, or intervention upon oneself, the question becomes: given the existence of such techniques, how will people work on themselves to attain happiness, or at least to diminish suffering?

In addition to the de-stigmatizing work associated with a biological explanation of mental illness, such optimism helps explain why patient and family support groups tend to support biological research into mental disorder. In North America and Western Europe, collectives based around a common disorder have been strong advocates for a biological understanding of mental illness. Over the last two decades, groups of patients and families have seen the shift to biological models as an opportunity to destigmatize these disorders and to develop new treatments.[10] They have helped to fund scientific research into the biological origins of mental disorder, and have mobilized to ensure that these illnesses be treated like physical illnesses by health insurers.

Rose suggests that the emergence of patient-advocacy groups as sites for the encouragement of self-management can be understood in terms of a broader shift in rationalities of government in Europe and North America, from welfare to "advanced liberalism."[11] This rationality disperses social planning from centralized bureaucracies to the actions of consumers, who are to make decisions based on a calculus of risk management. The aim is to turn social actors into subjects of personal responsibility, autonomy, and choice: to have individuals and communities take active responsibility for activities formerly performed by central authorities. Through such acts of choice, subjects are to maximize their quality of life. In the sphere of mental health, for example, the former psychiatry patient becomes a "consumer" of health services.

With the rise of the patient advocacy movement, what began as a behavioral norm to be implanted into citizens is turned into a demand that citizens make of authorities. Individuals become "experts of themselves" – adopting an educated, knowledgeable relation of self-care with regard to their bodies, minds, and behavior. As Rose puts it:

> Clients of expertise came to understand and relate to themselves and their "welfare" in new ways ... They organized themselves into their own associations, contesting the powers of expertise, protesting against relations that now appeared patronizing and demeaning of their autonomy, demanding increased resources for their particular conditions and claiming a say in the decisions that affected their lives.[12]

The rise of "bipolar self-identity" in the United States in the 1980s and 1990s is exemplary of the process Rose outlines: the biologization of mental disorder, the development of new techniques of self-management, and the support of biomedical research by affected groups and their families.[13] As we will see, the form of temporal orientation embodied in the treatment protocols and discourse around bipolar disorder points to the subject as a future-oriented risk-manager.

By the late 1990s, such patient-advocacy movements had not coalesced in Argentina, where a paternalistic model of physician authority remained strong. This is one reason why bipolar disorder was not widespread in the country, as we saw in Chapter 1. Nonetheless, a few doctors sought to generate advocacy and self-help groups for the mentally ill along North American lines. Experts with ties both to industry and to patient-advocacy sought to expand the diagnosis of bipolar disorder in Argentina. Alejandro Lagomarsino was one of the first psychiatrists to bring the issue of the under-diagnosis of bipolar disorder to the attention of Argentine psychiatrists. Lagomarsino is the founder and director of *Fundación Bipolares de Argentina* (FUBIPA), the Argentine bipolar patient and family support group. He is also one of Abbott Pharmaceutical's "opinion leaders," and now runs a thriving private practice after having spent the early part of his career working in public hospitals such as Romero.

Lagomarsino was originally trained in the era of dynamic social psychiatry – indeed, he was in the Pirobano residency with Jacinto Armando.[14] He says that he "converted" twenty years ago to a more biological view after seeing the successful effects of lithium treatment on a patient who could not otherwise be helped. The patient, who had been diagnosed as a schizophrenic and interned five times, asked him why he had never before received the diagnosis of bipolar disorder or treatment with a mood stabilizer. Such experiences convinced Lagomarsino to specialize in bipolar disorder, and to start an organization modeled on North American patient advocacy groups. "With 400,000 undiagnosed bipolars here in Argentina," he says, making an estimate based on transnational epidemiology, "I had to do something."

Lagomarsino is ubiquitous on industry-sponsored expert panels at professional meetings. One of his patients, a volunteer for the bipolar patients' group, proudly tells me: "he is very well known – you know, he gets $180 an hour – less for me, because I help with FUBIPA. He deserves it, though – he goes to the United States all the time, and the pharmaceutical companies pay him to go."

Among his colleagues, Lagomarsino promotes a model of the psychiatrist as a risk-manager, in partnership with the patient. At a panel on bipolar disorder at the Argentine Psychiatric Association (APsA) meetings, he speaks about tools, beyond pharmaceuticals, to achieve the final goal of a stabilized patient, one whose evolutionary diagram of sharp ups-and-downs softens gradually into a straight line. The course of the illness is one of the variables that determine the effectiveness of treatment, he says: it varies according to family ties, intensity of episodes, the pleasure of the euphoria. Reading aloud from Robert Louis Stevenson's *Dr Jekyll and Mr Hyde*, Lagomarsino emphasizes the feeling of power and liberty the narrator has as the "other." For this reason, the patient may not want to accept that this feeling is part of the illness. Here psychotherapy may be useful in order to get the patient to accept the illness, to recognize the necessity of medication.

In the talk, Lagomarsino suggests appropriate language for dealing with bipolar patients: do not say that the illness is "incurable," but that for now it is "controllable," and that given the achievements of neuroscience and molecular biology, we are not so far away from a cure. Also, analogies are helpful: tell patients that bipolar disorder is a chronic condition, like diabetes or hypertension. And use terms like "chemical circuits," so that the patient does not feel ill as a person: biologizing the disorder keeps it from affecting identity. It is not "I am depressive," but "I am a person with various dimensions," including this illness. The role of the psychiatrist that Lagomarsino outlines for his colleagues is that of a tutor in the art of self-management. As Rose puts it, "experts are now taught the techniques by which they can empower their clients, by which is meant according them the capacities for managing their own lives by way of acceptable logics of life strategy."[15]

I spoke with several leaders of FUBIPA, who testified in their role as patient-experts to their experiences with bipolar disorder and their methods for managing the condition. Miguel Perreira is an engineer in his late fifties who lives with his family in a middle-class suburb north of Buenos Aires. After his first episode at age thirty-three, he saw seven psychiatrists over a four-year period before he was diagnosed with bipolar disorder. Even when he was finally prescribed lithium, he tells me, it was not enough, and he had a traumatic second internment, when he was brought forcibly to a Buenos Aires psychiatric hospital. He was declared unable to work by military psychiatrists, and was fired from his job as an army engineer. He heard about bipolar disorder and FUBIPA after his sister saw a magazine article describing someone with similar symptoms. When I ask how he would describe the illness to someone who knew nothing about it, he says:

> It takes a great deal of effort just to be okay. One thing is the self, and the other is the illness. The idea of the ego and the superego is a lie: you cannot contain what you are doing, the mind cannot manage it, it is more powerful than your own self. Yes, it is a part of me, but it is also different – the manias have no limits to their power.

Perreira emphasizes the importance of distinguishing himself from the illness, as Lagomarsino recommends. This practice makes it possible for him to see himself as a monitor of his condition. The task of managing excesses of mood generates new kinds of relations with the self. Perreira speaks of looking after himself, of putting distance between himself and the illness: "You ask yourself why – what's the cause? You have to study yourself. It's not that I've forgotten the episodes – I remember each moment." His diagnostic identity becomes an art of self-government insofar as it encourages prudent vigilance over potential affective outbursts.

Here we can see that, as Luhrmann suggested, one implication of seeing psychotic symptoms as part of an organic disorder rather than a disorder of the psyche is the separation of self from illness. However, the fact that the site of illness is not in the self but in the body does not make Perreira less responsible, but rather indicates a different type of responsibility and a different range of possible interventions. Part of self-care will involve monitoring his moods, protecting against the excesses of the body. For Perreira, this separation between illness and self is not an easy task – rather, it is a project, and one that involves more than just medication:

> Even if I have an idea of what bipolarity is, everyone has their own idea. There are other factors – not just lithium. The family and work are central. You have to recuperate your self. In any other illness – cancer, or AIDS – the person does not lose this, but in bipolar disorder you lose the autonomy of your mind. The hardest thing is to put distance between you and the illness, to objectify it. After the internment, I had forgotten how to manage. It took a lot of internal strength to recover. At FUBIPA, I saw people who were much better than I was, and I learned about the history of psychiatry. It felt good – seeing other people gave me more hope.

FUBIPA coordinator Maria Fernandez works as a psychologist at a public hospital in Barrio Once. She is a feisty woman in her sixties, enthusiastic to tell her story. She has had a difficult, unfortunate life from very early on, she begins, telling me about problems with school and with love. When she was first treated, she was given a diagnosis of *neurosis phobica*. The most recent period began after the deaths of her sister and grandmother, and a friend's accident. She was interned for severe depression several times during this period. Two years later she changed her profession, beginning to work as a gestalt therapist, which she has now been doing for twelve years. When she had another low point several years later, she went to Lagomarsino, who diagnosed her with bipolar disorder.

She is taking tegretol and lithium. And also rivotril – she had many phobias. But medication is not the only answer, she says: "The table has four legs – medication, the psychiatrist, the help-group, and psychotherapy – the psychologist helps with balance in life, which is also necessary." Fernandez focuses on taking her medication, sleeping eight hours, and going to the psychiatrist for medication adjustment when she isn't doing well. Like Perreira, Fernandez does not adopt a wholly biological model of her illness, but rather integrates medication into a set of techniques of self-care, which include self-help. "Self-help – FUBIPA – provides security, you learn how many others suffer from the illness, you lose the sense of solitude . . . it's an interesting thing – after the crisis of bipolarity you encounter your own personality, your base personality – if you do not excuse yourself by saying 'I'm bipolar.'"

For Pablo Velicovsky, the diagnosis of bipolar disorder is a site where the epistemological question of how to see illness meets the ethical-political issue of the structure of authority between doctor and patient. He argues that the effectiveness of mood stabilizers should change the category of illness in which many patients are placed – from schizophrenia, a category that implies passivity and hopelessness, to bipolar disorder, a condition whose treatment involves a program of active self-monitoring. The two different categories also imply a different role for the psychiatrist: from custodian of a helpless patient to ally in the collaborative task of risk-management.

During Pablo's training, seeing the new generation of anti-psychotics and lithium work served as evidence of the inadequacy of what he calls the "schizophrenia paradigm." He describes his paradigm "conversion" in terms of specific cases in which he misdiagnosed patients as schizophrenic and medicated them badly, then later discovered that they had affective disorders. He tells the story of a young patient who was hearing the voices of his football fan club chanting to him: "olé, olé, olé, go kill yourself!" Pablo initially diagnosed schizophrenia and gave him the anti-psychotic Haldol. The patient began to suffer from severe tardive dyskinesia, a movement disorder that can be a side effect of anti-psychotic medication: he could barely walk without falling over. When Pablo finally got rid of the drugs, the patient improved enormously. "Why did the hallucinations go away?" asks Pablo. "Now I know: he had a major depression with psychotic symptoms that I had been sustaining with Haldol." Pablo sees the question of diagnosis as a battle of paradigms: "The only way to explain why it's so hard to see this problem is epistemological. That is, they are stuck in an earlier paradigm and so they don't see it, and this is a gestalt phenomenon very well applied by Kuhn, they don't see it and so the fight is ferocious."

Pablo argues that psychoanalysts have themselves been guilty of a kind of "dehumanization" by failing to provide the proper chemical treatments that can transform numerous patients from the dire category of chronic schizophrenia to a type of illness – bipolar disorder – in which normal functioning is possible. His approach is to name the illness in terms of the least damaging chemical intervention, and thus to begin with an affective rather than thought disorder diagnosis until proven otherwise. In turn, some of his fellow doctors accuse him of seeing bipolarity everywhere.

## Beyond DSM

In staff meetings in the men's ward at Hospital Romero, the doctors go over their patients much more quickly than in the women's ward. One resident explains that they do not have to spend a long time explaining things to each other because "they speak the same language." Despite this shared vocabulary, debates can be acrimonious. "Pablo has great clinical intuition," says Gustavo, then adds: "though he is often wrong." Their arguments are edifying, he says. This is the problem with the women's ward: they do not discuss their patients, they do not debate. And so there is no accountability. Several residents tell me that the most fascinating thing in men's ward meetings is the debating: this is where they learn something.

In one meeting there is a long discussion of a patient whose condition is described by one of the residents as a "disaster." The conversation begins by focusing on the meaning of the patient's belief that the devil is taking his soul. Pablo tries to shift discussion away from the thematic content of the patient's delusion to the form of the illness, asking about the patient's affect: "Is he depressed?" Pablo thinks it is a case of bipolar disorder. "This treatment with neuroleptics for schizophrenia isn't working," he says, "it's a messy case, with multiform episodes." Monica, one of the other staff psychiatrists, disagrees, as does almost everyone else there, and a heated discussion ensues:

"It's not that I think any hallucination is schizophrenia," she says, "but here it is the 'hallucinatory style' that is schizophrenic."

"This is the general error that everyone makes," Pablo responds. "There's no such thing. The treatment is not working – he's worse."

Monica retorts: "Many patients don't get better, there are schizophrenic patients of yours who've gotten worse."

"If we think of it in neuroscientific terms," says Pablo, "there are psychotic episodes rising and falling." He is seeing a cyclical pattern characteristic of bipolar disorder.

"But when he arrived," says Cecilia, a psychology resident, "he didn't have hallucinations." Her point is that the hallucinations are not the reason he was given a schizophrenia diagnosis: there are also symptoms such as social withdrawal and thought impairment.

"He was a megalomaniac!" exclaims Pablo.

"No he wasn't," responds Cecilia. Javier, a psychiatry resident, agrees with her. Monica points out that he was "disorganized" when he arrived, and he's been doing badly for two years.

"And there were conduct problems," adds Javier.

"What are you going to give him?" demands Pablo.

"Time," says Monica.

Pablo says he would try anti-depressants if it's a mixed depression and, if not, mood stabilizers. "He's a depressed patient with hallucinations, hearing voices."

Cecilia objects, citing the patient's clinical history.

Pablo argues that he has a "borderline intellectual deficit" – which would explain the apparent cognitive impairment. "It's probably an affective disorder," he insists.

"The 'clinic' doesn't make me think of bipolar disorder," says Monica, referring to her observation of the patient's behavior in the ward.

"But this strategy isn't getting results," protests Pablo.

"He is not explicitly depressed," says Javier.

"But to be 'explicitly depressed' requires an intelligent patient," answers Pablo. "With old folks and children, you have to look at the 'soft signs.'" He returns to the question of the content of the delusion, but now in terms of its affective implications. "What are these voices saying? They have to do with themes of ruination, catastrophe." He recalls a similar patient who was able to leave the hospital with anti-depressants.

Cecilia is blustering: "It's not what you are saying. He was kept interned in Tobar – not with a psychotic state but because of insistent sexual aggressiveness."

"That," pronounces Pablo triumphantly, "is a typical manic crisis with an intellectual deficit. He's worse with neuroleptics."

Pablo is convinced that giving neuroleptics to bipolars makes them look like schizophrenics because of the side-effects of the medication. Part of his argument is about social class: poor people from shanty towns are less educated, and therefore more likely to be diagnosed as schizophrenic. As he tells me later, "if you are crazy and *bruto* you are already more schizophrenic from the get-go."

Javier remains unconvinced. "Let's try him a bit longer with Lapenax," an atypical anti-psychotic.

"Why continue with this kind of thinking?" demands Pablo.

"It is not a cyclic type," says Monica.

"It's not working along this route," says Pablo. Referring to the patient's behavior in Tobar, the juvenile psychiatric hospital, he says: "the sexual aggressiveness is what would occur when this accelerates."

Monica objects: "He's in a *villa* – the intellectual deficit has to do with bad nutrition, a lack of stimulation."

Pablo agrees, but adds, "it's not that the whole *villa* population is like this. It's a completed course, the psychosis is not evolving. It accelerates with the neuroleptics." The patient's poor response to the neuroleptics helps Pablo to read the case as an affective disorder. "This mystic and Lujan, the guardian angel's voice: it all indicates a case of psychotic depression."

"But he is not sad," Javier insists. "Let's stick with Lapenax," the antipsychotic.

Pablo reminds Monica of another patient: "who had the same thing? Acute depressions in the afternoon after we gave him Lapenax."

"Well, there are fluctuations," admits Cecilia.

"If there are fluctuations," says Pablo, exasperated, "give him a mood stabilizer!" He leaves for another meeting. Silence.

"Well, it's true that he isn't responding well," Javier finally says.

"Okay," says Monica, "go with a little Trapax (an anxiolytic) so he will be less anxious."

Two weeks later, the patient is apparently doing better: he wants to go back to his house. His mood has picked up, and he is less psychotic. "Because we got rid of the neuroleptics," says Pablo.

After the meeting, a first-year resident tells me that she would not have known to see the patient as mentally retarded, with an affective disorder. "Pablo is not like the Borda psychiatrists," she says, referring to the old guard of Argentine biological psychiatry, still powerful in the city's large psychiatric hospitals: "he does not stay within 'the traditional.' He doesn't think in terms of brain lesions like the German school or in terms of DSM – he is creating a new space, something beyond DSM." Another resident says that while she respects Pablo, she thinks he is something of an extremist. She would have been more inclined to call the patient schizophrenic. Pablo has tunnel vision sometimes, is not very open. "It's good, if you're not sure, to think in terms of bipolar disorder," she says. "But Pablo sees bipolars everywhere. His passion is to do the best for the patient, which is to treat them with mood stabilizers, but this can sometimes be a problem." She gives an example. One time, she was on emergency room duty when a very manic bipolar patient was interned. He was huge, a personal trainer, and would get aggressive in his manic states. Meanwhile there were two other manic patients interned. They would spend all night fighting with one another, and she and another resident, both small women, would have to separate them – the nurse was afraid and would hide in her room. This patient began to threaten her, but Pablo refused to let her medicate him with neuroleptics, telling her instead not to leave the emergency room. He did not want to use Haldol, but mood stabilizers can take a month to work, and Pablo, thinking of the patient, was overly rigid.

Pablo's approach to diagnosis is nominalistic. He is not so much concerned with the question of whether there is really a coherent entity, "bipolar disorder." Rather, what matters to him is the form of treatment and the kind of identity that the act of diagnosis will foster. In the context of the Argentine public health system, he argues, to be bipolar is much better than to be schizophrenic – in part because of the kind of drug treatment one will receive, but also because the schizophrenia label orients clinicians toward long-term hospital confinement. For this reason, he thinks that one should look for "bipolarity" rather than for "schizophrenia" even if they are not clearly distinguishable things in the world. "Day to day," he says, "I diagnose bipolar disorder until proven wrong, because I don't trust the psychiatric clinic. It doesn't seem to me to be sufficiently powerful and exact to be very confident in it. The difference between being diagnosed as schizophrenic and being diagnosed as bipolar is enormous in its consequences." He is resolutely pragmatic in his use of psychiatric categories: "For me, it's operative: I diagnose what's useful for me to diagnose ... Diagnosis has to be made in terms of the possibilities for improvement of the patient. This is the only factor."

## The politics of classification

Pablo's attempt to expand the diagnosis of bipolar disorder is part of a strategy to increase an optimistic population: one whose treatment is less debilitating, whose prognosis is better. He is campaigning both for the disorder and for a specific treatment – the mood stabilizer – as an alternative to widely used older generation anti-psychotics such as Haldol. The bipolar disorder classification is a tool for changing the structure of authority between patients and doctors. Bipolar patients can be more active in their own treatment, and in the evaluation of their care, than schizophrenics, he argues. The diagnosis thus structures the doctor–patient relationship:

> What the diagnosis does is precipitate a series of therapeutic actions, pharmacological and non-pharmacological, and attitudes, implicit or explicit. So when I have a schizophrenic in front of me and I say, "this person is schizophrenic," what I expect from him is much lower than what I expect when he is a bipolar. Because of this I resist diagnosing schizophrenia from the start because if not, if I lower my expectations, I lower my demands.

Part of Pablo's strong advocacy for the expansion of the bipolar diagnosis has to do with his affinity for bipolar patients themselves, and his appreciation for the creativity and passion he associates with them. He doesn't think that bipolarity can clearly be termed an illness: he cites its links to intelligence and creativity, and enjoys speculating about whether various famous historical figures were bipolar.[16] What is called bipolar disorder probably represents a set of genetically influenced behavior patterns that can be either advantageous or disadvantageous depending on the situation, Pablo thinks. He describes "neurodiversity" as an evolutionary advantage that humans have as a species: "The neurosciences are demonstrating that between the enormous genetic diversity that there is and how enormously plastic the brain is, each subject is really different from the other in terms of cerebral structure."

"If anyone exists who has never been asked for his opinion regarding his treatment it is certainly the insane person himself," wrote Robert Castel in a history of psychiatry written in the midst of the anti-psychiatry movement.[17] Pablo's effort is to reverse this relation of authority by assimilating the results of biomedical research to the rights of patients. Given the opportunity to see hundreds of bipolar patients through the gene study, Pablo decided to conduct his own research on their diagnostic histories, giving out a long questionnaire that focused on the subjective evaluation of their experience of psychiatric care. Because the survey concerned patients' opinions as "health consumers" Pablo described it as a "marketing" study. It included questions like: how many years after first going to a psychiatrist before you were diagnosed with BPD? Were you ever diagnosed as schizophrenic? How many psychiatrists have you seen? Has a psychiatrist ever hesitated to give you a diagnosis?

In the survey, Pablo found that a large proportion of these consumers had received poor service. It had taken an average of twelve years for them to receive a bipolar disorder diagnosis. Many (38 percent) had been previously diagnosed with schizophrenia, especially those who had suffered delusions and hallucinations. This is due to the mistake of relying on such symptoms for making a diagnosis: the delusions experienced by bipolar patients cannot be differentiated from the "positive" symptoms of schizophrenia, says Pablo. 95 percent of bipolar patients experience such symptoms and so many are classified as schizophrenic. On the one hand, Pablo thinks disorders are only a question of names. But, on the other, because of what those names imply, making the distinction between these two disorders – even if it is a nominalist one – is something of a crusade for him.

The worldwide ratio of bipolar to schizophrenia is supposed to be one-to-one, he says, but here in Argentina schizophrenia is diagnosed fifteen to twenty times as often. He thinks that given a broader understanding of affective disorder, the diagnostic ratio should in fact be five to one, bipolars to schizophrenics. He links this discrepancy to the history of drug discoveries – there was a patent for the anti-psychotic chlorpromazine by Rhone-Poulenc but not one for lithium, and so schizophrenia was a more profitable diagnosis.

But also, he says, schizophrenics are submissive patients, as opposed to bipolar patients who are more inclined to challenge authority. Thus psychiatrists who want to remain in authority prefer to diagnose schizophrenia:

> I think that a lot of the relationships between psychiatrists and patients are based on a model of schizophrenia. That is, a high level of dependency, people with very little capacity to exercise subjective rights, to complain about the other's whims, and this has given them a model of the psychiatrist–patient relationship that is almost the model for psychiatry ... In contrast, a bipolar is a guy who sometimes comes from a very good socio-cultural position and once he is well, he is very demanding and insistent. So, they don't like patients to act this way because you begin to enter into a level of relation with the patients that has to be much more honest, on the other side. You can't lie to a bipolar.

The point to doing such a survey is to put power in patients' hands – many come to him after seeing half a dozen other psychiatrists and never having been given the right diagnosis or medication. He is treating the patients as consumers, therefore as agents in their own recovery. Pablo's focus on the agency of the patient invokes the anti-authoritarian discourse of the *salud mental* movement, but attacks the latter's anti-scientific stance. It will be through a scientific approach that patients will be given power in their treatment, he thinks. In framing the survey as a study of the subjective opinions of health consumers, Pablo indicates an understanding of mental patients as consumers with the right to quality care. In Pablo's point of view, the doctor enters a contractual relationship: he must recognize the disorder properly and design the best intervention strategy given the institutional, financial, and familial resources of the patient. Doctor and patient are to become partners in treating the condition.

## Being scientific

Pablo would likely disagree with Tolstoy's edict that science gives us no answer to the question "how shall I live?"[18] For Pablo, the neurosciences not only provide a guide to psychiatric research and practice, but also a way to understand and shape one's life. "I am slowly doing the exercise of living in a neuroscientific paradigm," he tells me. "That is, to be able to think some of my things and say, 'aha, here we have the inferential model functioning' or 'aha, here my working memory failed' ... I can think of myself in moments, when I'm concentrating, in a non-dualist way. That is, not to say 'my body and I' but to say, 'I am this: I am a bank of genes, a bank of ideas,' and so on."

He does not ask whether psychiatry is a science but rather points out why it should strive to be more scientific: in order to alleviate suffering, to improve lives, to use public health resources efficiently. Psychoanalysts do not have to put their terms to the test, Pablo complains: "they can stay at home watching television, then write up results." He works extra hours, often alone, trying to "do science," to come up with feasible clinical experiments. In all of Buenos Aires, which has the most psy-professionals per capita in the world, the men's ward of Romero is the only place doing "clinical neuroscience" research, he says. Other psychiatrists are afraid of doing science: they are scared that they might be wrong. And Argentines, he adds, do not like to be wrong. Instead they go to conferences elsewhere and bring back materials, acting as transmitters rather than producers of knowledge. He complains about the conformity of Argentine culture. People are slaves to fashion here, without diversity or individuality. There is no interest in science, no real university, journalism is at a very low level . . . and the corruption! "Argentines are storytellers – that's why psychoanalysis thrives."

Martín Beren is an ambitious and energetic psychiatrist in his thirties, a rising "opinion leader" at national and transnational conferences. In his bearing, Beren is a technician rather than a theorist: unlike his colleague Pablo, he does not provide a philosophical vision of the implications of neuroscience for human subjectivity. Rather, Beren speaks of the importance of building an institutional structure through which mental health resources can be rationally allocated. From 1970 to 1989, he says, psychoanalysis was hegemonic in psychiatric training in Argentina: "There was nothing else." In its heyday, a psychoanalyst could make a very good living, working forty hours a week and charging a hundred dollars an hour. "It was a pyramid scheme," he says, drawing a chart flowing downward from the study group leader to many derivatives, with money multiplying along the way. During his own training, he did not understand what the Lacanians were talking about: "they might as well have been speaking German." You could either spend all your time studying it or reject it, he says. Earlier, rejecting it would have completely marginalized him, but by the late eighties there were a few others around.

In the third year of his residency, Beren took a six-month rotation in a hospital in New York City. He describes a memorable experience there: a meeting in which the head supervisor announced to the residents, "just give me a few details of the case and I'll tell you the rest." The supervisor was able to do this not through an analysis of the patient's life history, but with a generalized, statistical knowledge of psychiatric patients' tendencies.

Given a piece of data about an individual, the doctor could infer a series of other characteristics, through a logic of statistical correlation. "*This* is medicine," thought Beren. In Buenos Aires the idea had always been to work on a case by case basis in the "clinic of the person." Beren was convinced that this other type of knowledge could be extremely fruitful, but that there was no place for it in psychoanalysis. It calmed him to encounter it: he had felt himself an orphan in Buenos Aires, where the "medical discourse" was only seen negatively. In the library in New York, he read American psychiatry journals compulsively, and upon his return he subscribed to several of them. Now he is interested in questions of health management and in generating epidemiological knowledge, which "doesn't exist here."

In order to build a national psychiatry, Beren tells me, you need to know what you have in the country. "Without data, you cannot have a politics." There is no national project of research, he says: the journals here are just "cut and paste" – they are derivative of others' research. At the department of pharmacology at the University of Buenos Aires he is trying to convince members that they need to actually do original research, not just import what is produced elsewhere. "To be an expert is not just a question of studying more than everyone else."

Beren and Pablo speak at a panel on basic research at a residents' training conference. Pablo says that he went into psychiatry because he thought that given the emerging field of neuroscience there would be a lot to learn, and so it would be easy to do research. But then when he began the residency, he quips, "I felt like I had bought a great set of ski equipment and then found myself in the middle of the Sahara." The importation of knowledge is an epistemological problem: "If you don't do research, it's like watching a sumo match without knowing the rules, just two fat guys bouncing off of each other. You can't translate a study from one place to another."

Beren is programmatic, specifying the problem and laying out a set of possible solutions – a way to bring mental illness into the realm of rational public policy. There is no politics, culture, or budget for research here, he begins. The problem is not how much money there is, but how it is spent. We have very few reference points, and there are no coherent problems for us to work on. Research here is not published in either national or international journals. The result is ignorance about the country's situation. For example: how many schizophrenics are there? According to transnational epidemiology, there should be 130,000 schizophrenics in greater Buenos Aires, given the population: so where are they? For Beren, the effective administration of health requires detailed knowledge about local conditions.

Beren continues: we need to increase our efficiency, to institute the practice of research – in residencies, laboratories, and journals. The national government should prioritize the rational assignment of resources: it must collect data. Entry into a teaching hospital post should be based on competitions that are decided on the basis of publications and research. The curriculum should be reformed so that students are taught to read and criticize scientific papers. We should establish journals, provide grants to go to congresses. Given the inability of the state to fund research, he suggests private–public partnerships: the pharmaceutical companies have plenty of money, given the recent success of the stock market. They can invest – 50 percent of research in the United States comes from the pharmaceutical companies. Joint ventures are possible.

## Administrative rationality

Beren's question – "where are the 130,000 schizophrenics of Buenos Aires?" – was an expression of frustration at the lack of administrative rationality in Argentine public health. There was very little data available on the prevalence of mental illness in the general population, or on public spending on mental health.[19] This absence of epidemiological data or accounting methods leads to reflection on the circumstances under which such knowledge is generated. Mental health policy in the Argentine public sector was not oriented toward the kind of auditing techniques that make relative rates of illness in the population visible and monitor spending patterns. Instead, as we have seen, what was important in the discourse of *salud mental* was the public provision of psychodynamic therapy. This can be contrasted with the situation in the North, in which "evidence-based" medicine, which relies on the generation of increasingly detailed statistical knowledge about rates of illness in the population, was becoming an increasingly dominant norm in the allocation of health resources.[20]

In a 1991 essay, sociologist Robert Castel sought to explain the expansion of such knowledge-gathering techniques in North American and Western Europe in terms of a broader shift in rationalities of government. He argued that in Western Europe and North America, these recent shifts in psychiatric knowledge corresponded with new formulas for administering populations, under an emerging "plan of governability appropriate to the needs of 'advanced industrial' … societies."[21] The new political rationality around health was oriented to managing risk rather than disciplining subjects. This transformed the interest of psychiatric expertise: it had shifted from a focus on the individual case to the study of populations. Castel noted a related mutation in techniques of intervention: direct therapeutic intervention in the clinic was minimized, supplanted by an increasing emphasis on the preventative management of at-risk groups. The task was no longer the surveillance of individuals, but of likely occurrences of disease: "The new strategies dissolve the notion of a subject or a concrete individual, and put in its place a combinatory of factors, the factors of risk."[22] As we saw in Chapter 1, the projected applications of genomics knowledge operate according to this rationality of gauging possible future dangers and bringing them into the present in order to make them manageable.

To find and track such risk-laden populations requires techniques for seeing illness in standardized ways across disparate spaces – and for convincing professionals to adopt these techniques. With its emphasis on cross-rater reliability, DSM serves as a tool for constituting populations, rather than generating the unique, incommensurable cases familiar from psychoanalysis. Such knowledge is administratively useful in that mental health professionals can justify the need for health resources through the display of numbers: the lifetime prevalence of depression in the population, the average yearly cost of hospitalization for schizophrenia, suicide rates among bipolar patients. Statistics such as "disability adjusted life years" (DALY) indicate what proportion of the population is likely to fall ill with psychiatric illness, what economic damage this will cause, and how much money might be saved through early diagnosis and intervention.

While this rationality of health administration, in which biomedicine operates to construct and administer risk populations, may have seemed increasingly prevalent in the North, for biomedical reformers in Argentina it remained an unrealized ideal in the field of mental health: there was little emphasis placed on techniques, such as standardized diagnosis, that could generate Castel's grid of administrative rationality. These psychiatrists argued that in Argentina such practices were especially necessary given the needs of what they called, with a certain irony, an "underdeveloped" country. Their goal, it might be said, was to generate a "biopolitics" in the field of mental health – a grid of visibility that would make possible the more efficient use of health resources and the ongoing measurement of their efficacy.

The difficulty biomedical reformers had in convincing their colleagues to embrace developments in cosmopolitan psychiatry indicates that, even in a globalizing era, the movement of knowledge-forms requires more than merely their availability. Such knowledge would travel only to a milieu of expertise where it was in demand, or where its adoption was enforced by professional norms. The fact that one could download abstracts from next month's *American Journal of Psychiatry* from the internet did not mean that one would – nor, for that matter, that its information would mean the same thing in Argentina as in the United States. These psychiatrists thought that epistemic transformation was unlikely to come about simply through paradigm "conversion." Rather, deeper changes in the structure of health administration that would lead to the regulation of professional practice according to biomedical norms would be necessary in order to shift the field away from its psychodynamic orientation.

New techniques of health administration seemed, to these doctors, to present a possible way to bring about responsible management of a bloated and indulgent mental health system. As it stood, they argued, the system tolerated waste and corruption and inhibited healthy competition and scientific thought. Given the condition of the public mental health sector, movements to rationalize the administration of health held the promise of a new accountability. This would involve embracing a logic of management oriented toward efficiency and a norm of "evidence-based" practice. Pressure to do so would not come from the Argentine public sector – but perhaps might come from such controversial international institutions as the IMF and the World Bank.

## Neoliberal reform

The World Bank's 1993 report on health in developing countries argued that inefficiencies of public sector programs hindered the delivery of services as well as the reduction of poverty, and recommended a series of administrative reforms in order to improve the situation. The Bank's recommendations were on the one hand exemplary of neoliberal political rationality – the attempt to improve efficiency and accountability by creating structures of competition and choice.[23] On the other hand, it incorporated aims not typically associated with neoliberalism: the reduction of poverty, an emphasis on extending access to health, and improving primary care. Its prescriptions for the health sector included the reallocation of resources, expanding coverage, creating a competitive environment, and introducing audit techniques: "Middle-income countries [such as Argentina] need to focus on at least four key areas of policy reform: phasing out public subsidies to better-off groups; extending insurance coverage more widely; giving customers a choice of insurer; and encouraging payment methods that control costs."[24]

The report recommended the promotion of prepaid health plans (*prepagos*) as a means for containing health spending and increasing the efficiency of health provision. With the development of a market in health, the Bank argued, not only would costs decrease, but through competition, care could improve: "Where social insurance covers services by government hospitals, competition with the private sector can improve performance." The report suggested that broader political reforms would be necessary as well, in order "to increase participation and to improve the accountability of governments for their health spending, service delivery, and regulatory performance."[25] Public sector monopolies were not sufficiently subject to norms of efficiency and transparency. The Bank recommended neoliberal reform not for the sake of economic growth or enterpreneurship, but in order to improve health services.[26] The *prepago* was to be a technique for improving the population's welfare.

The report's emphasis on accountability presumed that one could measure various therapies against one another in terms of cost-effectiveness. In order to make the kind of comparisons across broad populations that would make such evaluation possible, however, there must be agreement among professionals on what disorder is, and what improvement is. For psychoanalysts, as we have seen, the singularity of the individual subject eliminated the possibility of measuring a given treatment's efficacy against other treatments, or limiting the number of sessions that could be reimbursed. Many psychoanalysts associated the latter with attention to the superficial symptom instead of the deep structure. They linked the potential imposition of diagnostic standards to the kind of structural reforms proposed by the Bank. Neoliberalism, these critics argued, left no time for the deep exploration of human problems.

Whereas *salud mental* veterans were harshly critical of the possible implementation of managed care in Argentina, biomedical reformers saw in it an opportunity to bring accountability into an inefficient and ineffective public health system. Controversy over the technique of "brief therapy," which exemplified the ethos of price-based competition associated with managed care, raised the question of whether disparate forms of treatment could be compared with one another according to measures of efficacy and efficiency. The issue of what it meant to say that brief therapies had been proven to be more effective than psychoanalysis also highlighted the question of the task of therapy: did efficacy simply mean improvement on standardized measures of functionality? Or did therapy strive for something deeper and more profound?

Psychiatrist Javier Grinfeld works at a controversial clinic called "The Center for Private Psychotherapy," run by brief therapy entrepreneur Hugo Hirsch. The Hirsch clinic was often cited by psychoanalysts as exemplary of the dark forces of efficiency-based health administration that were challenging the supremacy of psychoanalysis. Grinfeld has a cautious, subdued presence, and is given to understatement. In Argentina, he says, where psychoanalysis has been dominant for so long, the measurement of efficiency "is looked at with a certain displeasure." It is true that the Center is coherent with the trend toward efficiency, he admits, but they use brief therapy with acute patients, which is different from the issue of chronic patients.

"People think that brief therapies to treat symptoms are superficial," Grinfeld tells me, "that the problems are deeper – but then they work on these for years and years and still don't decrease the symptoms. In one sense the psychoanalytic perspective is correct – there are other existential aspects left aside by brief therapies – but the primary object of therapy has to be to decrease suffering, to improve the symptoms." This emphasis on symptoms, rather than deep structure, is precisely what psychoanalysts protested as superficial.

In a lecture on anxiety disorders to a group of psychiatry and psychology residents, Grinfeld explains how brief treatment through cognitive-behavioral therapy works. The emphasis in the lecture is not on structure, but function. The psychiatrist confronts situations that provoke fear and forges tools to help manage them, he explains: you habituate the patient, for example with relaxation exercises. One of Hospital Romero's psychology residents interrupts: "But if you don't reach the problem at a deep level, won't it just return?" Grinfeld leaps at the question, citing results from biomedical research: evidence shows that no, it does not – in fact the patient feels more secure, has the means to deal with the problem. There may be some conflictive situation at the existential level, he continues, but the fact is that one can work directly on the symptoms successfully. Psychoanalysis treats the symptom as though it were a phenomenon from dream life, and seeks its meaning, whereas behavioral therapy goes at the problem in reverse, treating the symptom so that the patient may function. And empirical studies show that the reduction of symptoms through cognitive behavioral therapy lasts over time.

Biomedical reformers acknowledged that for most mental illnesses, psychotherapy of some sort was necessary; their demand was that such treatment be demonstrably effective, and not serve what they saw as the ongoing and indulgent propagation of psychoanalysis in public health. They sought to bring a "scientific" ethos – by which they meant one rationalized according to the norms of biomedicine – to psychiatric practice. Thus they did not so much contrast medication with psychotherapy as ask that each be tested according to biomedical criteria: if the efficacy of a specific form of psychotherapy could be demonstrated in comparison with other treatments, in given populations, then they would recommend it. As a form of knowledge based on the individual case, however, this was exactly what psychoanalysis would not demonstrate.

Anibal Goldchluk is a rare figure in the Buenos Aires *mundo psi*, highly respected both in the psychoanalytic and psychiatric worlds. He has the reputation of being not only an erudite analyst, but also a knowledgeable physician and an advocate for institutional reform. In an invited discussion with residents at Romero, Goldchluk begins with some reflections on his own background. He was in the storied residency at Hospital Pirobano before it was closed down by the army under the dictatorship and moved to Romero. "At that time," he says, "we believed in doing psychiatry completely through psychoanalysis – we didn't even have training in psychiatry. Now we are in an epoch of pharmacology and biology."

Goldchluk stakes out a position in favor of diverse approaches. "A pragmatic position takes advantage of each camp," he says, whereas "extremists insist on one pole or the other. When psychoanalysis was born, it was the only hope, but it cannot be applied to the whole world: there may be specific therapies for each illness." Thus with depression it is clear that a cognitive-behavioral approach is more useful than psychoanalysis, and that with phobia and panics, behavioral therapy works better, he says. "The problem here in Buenos Aires is the exclusive focus on psychoanalysis." When a psychology resident asks him whether the cognitive approach "erases the person," Goldchluk responds sharply: "Let me make something clear: when you discard the unconscious, you do not discard the person. We are crossing to more technical treatments – discarding subjectivity is not discarding the person."

Marielz Ruiz, a specialist in pharmacology who teaches at the medical school, is one of the few women among this group of progressive biomedical psychiatrists. Many of the city's psychiatry residents attend her course on psychopharmacology. In these classes, she teaches a technical approach to medication decisions: the evaluation of comparative risk and benefit, what dosages to use, what side-effects to watch out for. She decides whether published medication studies have been done well, and if so, she incorporates the information in a kind of mental chart linking situation to action. In her course, there is a sense of ongoing progress towards greater pharmacological specificity and improved prognosis for patients.

Ruiz tells me that when she entered the Hospital Romero residency in the late eighties, her superiors told her to ignore her medical training and learn psychoanalysis, but she rebelled at the strict Lacanian orthodoxy in the hospital. She didn't understand it, for one thing, and it seemed unscientific to her that this particular kind of psychoanalysis would be the only way to approach a patient. At the time, many students from the UBA Faculty of Psychology came to Romero to study psychoanalysis, listen to workshops, and watch patient presentations. "It was something of a business," she recalls: the analysts recruited their analysands from among the psychology student body. She tells the story of being a second-year resident under the supervision of a "fanatic" psychoanalyst who later became a powerful political figure in the Radical government. "The institution does not exist," he would piously pronounce, using the discourse of anti-psychiatry. One time in the hospital there was a depressed patient who had problems with vision. "There is something she does not want to see," the analyst surmised. But couldn't these be neurological symptoms, Ruiz asked him – couldn't she have a brain tumor? "Forget that you are a doctor," he admonished her, giving her a text by Freud on symptoms involving vision. The patient later died of brain cancer.

Why has the climate changed? "I like to think it's because we were right," she laughs. Patients did not improve, and doctors began to seek other solutions. Ruiz points to a disjuncture between the institutional task of the hospital and the ethical project of psychoanalysis. These are not psychoanalytic patients, she says: they are in hospitals, seriously ill with suicide risk. They are not choosing their treatment, paying for it, having it last years and years. "I am in analysis with a Lacanian," she says, "but I am not psychotic. It's my choice – it's a different thing." There is also an economic issue, she notes: people cannot pay for years of analysis, and the *prepagos* will not pay either. So now middle-aged physician-analysts are asking her to teach them psychopharmacology; otherwise, the new kids will take all of their patients.

Following Ruiz, a series of more biomedically oriented residents entered Hospital Romero. At this point, as her colleague Eduardo Reskin tells me, nearly all of the training there was still in psychoanalysis. While dealing with a patient with obsessive-compulsive disorder, Reskin became interested in a biological approach, and together with several other residents – including Pablo and Gustavo – started to discuss "neuroscientific" models. The other residents saw this as somehow immoral or de-humanizing, and nicknamed them "psychotrones." It was not that this group saw itself as rebels, Reskin recalls, but as more modern, more open to new scientific developments, without prejudices. "In the seventies," he reflects, "psychoanalysis was associated with the left, with anti-military activism, but now it could more accurately be called conservative."

Reskin is a specialist in obsessive-compulsive disorder. In a lecture to the city's psychiatry residents, he defines obsessions as recurrent images or ideas that the person tries to extinguish though compulsions – conduct that neutralizes the obsession. The difference between an obsession and a delusional idea is academic, he says: an obsessive idea can be an overvalued one, and therefore delusional. This calls into question the core psychoanalytic distinction between neurotic and psychotic structure. As far as Reskin is concerned, it is the capacity for functioning in daily life rather than the patient's connection to "reality" that is important.

He describes the first patient with obsessive-compulsive disorder he saw, in 1986 when he was a resident at Hospital Romero. This was a man who just stood in front of the wall, staring, "like the 'Man Facing Southeast.'" He had been diagnosed with schizophrenia and was being medicated with neuroleptics. When asked why he was staring at the wall, the man replied that he was obliged to focus on a specific point in the center. Reskin thought this sounded like compulsive behavior, and decided to change the treatment approach. He prescribed cognitive-behavioral therapy and a tricylic anti-depressant – the only "anti-obsessive" drug at that time. The staff doctors were highly critical of this approach, he reports, but it worked quite well. The results of drug treatment confirmed the initial diagnosis.

## Seeing bipolar disorder

Sebastian, a second-year psychiatry resident at Romero, tells me that he reads mostly "American" psychiatry: this is the future of the field, he says. When he first entered the women's ward, he was interested in psychoanalysis, but now he thinks that there is a defensive attitude there, that the staff doctors are dogmatic and exclusive. They are medicating patients with molecules that act on the central nervous system, altering their behavior, but do not read the studies on these medications. Psychoanalytic training involves reading only Freud and Lacan, he complains. "They were good for their time, but at this point ... If psychotic patients are well medicated, they can function." In the women's ward the doctors are intractable: you have to treat patients with interventions in speech. Now the people in the women's ward accuse him of having "converted" into a *biologista.*

A case presentation by Sebastian to the other residents at Romero provided a chance to see how young psychiatrists learn to see bipolar disorder. The case concerns a 25-year-old woman who had been interned in the hospital once before, after which she continued treatment as an outpatient. On her admission to the women's ward, she had megalomaniacal thoughts, was unable to sit still, was constantly dancing, singing, asking about Sebastian's personal life. She had been medicated with the anti-psychotic clozapine since her previous admission. She had also been undergoing treatment for thyroid cancer, but apparently had not been told about it. Her diagnosis upon admission was schizophrenia, which he changed to bipolar disorder.

Sebastian briefly tells the story leading up to her admission to the hospital: she dropped out of high school after marrying and having a child. At age twenty-one her husband left her, and her family found her in a mute and perplexed state. She was interned at a clinic for two months, and then withdrawn by her parents because she was heavily sedated and had not improved. She was first brought to Romero several years ago during a "depressive episode." At the time, doctors in the women's ward increased dosage of the anti-depressant imiprimine, but a week later she was interned in a "manic episode." She received various pharmacological combinations and a diagnosis of "maniform presentation within a case of psychosis." Her agitation and hyperactivity required emergency sedation. She developed severe parkinsonism from Haldol. Finally she was given the atypical anti-psychotic clozapine as her only medication, and was released from the hospital a few weeks later.

Sebastian suspended the clozapine treatment last year given his diagnosis of bipolar disorder and the lack of psychotic symptoms. A month later she had a depressive episode, and he added the anti-depressant fluoxetine (Prozac). A week later, in very bad shape, she had semi-paranoid thoughts, accusing Sebastian of trying to read her mind. The next week she improved, but a month later she had to be interned in a manic state with delusional ideas of persecution – that she was being filmed in the ward and that Sebastian was an actor in the movie. When her manic phase subsided she was released, medicated with valcote, a mood stabilizer, and clozapine. She has been in out-patient treatment since, living with her mother and maintaining friendships with people she met in the hospital. Sebastian describes her recent condition: lucid, cooperative, without perceptual alterations but with accelerated, scattered thoughts. In November he dropped the fluoxetine from the regimen, and adjusted the clozapine and mood-stabilizer levels. Since then she has been stable. Sebastian says that he has been guided in treatment by the diagnosis of bipolar disorder, and asks whether it might instead be a case of schizoaffective disorder. His question is about the relation of medication-response to illness entity: how should the stabilizing role of the anti-psychotic clozapine affect his diagnosis of bipolar disorder?

Sebastian's presentation leads to an initial debate among the residents about whether the presence of delusion in the case should lead to a diagnosis of "psychosis." Or instead, rather than focusing on the presence of psychotic symptoms, should the psychiatrist attend to cycles of affect? The residents raise a number of questions: Does she have "negative symptoms"? These could indicate schizoaffective disorder.

"What about the mood stabilizer," asks a psychiatry resident. "If she wasn't stable on it by itself, why did you drop the anti-psychotic?"

"I was thinking in terms of bipolar disorder," responds Sebastian. "I don't know if she was actually psychotic – it could have been a depressive episode. In her discourse, you don't see the self-referential phenomena typical of schizophrenia."

"Is there a difference between the psychotic symptoms in bipolar disorder and those of schizophrenia?" asks Manuel, a resident who works closely with Pablo. It is a rhetorical question: the implication is that in deciding between a bipolar and a schizophrenia diagnosis, one should not be concerned with "positive symptoms" such as delusion: even if the symptoms were psychotic, that should not affect the diagnosis.[27]

"No," responds Sebastian, provoking a din among the residents.

One of the psychology residents asks about what happened in the patient's life before the episode. "There was the operation," says Sebastian, "but she didn't know about the cancer." But she had to know, insist the psychologists.

The discussion then turns to the question of whether one can make a diagnosis via drug response – the question of the therapeutic trial: "Does bipolar disorder respond to clozapine?"

The chief resident mentions that the patient was extremely sensitive to the side effects of typical anti-psychotics when interned: this could indicate bipolar disorder. This leads Gustavo to the issue of the women's ward's initial diagnosis of "psychosis": "why was she given this diagnosis in the first place? Maybe she had psychotic episodes, but you cannot say that she's psychotic."

A psychology resident objects: "That's true if you think only in terms of symptoms, but there is another kind of criterion: metonymy – the order of the superego."

"Is that a modifiable structure?" asks Gustavo, alluding to the seeming immutability of psychoanalytic structures. As he understands it, there is no way to assimilate the "psychotic" symptoms of bipolar disorder into a psychoanalytic model, since they are the result of the irruptions of affect in the present and can be alleviated with medication.

The following week Pablo responds to Sebastian's presentation. How should one approach this case, he asks, beyond pharmacological treatment? She is young and does not have much insight. How does she manage stress – in her family, with a divorce, and motherhood? Looking at the patient's history, Pablo questions the initial schizophrenia diagnosis. He points at the first episode as a clear case of pure mania, which means that the case must be classified as an affective disorder – this is the only place for mania in DSM-IV. Also, with clozapine she decompensated. One has to look at the interaction of stress with anti-psychotics and mood stabilizers. What does each actually do? What is the neurophysiological model we are working with – the model of the illness?

Pablo goes over Sebastian's treatment decisions, analyzing the intersection of life events with medication response. The increase in the dosage of clozapine was good. He notes that the patient responded slowly to the anti-psychotic – a sign that it is an affective disorder: schizophrenic patients respond more rapidly, in five or six days. This is because different things are happening in each case. Affective disorders involve an alteration in time, in normal rhythm.

Pablo discusses the patient's encounter with the medical world in her cancer treatment: this would be terrible, especially for a mood disorder patient. He advises the residents to locate "stressors": often for young bipolar patients, relationship break-ups can set off the first episode. For schizophrenics, stress having to do with social ties is not as weighty – they have a "social tie deficit." Sometimes with an affective patient, when a potential stressor occurs, Pablo raises the dose of the mood stabilizer even without the appearance of symptoms. His interpretive technique requires an intuitive understanding of the relation between kinds of patients, their likely response to specific medications, and the interaction of such medication with life events.

Here Pablo brings the operations of the brain into view. What do mood stabilizers actually *do*? he asks. In psychiatry, you have to consider how you are affecting the whole brain: it is a physiological effect – this is the difference between psychiatry and neurology. So you have to think in terms of producing complex effects. Anti-psychotics block certain receptors, and eventually affect the calculating center. He draws a schematic chart of the brain. The basal ganglia sends outputs – projections – to the frontal area which must process them. It is performing a "search." With anti-psychotics the global performance lowers – the system functions less well. In bipolar disorder the patient doesn't have a problem in managing information. "But I still don't understand the initial schizophrenia diagnosis," Pablo puzzles.

"When she was interned," responds the chief resident, "she was very disorganized."

This inflames Pablo. He takes out his slides, pointing toward charts he has adapted from a North American textbook on bipolar disorder. "Look, acute manic depression shows more disorganization than schizophrenia. This error is malpractice. We've fallen into an epistemological trap in the last thirty years, and not just in this country but all over the world."

The chief resident again defends her initial diagnosis of schizophrenia: "In her first episode she was perplexed, inhibited."

Another resident explains this by saying that she was very "neurolepticized" – she was being given a high dose of Haldol.

"So she enters with a case of depression with a psychotic episode," says Pablo, "and the neuroleptics, which are central nervous system depressors, make her worse. The effects of being neurolepticized last for years, not months. She is bipolar: she cannot control her bursts of affect."

He draws a chart of the patient's evolution, based on her file, showing a sequence of highs and lows. The resulting longitudinal wave makes the condition indeed look like bipolar disorder. Looking at her history, he points out that in 1996 the patient had a "manic-switch" with an antidepressant – another sign of bipolar disorder.

"What about using two mood stabilizers?" he suggests. "You don't have to stay with just one drug. Still, nothing interferes with the diagnosis of bipolar disorder. 75 percent of bipolar patients have at least two first-rank Schneiderian symptoms [eg. delusions and hallucinations]. And on the subjective SAPS scale, 90 percent do."

Pablo then brings up the results of the survey of bipolar subjects he conducted during the genetic study at Romero. Here, among one hundred correctly diagnosed patients, 83 percent reported at least two first-rank [i.e., psychotic] symptoms. These people had personal messages from the TV, from the radio. It is the psychotic symptoms that always confuse the diagnosis, he says. So then: should this case be called schizoaffective because of the patient's response to clozapine? The boundaries between schizophrenia and affective disorder may not always be clear. What matters is not the name itself but what the label will imply in terms of medication, social services, employability. Think about it: if she were your child, which diagnosis would you rather she receive? It's better to be wrong this way than the other way around.

In tracking the course of the disorder, Pablo uses a longitudinal chart to follow the patient's cycles between lows of depression and peaks of mania. This chart represents a temporality of the wave function rather than of the developmental break. It is focused on the future rather than the past. Pablo does not probe the content of hallucinations for clues as to the patient's psychic structure, but rather monitors them as manic episodes according to this longitudinal scale. The goal is to lessen the amplitude and frequency of the wave, whose peaks represent irruptions of chemical imbalance. This diagram is the "form of life" generated by the treatment protocols for bipolar disorder.

This does not mean that the expert is not interested in the life history, the family context, the social environment of the patient. Rather, one is interested in these for different reasons than in psychoanalysis. The role of life events is not to shape psychic structure but to transform risk into active disorder. These events may take part in the formation of the illness but these do not have meaning except as "stressors." There is no need for a theory of the unconscious or for the hermeneutic labors of the analyst. The doctor's role is not to unravel hidden subjective traumas but to anticipate and manage the wave's potential fluctuations. If a potential stressor appears, Pablo says, he may increase the mood stabilizer dosage prophylactically, protecting against an episode. A well-managed patient's chart moves from a sharply oscillating wave of disruption gradually towards a straight line of stability.

# 5
# The private life of numbers

In August 2001, announcements of "Anxiety Disorders Week," an information campaign designed to bring patients to hospitals where they could consult with experts, appeared in a number of Buenos Aires newspapers. "One of every four Argentines suffers from them," one article proclaimed: "panic attacks, phobias. Specialists say that they are increasing; factors such as insecurity or incertitude with respect to the future can influence them."[1] The reference to uncertainty and insecurity was apt: the country was entering its fourth year of recession, the unemployment rate had reached 20 percent, the widely tracked index of *riesgo-pais* or "country-risk" was spiking to record levels each day. And the campaign was successful beyond the expectations of its sponsors: the city's hospitals were inundated with patients complaining of symptoms of stress. The articles did not mention that the campaign had been co-sponsored by the domestic pharmaceutical firm Bago, makers of Tranquinil-brand alprazolam. Since in Argentina it was still prohibited to market a drug directly to the general public, an alternative was to "grow the market" by making general practitioners and patients more aware of the illness. In an article that appeared two months later in the daily *Clarín* on the role of the growing economic crisis in increasing tranquilizer sales, a Bago sales manager reported that August had been a month of record growth for Tranquinil. The piece was subtitled, "Illnesses brought on by the crisis are increasing medical visits and anxiolytic use."[2] What might have been seen as evidence of the success of the Bago information campaign was instead interpreted as a sign of the nation's social and psychic crisis. The article cited data from the market research firm IMS Health:

> Total sales of prescription medications fell by 5.63 percent last year. But the number is not the same for all remedies. Tranquilizer sales grew by 3.86 percent

and sales of heart medication grew by 1.31 percent. The data does not seem coincidental.

It turned out that while tranquilizer sales were increasing, anti-depressant sales were rising even faster. While the Argentine pharmaceutical market as a whole shrunk over the years of hyper-recession between 1998 and 2001, income from anti-depressant sales jumped markedly: 16.5 percent from June 2000 to June 2001 alone.[3] How can we explain this – were these figures the result of the economic crisis, or of pharmaceutical marketing practices? This question has implications both for the question of how mental health "needs" are defined and met, and how the practices of experts in treating mental illnesses are managed. To approach the question requires an investigation of the structure of the Argentine pharmaceutical market, and more specifically, the character of the relations between doctors and pharmaceutical companies. I focus on a specific market research tool, the prescription audit, in order to show how the pharmaceutical market is constituted as a site of strategic intervention and a source of rectifying feedback. Through the numbers that pharmaceutical audit firms generate, market strategists are able to modulate the behavior of doctors, as well as to gauge the success of their own campaigns.

Relations between doctors and firms, mediated by the audit, take on an added importance in doctors' prescription decisions given other characteristics of the setting: the prevalence of unlicensed copies of drugs, the oversupply of doctors in the labor market, and – in the field of mental illness – an epistemological framework oriented toward social and psychic rather than neural explanatory models. As a form of knowledge about health practices that is used in guiding expertise, pharmaceutical audit data emerges as a kind of neoliberal epidemiology, whose trajectory I term "the private life of numbers."

## Private numbers

The pharmaceutical audit industry provides sales data that enables pharmaceutical companies to gauge the results of their marketing campaigns, as well as to monitor their relations with individual doctors. I first became interested in the uses of pharmaceutical sales data while attending editorial meetings of a leading Argentine journal of psychiatry. The editor of the journal, Juan Carlos Stagnaro, had complained at one of the meetings about sales reps from Eli Lilly who had rebuffed his request for sponsorship of his journal, saying: "Why are you asking us for help, when you only prescribe Foxetin?" Gador's Foxetin, a copy of Prozac, was at the time the leading anti-depressant on the Argentine market, while Lilly's patented original languished in sixth place.[4] Stagnaro, who was known for having been a militant activist in the left during the early seventies, was outraged: first at the extortionary tactics of the reps, and secondly at their in-depth knowledge of his prescription practices. How did they know what he prescribed? It turned out that there were database firms that microfilmed individual prescriptions in pharmacies, collated the data and then sold it to pharmaceutical companies. I was impressed at the detail of this private-sphere knowledge – especially in a country where in the public sector it is nearly impossible to find any epidemiological data on the prevalence of mental illness in the population or information on rates of pharmaceutical use.

The gathering of detailed knowledge about prescriptions that Stagnaro had stumbled upon is a window into a more general set of practices that informally regulate contemporary medical expertise, and which are particularly salient in countries – such as Argentina – where other forms of health governance associated with the state or with professional organizations are weak. The "avalanche of numbers" about the population's health status and practices produced by audit firms, and its stark contrast with the lack of data available elsewhere, direct analytic attention to the role these numbers play in shaping doctors' practices.[5]

Here it is useful to reflect briefly on the historical uses of statistical data about populations in guiding the political administration of health. In his genealogy of governmental rationality, Michel Foucault showed that sciences concerned with gathering knowledge about public health first appeared as part of an art of government whose aim was to improve the health and welfare of the population, in the service of increasing the strength of the state.[6] Fostering the well-being of subjects understood as a group of living beings gradually became a central task of government. Forms of knowledge about the health of populations – from statistics, which first referred to "the science of the state," to demography to epidemiology – have since been linked to a variety of modern state-building projects, as well as efforts to modernize colonial and post-colonial territories.[7] The gathering of detailed data about the condition of the population is thus crucial to modern forms of government, in that these numbers constitute the domains that become sites of its intervention – economy, society, and population.[8]

If sciences such as epidemiology emerged in the context of regulating the health of collectivities within a territory, how can we understand new forms of knowledge such as audit data with respect to the problem of government? What is being constituted through numbers, in this case, is not a population of living beings with certain biological regularities, but rather a market of consumers characterized by purchasing trends. It might be said that the role of the social scientist in the welfare or planning state – to constitute and intervene in the collectivity, understood as a national population – finds an analogue, in a post-'social' order, in the contemporary market strategist.[9] Gilles Deleuze hinted at this shift, describing the importance of marketing to the new form of capitalism oriented toward "meta-production": "Marketing is now the instrument of social control and produces the arrogant breed who are our masters," he remarked darkly.[10] Deleuze thought that predominant forms of power relations had shifted as well: disciplinary power had given way to "control," the problem of confinement to the problem of access. This new form of power operated through constant modulation and transmutation rather than surveillance or confession.

But where and on whom does it operate? In the case of pharmaceutical marketing, the figure who is modulated through the question of access is not the patient but the doctor. This complex, interactive control is made possible by audit data, the information collected on pharmaceutical sales and doctors' prescription behavior. In the Argentine milieu, these interlinked operations of knowledge and power work in a distinctive way to shape conduct. In this setting, the ethos of the "social" – described in Chapter 2 – is appropriated within a post-social technology for managing the behavior of doctors. In what follows, I focus on a different kind of expert than in previous chapters. Rather than the doctor or public health official, I look at the work of pharmaceutical market strategists. How do they understand and participate in the changing structure of the Argentine *mundo-psi*?

## Pharmaceutical relations

It is important to underline the distinctive roles of multinational and domestic firms in the Argentine pharmaceutical economy in order to understand the dynamics of the psychopharmaceutical market there. In the 1990s, the Argentine pharmaceutical market was a peculiar one: it was in an unlikely grouping with the United States, Germany, Switzerland, and Japan as the only countries whose domestic producers had a greater market share than foreign ones. But it was unique in that this thriving domestic production was based on high-priced, brand-named copies. The domestic pharmaceutical industry was founded in the 1950s according to the logic of import-substitution, producing copies for the internal market in a climate where patent rights for pharmaceuticals were not recognized. This was part of the developmentalist strategy of the postwar Argentine welfare or "planning" state, which engaged in state-led industrialization that, it was hoped, would lead not only to independence from external powers but would also provide work and affordable goods for the population.[11] By the early 1990s, political and economic turmoil, mounting debt crises, and hyperinflation had led to the abandonment of this model and the adoption, under the pressure of international lenders, of structural adjustment policies oriented toward reducing the role of the state.[12]

The pharmaceutical economy is a good place for looking at the uneven and contingent effects of the liberalization policies enacted by the Menem government in this period. Under neoliberal reform, controls on drug prices were dropped, the protection of local markets was eliminated, and the process of registration and authorization of medications was eased by giving automatic approval to a new drug if it had been approved by regulators in a "leading country" – that is, in Western Europe or North America. The idea was to regulate prices not by state-imposed controls but through competition structured by the free choices of consumers.

Argentina agreed to comply with the TRIPs accord on intellectual property that emerged from the 1986 Uruguay Round of GATT. Multinational pharmaceutical companies were encouraged to expand their efforts in the market through their local subsidiaries. This was obviously bad news for the domestic industry, which controlled most of the market but was dependent on the absence of an effective patent regime. To continue their operations domestic firms depended on the ability to freely expropriate intellectual property, and, during the 1990s, the domestic industry was able to repeatedly delay implementation of the patent regime.[13]

Under these circumstances, many domestic firms thrived in the neoliberal transition by turning exact copies of multinational drugs into local brands. Thus, of fifty-four marketed anti-depressants in 2001, there were fourteen kinds of fluoxetine (Prozac) and six brands of paroxetine (Paxil). This strategy should be distinguished from generic production: these products were marketed brand-names, sold at comparable prices to those of the multinationals. In other words, domestic firms took advantage of the value structure of the transnational pharmaceutical industry, which is based on patent protection, while at the same time defying such protection.[14]

In the spring of 1999, the United States brought a case against Argentina to the World Trade Organization's dispute resolution board for breach of the TRIPS accord.[15] The case was pursued on behalf of Eli Lilly, which accused the domestic firm Gador of unlicensed copying. It concerned Lilly's Zyprexa, a novel anti-psychotic, which was pitted against Gador's brand, Midax – the drug that was being "tested" in Humberto Garcia's department at Hospital Borda as a form of promotional exchange.[16] Lilly was enthusiastic to increase worldwide Zyprexa sales, since its blockbuster $2 billion per year anti-depressant Prozac was scheduled to go off patent in 2003. The brief submitted by the US lobbying group PhRMA claimed, as part of the case against Argentina:

> Argentina is widely recognized as the worst expropriator of US pharmaceutical inventions in the Western Hemisphere, as local firms dominate over 50 percent of the pharmaceutical market currently estimated at almost US $4.1 billion. Substantial and continuing loss of market share, in the range of hundreds of millions of dollars, is directly attributable to Argentina's defective intellectual property regime.[17]

In this context of widespread unlicensed copying, the Menem government's liberalization policies produced a striking change in the Argentine pharmaceutical market. Without price controls, drug costs rose sharply despite the lack of enforcement of patent protection, and while overall pharmaceutical consumption declined by 13 percent in the first five years after reforms, revenues increased by 70 percent.[18] This was in part the result of informal collusion between drug firms and insurance providers, and the systematic blockage of the emergence of a generic industry. But it also had to do with the role of doctors as gatekeepers to consumption, since they, rather than purchasers, made the decision as to which drug would be used. Doctors' prescription decisions are not shaped by price competition. In this sense, the model of rational consumer choice assumed by the strategy of deregulation is clearly an inappropriate one for the pharmaceutical market, which is inherently "imperfect": the one who chooses the drug is not the one who consumes it, and the one who consumes it is not (or often is not) the one who pays for it.

Since the pharmaceutical economy is a restricted sphere of market exchange, it is not obvious who should be assigned the position of the pharmaceutical "consumer" in economic terms. Doctors rather than patients are the target of most advertising. In Argentina it remains illegal to advertise directly to consumers.[19] Doctors can be put in a category of "expert-purchasers": while pharmaceutical advertising is directed to them, they are to select products based not on desire, taste, or self-identity, but on expertise. This means that marketing and science are closely linked: companies use the results of biomedical research to convince doctors to prescribe their products. They also fund such research and sponsor travel to professional conferences and workshops to disseminate the results – so long as these are favorable.

The fact that drug research is both structured by, and structures marketing practices does not in itself de-legitimate knowledge produced and disseminated about pharmaceutical safety and efficacy. Rather, it directs us to consider how doctors come to invest authority in the information that comes to them via pharmaceutically mediated circuits.[20] This requires investigation of the character of the relationships between pharmaceutical companies and doctors. While such relations are strengthened through exchange, the form of trust involved is potentially deliberative: there are structures of accountability on each side.[21]

The ubiquity of gifts from pharmaceutical firms to doctors and researchers has recently drawn increased scrutiny in US professional and ethical discourse.[22] The anxiety provoked is of a "conflict of interest" between the doctor's duty to the patient and a reciprocal obligation to the pharmaceutical company that might compromise doctors' professional integrity. This concern about the danger of the influence of marketing practices on pure science presumes that a clear distinction can be made between rational pharmacology and drug promotion. However, marketing and expertise cannot be so easily distinguished: pharmaceutical companies are producers not only of pills but also of knowledge about their safety and efficacy, and their gifts to doctors of travel to conferences and workshops provide access to the latest expertise.[23] The fortress that is supposed to guard against the crude logic of profit – biomedical expertise – is itself ensconced in the market.

We thus need a more supple understanding of how industry gifts work to shape the practices of doctors. Gift exchanges, as anthropologists have long noted, are not merely a matter of the exchange of goods, but rather work to forge social ties. In the case of relations between doctors and drug companies, the gift should be understood not as a commercial transaction – you prescribe my drug, I send you to your conference – but rather as the construction of an ongoing relationship between the doctor and the company.[24] Rather than a direct transfer of goods, this relationship involves something more like the reciprocal provision of access to guarded resources. From the vantage of firms, these relations enable access to patients – either as drug consumers or as subjects of clinical trials. From the perspective of psychiatrists, the kinds of gifts that are offered – computer equipment, travel to international congresses – represent the possibility of engagement with centers of knowledge production and professional authority. This is especially important in Argentina: given a lack of other means of accessing cosmopolitan systems of expertise, pharmaceutical relations become portals to the global biomedical infrastructure. In their relations with pharmaceutical companies, then, it is not so much that doctors are faced with a conflict of interest between science and the market as that they are embedded in an atmosphere of *interested knowledge*.

## Post-social regulation

Given the presence of so many copies in the Argentine market, and the prohibition on direct-to-consumer advertising, there was intense competition among both domestic and multinational firms for the loyalties of doctors. Meanwhile, there was an oversupply of medical professionals. Doctors had difficulty finding enough private patients to subsist and received abysmally low salaries in public hospitals or social insurance-based clinics. With no research costs, domestic firms could reinvest their earnings directly back into marketing – and the key strategy was to build reciprocal relationships with doctors through gifts.

In Buenos Aires, public hospitals provided important opportunities for access to doctors who commuted to private practices in places like Palermo in the afternoons, and to patient populations for use in clinical trials. Sales reps were ubiquitous in public hospitals. In Hospital Romero, reps lingered outside of the cafeteria, waiting for doctors to come by. Among psychopharmaceuticals, tranquilizers vied with anti-depressants. One month, Roche sales reps made free copies of doctors' keys to advertise a new anti-anxiety medication. A few weeks later, a representative from SmithKline handed out little poetry booklets, entitled "Melancholia," to promote a new anti-depressant. The booklet featured three artistic figures who were supposed to have suffered from depression. The Comte de Lautréamont – Isadore Ducasse of Montevideo – was featured, along with Antonin Artaud and the poet Alejandra Pizarnik.

But more important were major gifts, such as trips to international conferences: at the 2001 American Psychiatric Association (APA) meetings in New Orleans, the largest foreign contingent was from Argentina, with over 500 psychiatrists attending, most of whom had received sponsored trips from pharmaceutical firms. The goal of the sponsored conference trip and other major gifts from pharmaceutical companies was to forge a relationship of loyalty between the doctor and the firm. Two kinds of doctors were particularly sought after for such relationships: prescription leaders and opinion leaders. The basic strategy of building brand loyalty among doctors took different form depending on whether the doctor was an opinion or prescription leader. The delicate work of forging ties with opinion leaders was the job of the sales director or product manager. The key figure in relation to prescription leaders, on the other hand, was the sales rep – to which the Argentine pharmaceutical industry devoted 15 percent of its total revenue, $3.6 billion in 1996.[25] As of 2001, there were 90,000 physicians and 8,000 reps in the country.[26] The rep's task was to work within an assigned territory to increase the market share of his company's products. Strategies for gaining loyalty differed somewhat between domestic and multinational firms. Multinationals relied on their links to prestigious knowledge centers, and regulated themselves (at least in appearance) according to transnational norms; domestic firms, as we will see, invented tactics based on knowledge of the local terrain.

As I explored this milieu, my interest was in recent changes in psychopharmaceutical sales in Argentina, but it was quite difficult to get hold of actual numbers and trends. During my visits to pharmaceutical company offices, I was sometimes allowed to surreptitiously glance at the huge binder from the market research firm IMS Health that listed monthly sales figures, but not to make copies. One sales director I met with in a café had written them down on a piece of paper before coming, let me look at them, and then tore up the piece of paper. Sales data were private numbers. They were quite valuable: it cost pharmaceutical firms up to $150,000 per year to subscribe to the IMS service, which was only one kind of audit. The other service, Close Up, which collected prescriptions from pharmacies, provided a different and complementary set of data, which was equally difficult to access. Both came with software that allowed one to move through their databases, breaking down the information into its significant components: for what pathology did doctors generally prescribe a given drug? Who were the leaders in a given therapeutic class over the last twelve months, and what was the pattern of change? And more impressively, how did sales break down by region – by city, neighborhood, or even postal code?

IMS Health is a multinational firm headquartered in Britain with a subsidiary in Buenos Aires. It is the leading collector and distributor of pharmaceutical sales data in the world. The firm's "primary material" is standardized information on overall sales and specific therapeutic classes, listed in terms of units and value at the level of both regional and global markets. IMS information can also be specified down to the level of the zip code of the pharmacies where drugs are sold. In Argentina IMS buys this information from wholesale drug distributors. As an executive at IMS Argentina told me, they provide only the "pure information" and it is up to the companies themselves to figure out what the numbers mean.

Audit numbers work to make the pharmaceutical market palpable as an entity that can be both a target of strategists' intervention and a source of rectifying "feedback." They provide a vision of the territory as containing a market rather than a population. While the notion of a sales territory is not new, information technology makes possible an immediacy and detail of knowledge that changes the character of territory management.[27] A veteran psychopharmaceutical marketer told me how he used such data to find prescription-leaders, referring to an upper-middle-class neighborhood of Buenos Aires: "You know that Palermo's postal code is 1425 and so you say, 'I want anti-psychotic prescriptions from Palermo.' You find the five best prescribers, and how much they prescribe of what. These are often doctors who are affiliated with high volume insurance plans." The strategist can then do targeted marketing.

In looking at the practices of market strategists, it is possible to see how specific drug markets are both constituted and transformed through the use of such audit data.[28] The market is both that which directs strategy and that which strategists try to re-shape. Firms such as IMS, which generate the numbers that make the market and its transformations visible by auditing drug sales, are crucial to this reflexive loop. Information from IMS makes it possible to grasp the market as a kind of living entity, evolving in unpredictable but measurable ways. In the binder displaying IMS' accumulated data on monthly drug sales, the market's recent evolution becomes visible. Gabriela, product manager for a new anti-depressant that had 33 percent growth in 2000, showed me how strategists distinguished between markets according to therapeutic class:

> Studying the market in the past, we deal with the sales statistics to see what specialties use our products, and seeing, for example the evolution of the numbers I was just talking about. Which are the markets that evolve most rapidly or which are the markets that are growing? I have a general market that is shrinking and this market is growing [pointing to the anti-depressant sales column in the IMS binder], this one is attractive.

A given market could also be seen as a foe, an antagonist. Martín, CNS sales director at a multinational firm whose anti-depressant was struggling in the overcrowded field, told me how he used audit information to design a market strategy:

> First you analyze the market ... What volume it has, how it is evolving, who are the companies that participate, what percentage that company has in sales of its products in the market ... this means: whether I'm going to attack it, whether it's going to react or isn't going to react, how it's going to react, what is the age of the products, what is the index of penetration of the new products that were launched onto the market, what differentiation do you have with what already is there, who are the doctors that prescribe the products in this market, how many there are ...

Along with its primary material of standardized sales data, IMS also collected "qualitative" information through focus-group interviews with panels of experts. The IMS executive explained how to use this qualitative knowledge to plan a marketing campaign: "So: I'm thinking of launching a tranquilizer. The first thing I'm going to do is enter [the database] by pathology, and what am I going to see? From my information, which products do doctors use, which brands, what do they associate it with, in what cases do they use them?"

## Integrated control

An executive at Close Up, an Argentine firm that audits doctors' prescriptions, competing with IMS for the business of pharmaceutical industry clients, explained why IMS' data on territorial sales alone is not sufficient. One must also have individual doctors' prescription numbers at hand, she told me: "It's sort of an integrated control. We don't claim that the pharmaceutical companies don't have to see the territorial sales, but they also have to see the prescriptions. They ... have to be analyzed at the same time, to be able to have more coherent and more precise explanations of what is going on in the field." With a subscription to Close Up's databases, the sales director can look up which doctors prescribe his products, which prescribe competitors', and how much each doctor prescribes. To get this information, Close Up buys or barters microfilmed copies of actual doctors' prescriptions from pharmacy chains. They claim to cover 18 million (out of an estimated 300 million yearly) prescriptions in Argentina, and to have profiles on the behavior of over 90,000 physicians, including nearly

2,000 psychiatrists in the city of Buenos Aires. Their data, in the hands of Lilly reps, was the source of Stagnaro's ire.

Close Up's promotional material makes it clear that the task of the sales strategist is to manage the practices of doctors. One of their brochures advises: "success, for a pharmaceutical company, depends on a primary factor: The physician's prescriptive behavior." How do these numbers work to keep track of and influence such behavior? The Close Up literature provides a rather sinister vision of government by surveillance, targeted specifically at doctors. It seems to confirm recent analyses of audit cultures in terms of the prevalence of "technologies of mistrust" – means of monitoring and shaping behavior that otherwise cannot be checked.[29] If you use Close Up, they tell prospective clients, you will know "what the doctor does, not what he says he does." Their "Audit Pharma" database could be loaded onto hand-held computers which reps consulted while in the field. As one psychiatrist told me, "You feel like you're being watched by the CIA."

But why do sales reps need to find out whether doctors are lying to them? It is a way of checking whether their gifts are actually paying off. As Gabriela told me, "so if [the doctor] says, 'why don't you pay for my trip to the APA [American Psychiatric Association] because I'm prescribing a lot of this product,' to see if it's true or not ... because the doctor can tell all the laboratories that he's prescribing a lot of every product." And thereby get a lot of trips. Sometimes this negotiation between the firm and the doctor is quite direct, Gabriela said: "'Doctor, if you get me twenty more prescriptions a month, I'll send you wherever you want to go.'" But usually the interaction is subtler: "'How can I help you?'" the rep might ask.

## Territory management

But doctors are not the only parties subject to audit surveillance. While reps track doctors' behavior armed with knowledge of their actual prescription practices, sales managers monitor how their reps are doing. Gabriela pointed to a number in her IMS binder and explained:

> This statistic shows the "market-share" of each visitor in each zone. So you know that you have a visitor in Santa Fe and you see the market-share of each product in this zone, so you see how this visitor is doing in the zone. And you are doing what is called "Territory Management," you are seeing the profitability of each zone or how each visitor is doing.

The fact that sales performance is constantly monitored colors the interactions of doctors and reps. Reps, who try to form relationships of "friendship" or at least mutual obligation with doctors, plead for help from doctors in raising their territorial sales figures. Meanwhile, with this information on their own salespeople, the audit becomes a reflexive technique for the firm, a way of directing strategy but also a form of self-modulation, given the precarious uncertainty of the market. Close Up claims that its service for measuring reps' productivity, called "Feedback" (in English), allows the product manager to know exactly what is happening in the sales territories:

> Measure the prescriptive productivity of each one of the representatives and their supervisors, through prescriptions captured from the visited doctors. Eliminate the deviations of productivity measurement according to territory [this is a dig at IMS]. An objective and valid measure of the results from promotion with visited doctors. Feedback is the only technical report that makes it possible to make precise decisions to identify market opportunities.

How well was a given campaign – of samples, information-diffusion, symposia – going? The reflexive loop provided by the audit database allowed for self-evaluation and transformation. As Martín said upon getting the disappointing results of his new campaign: "We thought we would grow 15 percent this year, and we're getting there, we're doing pretty well. But one has to be permanently monitoring what's happening." The "market" – here, the accumulated prescribing decisions of the country's 90,000 physicians – was a semi-controllable entity that on the one hand was what one wanted to act upon but which also reacted – reinforcing successful decisions and throwing unsuccessful ones into question. The modulation was interactive – pharmaceutical marketers regulated doctors, but doctors, as a collectivity represented in the market's monthly evolution and the inevitable bell curve of any specific product's life-cycle – shaped the actions of marketers as well.

## Opinion leaders

While directly surveying prescriptions helps sales reps to manage relations with prescription leaders, with whom one can make arrangements of exchange, a more subtle set of dynamics occurs with opinion leaders. Explicit negotiation and direct exchange are not typical of the relationship between the opinion leader and the firm. In fact it can be counterproductive to bring sales numbers into these relationships. Here the main technique for the company is to develop trusting relationships with well-known doctors. This task is not left to the reps in the field, but is the responsibility of the sales director or product manager. Audit numbers play a role in the process, but in a more subtle way. Gabriela, the young CNS product manager at an upstart European firm, told me how they decide with whom to develop contacts:

> We work with doctors with high prescriptive power, very prestigious doctors, who can establish some trend in the use of psychopharmaceuticals, either because they have a lot of patients or because they are well known, for example, they are "speakers" [in English]. Or because they decide on purchases, for example in hospitals, or they participate in some important institution or in the psychiatric associations, so these doctors are those that enable us – through a good, fluid contact and relation with this doctor – to get the message we need out to the doctors who follow his trends.

In the case of opinion leaders, it is not a question of monitoring prescriptions, but of developing alliances – of having these respected figures available for seminars, symposia, the authorship of "scientific literature" to be disseminated. The role of the opinion leader is something like a brand spokesman – although opinion leaders are typically allied with multiple firms. There is a hierarchy of opinion leaders, and of firms. Market strategists know as well as anyone who the key players in the field are – and in fact can play a major role in making them into opinion leaders. Through these relationships, companies are able to ally themselves with experts who command respect and have the trust of other doctors. Conversely, these experts are able to reaffirm their authority and to disseminate their knowledge through their relationship with pharmaceutical firms – such as Marielz Ruiz, whose book on psychopharmacology was sponsored by Gabriela's firm and introduced by the head of Pharmacology at the University of Buenos Aires.

I ask Ruiz about the role of pharmaceutical companies in the dissemination of knowledge about medication. Her training in pharmacology gives her a distinctive way of thinking, she says, but for those without such training it is more difficult to keep up with new developments. As soon as she looks at an article, she can see if it is serious or not, but others are more credulous. "There is a lot of pressure, a lot of marketing," she says. "If people don't know what they are doing, in psychopharmacology, the results are not obvious – this is not intensive care, you cannot kill patients. So there is more space for error, and a lot of *chantada*. One has to be very stupid to cause harm. In this sense, the laboratories also perform a noble role – they fund training, sending people to congresses."

But don't the psychiatrists have to prescribe a certain amount to get these favors? "Yes – but there are two kinds of marketing strategies – one for prescription leaders, and the other for opinion leaders." She is one of the latter. So she does not have to sell the drug, and besides, she could go to the conferences anyway, without the help. If they invite her to give talks about the drug, she doesn't accept, even if it is a good drug. But it's helpful – if there is a two-day symposium in Miami, she can go, help her training, get up to date. I ask if she is going to the upcoming APsA meeting in Mar del Plata. No, she already has a full schedule: first the American Psychiatric Association meetings in Washington and then the World Psychiatric Association in Hamburg.

Another technique for forging links with opinion leaders is to offer them a marketing-oriented "Phase IV" clinical trial. This is a trial of an already approved medication intended for promotional purposes rather than to actually glean information on the efficacy of the drug, as we saw in Chapter 2. The ostensible study results in a "poster" that is presented at an international scientific congress, with travel expenses paid for by the company. For young doctors, this is one way to begin to appear in circuits of expertise as an emerging opinion leader.

Among his cohort, Martín Beren has a reputation for having "close relations" with the laboratories. Recently Janssen sent him to a high-profile conference in France on Risperdal. The pharmaceutical companies present in Argentina can be divided along two axes, he tells me: international versus national, and those that are interested in psychiatry as opposed to those that are not. The international companies are huge, like Coca Cola, and the people who work for them are dull, uncreative: there is not much flexibility in working for them and they have many norms that don't work here. These companies often don't understand the rules of the game in Argentina, so, for example, they have gone after the patent issue.

Firms have to tread lightly with opinion leaders. As a veteran strategist tells me: if he is putting on an event, he makes sure to invite all the most important opinion leaders. If you leave someone out, they'll be upset and won't prescribe your product. The opinion leaders are very sensitive, he says: "they want to feel important." In this respect multinational firms have an advantage given their ability to link local opinion leaders to their networks of prestigious transnational experts. Companies strive to develop a reputation for taking good care of their opinion leaders. Gabriela, the product manager, says of her company's efforts at conferences: "If there is something that distinguishes us it's that we don't make huge investments of money but we do make high quality investments, we are with them all the time, it's not that we invite them and then they go alone. We are very careful with the relationship of the doctor with the laboratory, because we don't have such a big [sales] force." And the psychiatrists care about how they are taken care of as well. At one of the editorial meetings of the psychiatry journal two members of the board spoke about their upcoming trip to the APA meetings in Washington, DC: the younger of the two was going early to attend a Lilly course on Zyprexa and depression. "Oh, it's marvelous," enthused the more experienced one, "you're going to love it, and they look after you so well."[30]

The opinion leaders I spoke with generally told me that they never endorse a specific product, and only accept offers from reputable companies whose products they believe in. The reputation of the firm then becomes a means of ethical regulation. Firms that wish to ally with prestigious opinion leaders have to maintain a image of propriety: they do not give out samples ("like the others do"); they provide access to information, sponsor studies, help patients.

A former Janssen marketing director described a campaign he ran for the anti-psychotic Risperdal that won a prize from an international patient organization. Its theme was "reinsertion" – an attempt to go further than just medication, toward resocialization. Ten patients from a schizophrenic patient support group were hired at Janssen for short periods to do simple tasks like photocopying, were paid small salaries and then received scholarships for training and certificates for having worked. The program showed that these patients needed less medication and had fewer relapses – that they could be successfully "reinserted" into society. More than being directly about sales, he said, the campaign was about shaping the image of the company as one that was interested in the "quality of life" of patients.

The CNS sales strategist for Abbott Argentina told me that there is a "symbiotic relation" between the representatives and the doctors: representatives provide samples as aids in trying a new medication. Samples also serve a "social" function, he says: by giving them out Abbott tries to minimize the monthly cost for needy patients. They even provide free medication to some – people who have lost their job, who have social problems. "It's good for the doctor–laboratory relation to give the patient a hand," he explains.

## Local knowledge

The Risperdal campaign was ingenious in its awareness of the importance of issues such as social reintegration to the epistemic milieu that it targeted,

Argentine mental health. Psychiatry is distinct from other biomedical fields in the multiple forms of expertise that coexist within it, each of which has a distinct model of the cause, site, and optimal modes of treatment of disorder. As we have seen, whereas in the United States, psychiatry had recently shifted toward a neuroscientific approach that considered mental illness to be a discrete disease located in the brain of the patient, in Argentina social and psychoanalytic explanations remained strong. For many members of the *mundo-psi*, biomedical psychiatry was associated with the political right, and with the violent 1976–83 military dictatorship, which persecuted psychoanalysts and social psychiatrists as subversive to the traditional moral order.

As a result, the critical social psychiatry associated with *salud mental* was predominant in public mental health discourse. This ethos posed a challenge for pharmaceutical companies accustomed to campaigning to psychiatrists in terms of serotonin levels and synaptic receptors. How, for example, might one appeal to former *salud mental* activists? Consider Stagnaro, a staunch critic of globalization who associated the new biomedical psychiatry with American imperialism, and who linked the global extension of diagnostic standards to the power of the pharmaceutical industry. As he told me: "In Argentina, the boom of the pharmaceutical industry in the last fifteen years has been notable, more or less coinciding with the beginning of the reading of DSM and the arrival of Friedman and Kaplan's manual."

Here we can distinguish between the types of knowledge about the market that strategists gathered. One was quantitative, grid-like, evolving over time, displaying trends, providing a picture of the market – this was what IMS and Close Up provided. The other type of knowledge was local, qualitative, picked up gradually through interactions with doctors. It showed an awareness of the ethos of the market. This distinction helps answer the question of why Gador's generic fluoxetine was the leading anti-depressant in 1998, while Lilly's Prozac remained far behind.

A CNS market strategist I spoke with at Gador was something of a legend in the field. In our interview, he argued that quantitative audit data was only necessary if one did not already know the market – "they are orienters, but they are not [so] important ... We don't apply some of the tools that other companies do, because our strength, in the case of the sales force, is very different, this is a totally atypical company." In what sense? "In the average seniority of our men ... in each of their zones ... our man has a lot of stability and is someone who inspires trust." In other words, sustaining close, long-term relationships with doctors was one of Gador's chief tactics.

The strategist spoke angrily about Lilly's protest before the WTO: Gador was not a pirating firm, he explained; they had tried to license the rights to sell olanzapine locally, but Lilly refused, insisting on its exclusive rights. He told me about some of the company's contributions to the training of Argentine psychiatrists. Not only do they provide drug samples, sponsor studies and local conferences, and disseminate published research, they also cultivate a network of opinion leaders, whose trips to foreign conferences they pay for. Moreover, they print and distribute Spanish-language editions of DSM-IV.

Gador's recent CNS ad campaigns illustrated the company's understanding of their target market, Argentine psychiatrists. Gador strategists intuited that unlike the United States, lock-and-key illustrations of neurotransmitter re-uptake inhibition might not be the most effective technique for pitching psychopharmaceuticals in this milieu. As an alternative, Gador took up the social analysis of the effects of economic crisis on the nation's mental health as the basis for its CNS marketing campaign. The campaign used "globalization" and the anxieties it provoked to promote its extensive line of anxiolytics and anti-depressants. One ad featured a series of grim figures traversing a map of the world, suffering from symptoms of globalization: "Deterioration of interpersonal relations," "Deterioration in daily performance," "Unpredictable demands and threats," "personal and familial suffering," "loss of social role," "loss of productivity." Gador's explicit articulation of pharmaceuticals as a means to alleviate social suffering indicates how medication can operate in distinctive ways according to its milieu of use.[31]

I asked the strategist how he had come up with the "globalization" campaign: "For as long as Gador has been putting together molecules, the work has been, in some way, to establish clearly the niches to which each one of these molecules is directed and, in this sense, globalization as a cultural concept – it is too strong not to use it." He told me about the next phase of the campaign: "Right now we are in a later stage; we realized that the medical audience and even the users are absolutely conscious that globalization brings all these problems and we are in a campaign that is in the next stage, and this is that of *vulnerability*." Another firm's CNS product manager noted the cleverness of Gador's word choice, pointing out its resonance with a popular Argentine television series, called *Los Vulnerables*, about an eclectic group of patients involved in group therapy. The Vulnerability campaign was kicked off by a Gador-sponsored symposium in October 2000 called "Stress, anxiety, and depression: A progressive clinical sequence," at which a number of important local opinion leaders spoke. Among the organizers of the symposium was Stagnaro, the journal editor who had been so irate with Lilly's reps: Gador had succeeded where Lilly had failed – by approaching the opinion leader on his own terrain.

## High contact

Let me return now to the question with which I began the chapter: why were anti-depressant and anxiolytic sales rising so markedly while the rest of the Argentine pharmaceutical industry was in recession? Were Argentine patients being prescribed psychopharmaceuticals in increasing numbers as a palliative for the stress caused by the economic crisis? When I posed the question of why anti-depressant sales were increasing, market strategists gave the same response I had seen in the media: they pointed to turmoil caused by the deteriorating social and economic conditions of the country. The Close Up executive suggested a couple of reasons for the phenomenon: on the one hand, older anxiolytics were losing market share to anti-depressants; but also, a tremendous increase in panic attacks, especially in Buenos Aires, was driving up anti-depressant sales. Why were there more panic attacks?

> Because there is a totally confusing situation in this country ... a very stressful situation; there's a huge amount of unemployment, there's under-employment, and on the other hand we Argentines are in a dead end. It seems like we don't have or we can't find the way out ... You're an anthropologist, you understand well. Problems of social relations are being added to personal problems.

The overwhelming sense of insecurity linked to the ongoing economic crisis was generally the first answer pharmaceutical executives and strategists gave me to the question of why anti-depressant sales were increasing. When I asked the executive from IMS Argentina about recent sales trends, he said:

> You've been here for a month. You must know by now ... the socio-economic situation and the politics of the country make it so that people are consuming more anxiolytics all the time and are going to the psychiatrist more all the time ... Imagine a man who works, who has ... who had a decent quality of life and has an income around a thousand or twelve hundred dollars a month. A few years ago he could live on this, now it's not enough to live on, so he becomes anxious. Don't forget that everyone in Argentina, everyone, has a tremendous fear, which is to be left without work.

As the crisis in Argentina reached its zenith toward the end of 2001 with the fall of two presidents and the record default on its $132 billion national debt, the growth in psychopharmaceutical sales became a subject of increasing interest to the press. A Spanish-language *BBC online* article in January 2002 cited reports from the pharmaceutical industry that while overall sales had decreased 10 percent in the previous year, anti-depressant sales had increased 13 percent and tranquilizer sales 4 percent.[32] *The Observer* cited similar statistics in a piece called "Argentina Hits Rock Bottom," again linking the crisis to increased symptoms of anxiety and increased suicide rates.[33] In general, these sales data were interpreted as evidence of the effects of the economic crisis on the mental health conditions of the population. After mentioning an increase in stress-related medical visits in the wake of the crisis, the BBC article quoted an Argentine psychiatrist: "Argentines feel devalued. People feel lost. The rules of the game have changed. Working hard for many hours doesn't mean economic security any more."[34] "Devaluation" here referred to the uncoupling of the dollar-peso peg, which for ten years had provided Argentines with a tenuous sense of economic security, while at the same time hampering the government's capacity for macro-economic intervention to promote growth.

The social analysis of psychopharmaceutical sales patterns was almost second nature to market strategists. A veteran pharmaceutical sales representative told me his theory of the relation of social change to drug consumption:

> In the seventies you had the Cold War, and a heightened sense of tension and nervousness – so valium sold well. Then in the eighties with the phenomenon of the yuppies and their emphasis on career success, the drugs of choice were anxiolytics. In the nineties anti-depressants became popular, for two reasons: first, there were those who had failed to meet their expectations in the eighties and so they were depressed. But pharmaceutical marketing strategies also had to do with it.

To interpret increased psychopharmaceutical sales over the period of economic crisis as an instance of the medicalization of suffering, though tempting for a critical social scientist, was somehow redundant in this context: it was a part of assumed knowledge that increased symptoms of anxiety and depression were linked to social and political phenomena. So much so that the very salience of social accounts of suffering served not as a *critique* of the role of pharmaceutical marketing but as its *basis*, as could be seen in the case of Gador's "globalization" campaign. Even central nervous system product managers did not subscribe to a biological model of depression. Thus Martín, in discussing the question of the sources of depression, protested the predominance of psychoanalytic explanations in Argentina – in favor of a social one:

> It's not necessarily the case that the current modification, which is the cause of the depression, has its origin in what happened to me during my infancy. It's very likely that this marks us, but also the context and this sense of feeling ever-more vulnerable before change … The world is changing very fast, too fast for all of us. Today I was talking with someone about this issue and how we're stuck now – the deficit, the default or not, devaluation or not, it's such an uncertain horizon.

Media pundits, sales directors, and market research executives agreed: a generalized sense of insecurity linked to the economic crisis was driving up psychopharmaceutical sales. But in fact it was not clear whether it was the effects of the crisis on the nation's psychic state or the promotional strategies that harnessed these ostensible effects that were the primary cause of changes in the psychopharmaceutical market. Sales data at first seem to provide evidence of the growing medicalization of social disorder, but it is instructive to distinguish between actual data on the transformations of the market from the stories that were being told about these data.

While mass media attention to psychopharmaceutical consumption appeared to increase toward the end of 2001, such stories about the relation between such consumption and social transformation were not a new phenomenon. In 1996 – a moment that five years later looked like the height of the 1990s economic boom in Argentina – a piece called "The Ranking of Remedies" appeared in *La Nación*.[35] In it, the President of the Argentine Federation of Pharmacies hinted at the role of social crisis in shaping the consumption of pharmaceuticals: "Perhaps what is most notable is the boom of the anti-depressants, whose massive consumption took off in our society at the beginning of the seventies. And not by chance, as will be understood." The author of the article commented: "Of the five products most sold annually in our country, one is an antibiotic and the rest are a faithful reflection of the two great maladies of our time: stress and *nervios*." More pharmaceutical industry representatives added their interpretations: "Who isn't *nervioso* in Argentina today?" asked the Executive Director of the Council of Multinational Laboratories. The President of the College of Pharmacists also provided a sociological explanation of psychopharmaceutical sales data: "Life conditions are getting worse … and we live in a permanent state of alteration. In 1994 alone, more than 16 million boxes of psychotropics were sold." This narrative, in which sales of anti-depressant and anti-anxiety medications were increasing as a result of economic crisis, cohered with the "social" model of the sources of psychic suffering: conditions in the social environment could best explain psychic ills – and with the message of Gador's "globalization" and "vulnerability" campaigns.

However, it was not certain that the actual consumption of medication had changed significantly during the economic crisis. Martín told me: "the quantity of patients treated with anti-depressants hasn't increased that much; what has changed is the average *price* of anti-depressants." This would make sense given the pattern in the early nineties in the rest of the Argentine market – an increase in revenue generated not by an increase in consumption but by the use of newer, more expensive drugs. In this case the explanation for increasing anti-depressant sales revenue could be a gradual switch, especially among non-specialists, from tranquilizers – still used far more than anti-depressants – to the new SSRIs.

In fact, Martín thought that the market was still relatively untapped. "I think it's the tip of the iceberg, what we have today. Today the anti-depressant market, even though as you said it's growing, I think that the potential is easily ten times more than what it is now." How did he know the potential since no data were available on the prevalence of depression in Argentina? He used transnational epidemiology, combining it with audit firms' data on drug sales: "If you take the index of the prevalence of depression in any country in the world, which is around – let's take a conservative number, 3 percent – you would be talking about a million or so people ... in reality that would be pure depression, but if you begin to take the different types of depression, dysthymia, we're talking about three million people ... And today you have, treated patients, 350,000, more or less." I was impressed by the number – not because it was low, or because it was right, but because I hadn't been able to get even an estimate from anyone before – not from the health ministry, which didn't have them, nor from the database firms, which wouldn't give them away.

Martín's argument that it was higher prices more than the actual number of patients treated that was driving up sales revenue was substantiated by a study I initiated, given the paucity of other available data, with a group of pharmaco-epidemiologists affiliated with the University of Belgrano and an Argentine pharmacy benefits management firm. The study compared the pattern of tranquilizer and anti-depressant use over the period from 1997 to 2000 among members of four separate health plans, comprising a population of about 600,000 people.[36] It turned out that over this period there was a sharp *decline* in tranquilizer exposure in this population, from 21 percent to 14 percent, and a slight increase in the number of patients taking anti-depressants, from 3.6 percent to 4.5 percent of affiliates. What this meant was that the health plans were reimbursing many *fewer* patients overall for such medications. These results are striking in comparison with the steep rise in psychopharmaceutical sales figures cited by the media as evidence of the effect of the economic crisis on the population's mental health. They are substantiated by data obtained from IMS Health on changes in psychopharmaceutical unit sales volume in Argentina over the last five years, which indicate that overall tranquilizer unit sales declined by 5 percent between 1997 and 2001, while anti-depressant unit sales increased by 9 percent over the same period – but from a much smaller base.[37]

If we add to the results of this study another piece of privately held information we can be more precise about what was happening in the market: it turned out that the impressive growth in anti-depressant sales revenue in Argentina between December 1998 and June 2001 – from 45 million dollars per year to 54 million dollars per year – could be mostly accounted for by sales of Paxil and Zoloft alone, which leapfrogged Gador's Foxetin to become the market leaders in the SSRI field.[38] This was due to intensive contact between reps and doctors, and to the enviable position of these drugs within the product life-cycle. Thus Glaxo and Pfizer had apparently been successful in convincing doctors to switch from tranquilizers to their SSRIs – which were now indicated for anxiety disorders as well as for depression.

Rather than a precipitous increase in overall psychopharmaceutical consumption caused by the economic crisis, the growth in anti-depressant revenue could best be explained in terms of a specific tactic: the work by sales reps and opinion leaders to convince doctors to prescribe the newer SSRIs instead of tranquilizers for symptoms of stress, anxiety, and depression. It is worth noting that such a shift is in accord with the recommendations of leading health authorities, who have expressed alarm at high rates of tranquilizer use, often tied to addiction and self-medication, in countries such as France and Argentina. In other words, "high contact" – the intensification of relations between pharmaceutical companies and doctors – worked in this case to shape prescription habits more or less along the lines that officially sanctioned expertise would authorize. Thus, the increase in anti-depressant sales as a result of marketing practices does not necessarily indict the pharmaceutical industry for its dangerous influence on scientific medicine. Rather, it demands an understanding of the transnational biomedical infrastructure that links knowledge, regulation, and the market – and which does so in different ways depending on divergent economic, institutional and professional contexts. In Argentina in the late 1990s, "interested knowledge" – the conjuncture of marketing and biomedical research – directed doctors' prescriptive behavior along the lines public health authorities advised, but through the regulatory technique of the audited pharmaceutical gift relation.

## The regulation of specificity

What can the dynamics of marketing psychopharmaceuticals in Argentina tell us about the controversies these drugs have provoked in the North? One issue has been whether the availability and promotion of the new anti-depressants (SSRIs) illegitimately "produce" the illnesses they are meant to treat. In other words, is the apparent increase in the prevalence of conditions such as depression a result of pharmaceutical industry marketing?

The legitimacy of the demand for anti-depressants has been a question in part because the curative properties of these drugs seem to transmute depending on what illness they are supposed to treat, and also on the expert's model of disorder. There is, then, a dynamic interaction between the illness population and the drug itself. The World Health Organization (WHO) and other international bodies have pointed to an apparent epidemic of affective disorders worldwide, citing figures indicating that 10 percent of the population is expected to experience depression at some point in their lives.[39] As David Healy and others have pointed out, this is an especially impressive figure given how rare a diagnosis "depression" was in cosmopolitan psychiatry as recently as three decades ago.[40]

There are various ways of interpreting the apparent rise in depression's prevalence in Europe and North America over the past few decades. The position of cosmopolitan psychiatric epidemiology is that the disorder has remained more or less constant over historical periods and across geographical divides, but that its "true" prevalence is only now at last being recognized. Another approach is to suggest that the growth in depression is a sign of changing cultural models of the self, given recent social transformations and new personal demands.[41] A third argument is that the rise in diagnosed cases of depression can most likely be attributed to the success of marketing practices that promote the expansion of the diagnosis of depression in order to increase the prescription of anti-depressants.[42] As Healy puts it, "we are at present in a state when companies can not only seek to find the key for the lock but can dictate a great deal of the shape of the lock to which a key must fit."[43] That is, companies design not only medication, but also the conditions that the medications are supposed to target.

The Argentine case suggests another interpretation, though one related to the latter argument: that the source of the rise in depression in Northern countries has to do, not only with such marketing pressure, but also with the regulatory demand that prescription drugs correspond to specific illnesses. In Argentina, one finds the rapid expansion of anti-depressant sales without, it seems, a concomitant increase in the diagnosis of depression as a discrete clinical entity. What is striking there is the general absence of the notion of "depression" as a biological condition located in the brain that is the target of anti-depressant action. The same drugs that in North America are associated with intervention into the biological condition of depression in Argentina are prescribed as treatments for socially induced stress.

In the North, the ambiguity of anti-depressant action, in combination with a medical system structured by the specificity model, has led to the expansion of the depression diagnosis. As Mikkel Borch-Jacobsen writes: "If depression has spread to the extent that it has, it's because it is that on which antidepressants have an effect."[44] But while anti-depressants may "recruit" depressive patients in the United States, SSRI sales in Argentina were thriving in the absence of a notable increase in "depression" as a diagnostic entity and mode of self-identification. The Argentine case indicates that not only marketing practices, but also regulatory demands and epistemic cultures play a key role in the growth of flexible diagnostic identities such as depression. The missing ingredient for the growth of the category of biomedical depression in Argentina was not pharmaceutical marketing but the regulatory bodies – government and third-party payers – that demand specificity of effect in order to authorize pharmaceutical prescription, and the use of DSM-based protocols in the clinic that embed the model of specificity.

In the United States and Europe, regulatory and professional demands that medication be targeted at a specific illness located in the brain shaped the marketing of biomedical "depression" as that which anti-depressants are meant to treat. In Argentina, in contrast, the new SSRIs did not need the specific illness entity of depression in order to circulate. Without the imperative to diagnose according to the specificity model, the diagnosis of depression did not spread. So one could have an intense set of operations and dynamics in place for the circulation and distribution of pharmaceuticals – and SSRIs could markedly expand their use – but this could occur somewhat independently of the extension of a biomedicalized psychiatry, and independently of the diagnostic category of depression. SSRIs found a different means of entering the professionally mediated marketplace: doctors understood and used them not as a treatment for a lack of serotonin in the brain but for the suffering caused by the social situation – the sense of insecurity and vulnerability that the recent economic and political crisis had wrought.

# 6
# The segmented phenotype

In April 2003, the United States Patent and Trade Office awarded a patent to Genset for its invention of a gene associated with psychiatric illness. "The invention," read the patent, "provides means to identify compounds useful in the treatment of schizophrenia, bipolar disorder, and related diseases, means to determine the predisposition of individuals to said disease, as well as means for the disease diagnosis and prognosis."[1] The patented gene, on the long arm of chromosome 13, had been identified using DNA extracted from schizophrenia patients in a Quebecois population as part of a collaboration between Genset and Janssen Pharmaceuticals.

In the short term the implications of the patent, and related findings published in scientific journals, were unclear.[2] For one thing, the same genetic variant had also been found among Genset's Argentine bipolar samples. Thus, rather than stabilizing the diagnostic entities – schizophrenia and bipolar disorder – that had been used in the company's search for genes linked to susceptibility to mental illness, the finding seemed to undermine them. Moreover, the basic unit of information that was the object of the patent was elusive: the list of possible entities ranged from "gene," to "biallelic marker," to "susceptibility locus," to an "isolated nucleic acid" comprising the "open reading frame" that encoded the gene's protein product. Indeed, the meaning or usefulness of the word "gene" was no longer certain in the field of molecular biology: the postwar paradigm of the genetic code or blueprint was in question in the wake of the completion of the Human Genome Project.[3] One might say, following Evelyn Fox Keller, that at the turn of the twenty-first century, the gene was a site of "productive uncertainty."[4] As a patentable informational unit, the notion of the gene provided an economic and scientific framework from which to proceed, rather than a clearly identifiable entity, much less a causal basis of mental illness.

Findings like these marked the beginnings of a new phase of inquiry rather than a solution to the problem of the sources of psychic distress. Multiple actors were at work in shaping the future uses and meaning of psychiatric illness genes. For companies like Genset, the question was how the gene could be made productive of value – simultaneously biomedical and economic. The economic value of genomic information relied on its projected biomedical uses. The Genset patent listed a number of possible applications for the schizophrenia-bipolar gene, including: knowledge of illness etiology that could lead to new drugs directed against the cause of the illness; early identification of subjects at risk of developing the illness; the efficient design and evaluation of suitable therapeutic solutions including individualized strategies for optimizing drug usage; screening of substances modulating the expression of the gene; tools for associating genomic markers to the disorder; and tools for associating these markers to the effects of medication.

These various possible uses can be framed in terms of two basic domains of application. One was in the generation of new targets for drug development. The other, with more imminent clinical possibilities, was in creating diagnostic instruments, either by locating susceptibility genes or by finding genetic markers linked to medication response. This last application is recognizable as "pharmacogenomics" – which, according to many biotech analysts, was one of the more promising potential sources of value to emerge from the Human Genome Project. Pharmacogenomics sought to link genetic markers directly to pharmacological intervention – finding the right treatment for a patient according to his or her genotype. I will return below to this idea – but first I want to illustrate its potential significance for psychiatry, given the uncertainties that pervade its everyday operations in the clinic.

## The therapeutic trial

The logic of pharmacogenomics – the configuration of disorder in terms of already existing treatment – is similar to that of the "therapeutic trial." In the absence of physiological indicators directing doctors to the appropriate chemical intervention into mental illness, doctors may use an intervention technique to determine a diagnostic entity. The therapeutic trial proposes that the patient's condition may be surmised given his or her capacity to respond to a specific treatment. However, in the case of mental illness, the trial's capacity to delineate an actual illness entity is controversial.

This can be illustrated by looking at a famous moment in the history of psychoanalysis. Freud and Breuer's classic *Studies on Hysteria* recounts the authors' invention of the cathartic technique – the talking cure – to induce the recollection of repressed traumatic events. In the book, Freud and Breuer argue that a successful cure through speech can be used as a therapeutic trial to determine a diagnosis of hysteria. As they report of one patient, a girl who had suffered for years from attacks of general convulsions that were thought to be epileptic seizures, but which they diagnose as hysteric:

> She was hypnotized with a view to a differential diagnosis, and promptly had one of her attacks. She was asked what she was seeing and replied "The dog! The dog's coming!"; and in fact it turned out that she had had the first of her attacks after being chased by a savage dog. *The success of the treatment confirmed the choice of the diagnosis.*[5]

For Freud and Breuer, the effectiveness of the cathartic method proves the hypothesis of hysteria, whose source is the repressed traumatic memory – the attack by the dog. The therapeutic trial addresses the problem of diagnostic uncertainty by approaching the illness in terms of its specific intervention. However, critics have argued that such a trial does not resolve the question of the existence of the putative disorder – in this case, hysteria. As Mikkel Borch-Jacobsen writes: "Like so many other 'neuroses,' 'mental illnesses,' or 'psychosomatic disorders,' but more blatantly and spectacularly so, hysteria is an illness that exists for the sake of the cure."[6] In his revisionist account of the central case described in *Studies on Hysteria*, Borch-Jacobsen argues that Anna O.'s "hysteria" and its traumatic etiology was actually a collaborative production between Breuer and Anna O., a kind of "folie-a-deux" in which the doctor's expectations shaped the patient's performance. He suggests that Breuer's technique of intervention, hypnotic suggestion, in combination with his model of illness, actually brought Anna O.'s symptoms into being.

David Healy and Philippe Pignarre have made a similar critique of contemporary biomedical psychiatry, focusing on the relation between depression and anti-depressants. They suggest that through a complex elaboration between the effects of these drugs and the patient's understanding of what distress signals are supposed to look like, "depression" has come to be a general term for a number of disparate forms of suffering whose only commonality is that they respond to "anti-depressants." This phenomenon, they argue, explains apparent recent increases in the prevalence of depression in North America and Europe.[7] Here the movement from intervention to illness is something like the relation of catharsis to hysteria in Freud and Breuer's work, except that in contemporary psychiatry the intervention that shapes diagnostic representation is not hypnotic suggestion but psychopharmacology. And the medium in which this dynamic elaboration takes place is not the unconscious but the brain or the genome.

This critique points to the problem of the legitimacy of the therapeutic trial for delineating actual illness-entities. Given that the class of medications known as anti-depressants have a wide range of possible effects, critics argue their capacity to alleviate symptoms in a given case does not mean that "depression" is the specific illness entity being treated. The indication-expansion of the newer anti-depressants still under patent protection – for the treatment of panic disorder, social phobia, pre-menstrual dysphoria, and other conditions – points to this ambiguity: the multiplicity of potential effects of the drugs combines with the regulatory demand for illness-specificity to produce novel illness-entities, or to expand existing ones. This critique does not suggest that the drugs do not "work"; but rather that how they work, and what they work on, depends upon the milieu of their use – as we have seen in prior chapters.

The analogy between late nineteenth-century hysteria and early twenty-first-century depression is useful in order to clarify the operations of the therapeutic trial in contemporary psychopharmacology, but needs to be qualified. While the diagnosis of hysteria multiplied in the nineteenth century through extended doctor–patient encounters in the clinic, depression and other contemporary psychiatric disorders are embedded in a more complex set of relations, involving not only the clinic, but also insurance reimbursement protocols, professional training practices, biomedical research, and governmental regulation. The norm of specificity – of coupling diagnosis directly to intervention – links these disparate domains. And yet, as the case of anti-depressants and depression illustrates, the legitimacy of the disorders generated in the process remains in question. To understand the stakes involved in the question of whether a therapeutic trial is a valid means of identifying disorder, it will be helpful to return to the Argentine milieu.

## Case presentation

A central theme of this book has been the question of how expertise recognizes and intervenes in pathological human behavior and thought. I have argued that psychiatry's difficulty in stabilizing its objects of knowledge and justifying its treatments has been an ongoing problem for its legitimacy as a biomedical discipline. As we have seen, the field's aims, objects, and modes of authorization vary according to the social and political milieu in which it is practiced. The context in which expertise is called for structures how illness is seen – and divergent systems of knowledge can lead to quite different modes of intervention. The setting of this study in the Argentine *mundo-psi* has demonstrated the epistemological and political challenges faced by any attempt to generate universally valid techniques for identifying and intervening in mental illness.

The question of the validity of a therapeutic trial in determining a diagnostic entity is the topic of intense debate in a session I attend at the *Asociación Psicoanalítica Argentina* (APA). Two psychiatry residents, Adrian and Valeria, present a case to a gathering of members of the APA. The discussion following their presentation concerns the distinction between two disorders that belong to incommensurable epistemic systems: DSM-IV obsessive-compulsive disorder and the psychoanalytic category of psychosis. At issue is the relation between psychic structure and medication: specifically, whether the results of drug intervention can lead the expert to a diagnosis of the illness – the issue of the therapeutic trial.

Adrian begins: the case involves a girl in her teens, who was referred to the residents by her therapist for possible drug treatment. In the referral, the therapist – a Lacanian analyst – told the residents that she could not do anything more for the girl's suffering, and that the girl needed anti-psychotic drug treatment to stem her delusions. The girl's delusions are centered around a voice that gives her orders, explains Adrian. She first heard the voice when she was nine years old, when it appeared as though it were in her thoughts – giving orders, controlling her, threatening to do bad things to others, like stab her mother to death, if she did not obey. The orders took the form of time-intensive rituals, such as making her bed in a specific way. She says that she knew that nothing bad would really happen, but that she nonetheless had to perform these acts. Later she got better, she told Adrian and Valeria, because she learned what she had to do. She sees her illness as something in her head. Her discourse is not delusional, says Adrian, but she does have "overvalued" ideas. The semiology of the voice is best understood as a kind of intrapsychic hallucination tied to her compulsions. "It is neither a person nor an object," he says, but is more of a companion, like a lost dog. The voice is accompanied by an image – a face, bearded, of a man in his forties, not attached to a neck or a body.

In the hospital, the therapist diagnosed "psychosis" based on the presence of the delusional voice and image, which led to a dispute between the therapist and the residents. If it is a psychosis, the therapist argued, the patient needs anti-psychotic medication, and if not, she should not be medicated at all. Adrian and Valeria, on the other hand, diagnosed obsessive-compulsive disorder beginning in childhood, and prescribed the anti-depressant fluoxetine (Prozac). They pose the question to the audience at the APA: is it a case of obsessive-compulsive disorder or of psychosis?

Lía Ricón agrees with her students that it is probably obsessive-compulsive disorder. "At any rate, one shouldn't begin with anti-psychotics," adds Valeria. The potential side-effects of these medications, which are given to stem hallucinations, are much more severe than those of the SSRIs, and can include crippling movement and thought disorders. The more recent anti-psychotics such as olanzapine, whose side-effect profile is more mild, are still far out of the range of affordability for most Argentine families.

"When you say 'obsessive-compulsive disorder,'" Gustavo asks the residents, "do you mean an anxiety disorder or an obsessive-neurotic structure?" He is asking whether they are thinking in the terms of DSM or of psychoanalytic structures. Valeria says they were concerned with the question of medication, so they used DSM-IV, diagnosing psychotic symptoms existing within obsessive-compulsive disorder.

José, a Lacanian analyst, speaks up at this point. "This symptom is complicated. Is it an obsession or a hallucination?" As a structural diagnosis, he says, he would propose "restitution, in an obsessive manner, of an infantile psychosis." The question is whether the voice is part of herself.

"At first," answers Adrian, "the voice was the devil. Then later it was God. She says it is the voice of a man with big ears, appearing more often in one place than another."

"Is it out loud, or is it thought?" asks Ricón. This will be a critical question. "It may be a mixed case," she suggests, with aspects of both hallucination and obsession. Depending on the semiology of the voice, then, it may be a case of schizophrenia. "Before the era of psychopharmaceuticals," she says, "cases of schizophrenia were described that began with obsessions and that were extremely serious. When the patients lost their power over them, the delusion appeared."

José returns to his structural interpretation: "It is a restitutive obsession following an infantile psychosis." He describes a process of foreclosure, and the patient's subsequent lack of a superego. "This face is not an obsessive kind of thing," he says. "The face is of someone in his forties – it concerns the paternal function. In psychoanalysis," he explains, "the psychotic symptom is an attempt to restitute." For José, the symptoms clearly point to psychosis: "For an obsessive neurosis, it is extremely rigid. I have never seen a neurosis with such strong hallucinatory symptoms."

Ricón disagrees. "From the clinic," she says, "it is not clear whether the voice is hallucinatory. The symptom is the obsession. According to the phenomenology, it is not the established delusion of a chronic psychosis."

Gustavo asks the residents a question that is directed at José's comments: regarding this supposed "restitution," is the patient deteriorated? He is implying that a valid diagnosis of psychosis, or of schizophrenia, should be accompanied not only by symptoms of delusion, but also by "negative" symptoms: social withdrawal, cognitive difficulties. If it were an infantile psychosis, she would have to show deterioration.

No, they answer, not at all. Adrian takes out some of the patient's figure drawings. There is one of a woman who has no eyes. He challenges José to say what type of infantile psychosis it would be: when and how did it happen?

"Is the symptom neurotic then?" José rejoins. "How so?"

"I don't know if it is one or the other," responds Adrian, "we are at the borderline."

"What is not common for neurosis," says Ricón, "is the voice in the head. There is a long time with no change, without producing anything else, and no deterioration. Is it neurosis? Is it psychosis? Why do we have to have such a mechanistic concept?" She thinks that the names of disorders are theoretical constructs, rather than things out there in the world.

This is anathema to José, who snaps back: "Why? It defines the medication!" He continues with his analysis: "The symbolization of the voice, if it is heard" would imply a psychosis. And as for treatment: "The diagnosis defines the strategy" – that is, anti-psychotic medication.

"But we don't know if the voice is heard," objects Ricón.

"It doesn't seem hallucinatory," adds Ricardo, another analyst.

José continues: "But the necessity of giving it a face, or imagining the look, it symbolizes a break. I don't think it could be a neurosis."

"Did anything improve with twenty milligrams of fluoxetine?" asks Gustavo. He is hinting at the possibility that medication response could be a means of confirming the residents' diagnosis, since SSRIs are indicated for obsessive-compulsive disorder and, presumably, would not change the key symptoms of a psychosis.

"She began to want to know what was happening to her," answers Adrian. "The patient had an alleviation of her symptoms, and at minimal doses. Her relationship with her brother improved as well."

According to Ricón, the fact that the evolution has changed makes one suppose that the illness is at a correctable level – and therefore is not a psychosis. "You cannot correct a delusion except with an anti-psychotic.

With an SSRI, no." She is making a structural diagnosis via drug response: it cannot be a psychosis because an anti-depressant worked on the symptom.

"Have you ever heard of psychotic patients saying that they don't want you to get rid of the voice?" asks Gustavo.

"Sometimes they don't want you to get rid of them – these are similar to paraphrenias," says Ricón, referring to classical European nosology, "or to Ballet's delusions in which there is an hysterical participation, they don't want to lose them. If it is a defense mechanism, you have to be careful not to get rid of it."

This is José's concern. "In an infantile psychosis, you have to think that there is a foreclosure that she is trying to resolve. It is difficult for it to improve," he says. The psychic structure, once in place, seems immutable according to José's scheme.

"When listening to the Lacanian model," argues Ricón, "we have to figure out which of the structures are being talked about. All of us have foreclosures, but we are not all psychotics. It's fine to think in these terms, but in this case to claim a psychotic structure is dubious."

José is upset: "There are elements – the mother with depression, the figure drawings, the face – it is a fragmented body, at the limit of the symbolic. There are cases of psychosis without deterioration, of defenses that are sustained for many years."

"Diagnosis is important only insofar as one is going to change the case," argues Adrian.

"One can leave the diagnosis in suspense," says Ricón, "and watch the development, or not, of the disorder. The response to medication can be, as Freud called it, a therapeutic trial." Ricón's suggestion here involves a surprising juxtaposition of techniques and knowledge-forms: She refers to Freud's use of the therapeutic trial to legitimate the use of an anti-depressant in differentiating between obsessive-compulsive disorder, a DSM category, and psychoanalytic psychosis.

## The future of health

How might new developments in the life sciences, such as pharmacogenomics, address the question that was at stake in this discussion – the problem of identifying disorder in order to know how to intervene? Let us turn back to the potential uses of Genset's patented gene linked to schizophrenia and bipolar disorder. Beginning in the late 1990s, pharmacogenomics became a potent buzzword in promoting the benefits to human health that the completion of the Genome Project would bring. Pharmacogenomics underpinned a projected future of personalized medicine, in which gene chips would guide physicians to the most appropriate pharmaceutical intervention, bypassing wasteful medication trials and avoiding harmful side-effects. It was directed toward characterizing, at a genomic level, distinctive medication-response phenotypes. In the process, a new way of grouping people – according to their "medication-response profile" – emerged. As GlaxoSmithKline executive Allen Roses wrote: "Pharmacogenetics will enable individuals to be classified according to their likely response to a medicine."[8]

Whether or not this vision was an accurate portrayal of the future of health, the promise of personalized medicine structured the potential value of inventions such as Genset's schizophrenia-bipolar gene. And given the company's need for capital from investors and partnerships with major pharmaceutical companies, it was such potential value that made possible the company's research endeavors in Argentina and elsewhere. The vision of personalized medicine illustrates how an anticipated future structures the present value of genomic information. In looking at a series of industry documents and media pronouncements from the late 1990s about forthcoming developments in health care, it is possible to glimpse a part of the process of generating and stabilizing such a "present future" – in this case, a future of individually tailored, predictive medicine based on knowledge of each individual's genome.[9]

Strategic consulting, which Nigel Thrift calls "reflexive business knowledge," is one place where the future is brought into the present and made a field of possible intervention.[10] Strategic consulting responds to a firm's need to know about itself and its milieu in order to adapt to changes in its surroundings. In the 1960s, the field emerged as a new kind of expertise: the ability to broadly survey a field of competition and guide organizations in orienting themselves to a changing terrain. One of its early pioneers, the Boston Consulting Group, honed the message that for a company to attain competitive advantage in a given field, it needed in-depth knowledge of the company itself, its competitors, and the economic structure of the industry as a whole.[11] Over the past few decades, strategic consulting has become an ever more prominent force in global business practice.

These consultants do a number of things: advise organizations on restructuring, provide guidance on alliances and mergers, and shape visions of the future that permeate the business media and direct the planning decisions of managers. While some of its methods resemble the social sciences – interviews, surveys, even ethnography – strategic consulting is a "post-social" science in that the central object that its knowledge constitutes and intervenes in is not "society" but the market. The collective entities it concerns itself with are not social groups but rather market segments, and its individual actors are not social subjects but consumers.

An example of how the field has reconfigured the organization of health is the concept of "disease management," introduced by the Boston Consulting Group in its work on marketing new diabetes monitoring devices in the 1980s, but which was soon extended to chronic diseases in general – from asthma to heart disease to Alzheimer's.[12] This concept helped to structure an ongoing relationship between producers of health interventions, especially pharmaceutical companies, and their consumers. In similar fashion, the novel concept that I describe here – "personalized medicine" – is an innovation linking production and consumption through the invention of a new need.

Consulting knowledge does not aim at finality: following Niklas Luhmann, the worth of its prognoses lies, rather, in "the quickness with which they can be corrected."[13] In forecasting the future, consulting expertise also helps to shape it. As Reinhardt Koselleck writes, this form of prognosis "radiates time" – it enters into calculation in a way that alters the very conditions of the prognosis.[14] The vision of personalized medicine as the *telos* of private sector genomics research crystallized in the late 1990s. We can look at a series of consulting industry artifacts to see how it took form. These documents serve as indicators of a generalized change in the understanding of the pharmaceutical field, a shift mediated by consultants, stock analysts, and life science entrepreneurs, among others. In January 1999, the Boston Consulting Group released an influential report arguing that the pharmaceutical industry was facing a period of rapid transformation:

> The 100-year-old pharmaceutical industry is at an important crossroads and is facing a period of radical change. The next twenty years will see a revolution in care, characterized by both a surge in medical treatments available and a bigger emphasis on the individual patient playing a leading role in the healthcare system.[15]

According to the BCG report, the pharmaceutical industry's classic strategy of mass-marketing blockbusters to broad segments of the population was entering into crisis due to patent expirations, the lack of replacement products in the pipeline, and changes in the "healthcare environment" – including price controls coming from third-party payers. There were new opportunities as well, the report argued, stemming from two new developments: first, the rise of a new, educated healthcare consumer demanding tailored treatment; and secondly, technological innovations coming in the wake of the Human Genome Project. Meanwhile, the report warned that pharmaceutical players faced an emerging threat from agile new biotech firms branching into pharmaceutical development. BCG proposed a solution that would meet these new demands and threats, shaping a post-blockbuster pharmaceutical economy: personalized medicine, using the technological platform of pharmacogenomics. In the report, the future was a field of contemporary reflection at two registers: first, in its vision of where the health industry was headed; and second, in the very technology that it described – a technology for predicting patient responses to medication:

> "Pharmacogenomics" – a science that combines the knowledge and study of genetics with the process of developing new drugs – will enable pharmaceutical companies to create treatments geared to distinct genetic variations of any particular disease. Companies will, in essence, be able to predict which patients are likely to respond to which "suites" of medications. With this capability, a pharmaceutical company will have the opportunity to market to specific patient subgroups.

BCG's vision was of a future in which drugs would be targeted toward sub-populations of patients who were genetically "responsive" to these medications. Since it proposed to break up current illness categories and reformulate sub-populations in terms of medication response, what pharmacogenomics aimed for is better described as "segmented" rather than "personalized" medicine. Millennium Pharmaceutical's vice president of product development described his company's plan to bring personalized medicine into being: "We are focused on integrating genomics-based diagnostics and therapeutics with the ultimate vision of linking the right drug to the right patient."[16] Diagnostics would be linked to therapeutics, representation to intervention, through the technological platform of pharmacogenomics.

In its goal of reorganizing the field of health through the delineation of new sub-populations, personalized medicine promised a biopolitical innovation – that is, a novel way to rationally manage the population's well-being.[17] This form of rationality operated according to the norm of pharmacological specificity. The technology of pharmacogenomics sought to operationalize human genetic variation by matching patients to the most appropriate pharmaceutical intervention. It would directly link illness populations to market segments, calibrating health need and consumer demand. Biopolitics and the market were to be brought together through the application of genomic knowledge.

The BCG report spelled out what would become a number of truisms in life science industry analyses in the ensuing years, including: the failings of the old "one-size-fits-all" medicine, the powerful new role of the health-care consumer, and the coming era of personalized medicine. Along with this vision came increasing publicity around a new set of public health problems for which pharmacogenomics was the solution: an epidemic of toxic responses to drugs, the high percentage of patients who failed to respond to their prescribed medication, and the many promising drugs that had been taken off the market due to side-effects in a small number of patients.

At this point, companies whose technology might help to bring this future into being were highly valued by investors. One example was Genset, which sought to find and patent genes linked to common illnesses using its proprietary SNP (single nucleotide polymorphism) map. The SNP map was seen as especially valuable since it could guide researchers efficiently to genetic mutations linked to risk for common, complex illnesses. After a 100-million-dollar initial public offering in 1996 and a much publicized 42-million-dollar pharmacogenomics alliance with Abbott in 1997, Genset was valued at seven hundred million dollars by mid-1998, its stock trading as high as forty dollars per share.

The BCG report urged pharmaceutical industry managers to be attuned to such developments: "the opportunity inherent in the new era of pharmaceuticals will be available to only the most flexible and visionary players, which must invest today to benefit from future opportunities." Given the prospective transformation of the health industry, innovative genomics companies such as Genset seemed poised to conquer terrain ceded by slow-moving pharmaceutical giants. In response to the threat posed by these upstart biotech firms, a group of major pharmaceutical companies created an institutional innovation designed to block value creation around genomic information.

A few months after the BCG report came out, in April 1999, ten major pharmaceutical companies along with the Wellcome Trust announced the formation of the SNP Consortium, whose goal was to create a SNP map and make this data publicly available. The anticipated future of personalized medicine was the stated rationale for the Consortium – which promised, in turn, to help bring this future into being. In a *Wall Street Journal* article about the Consortium, Allen Roses of Glaxo clearly articulated the rationale of personalized medicine: "in the future, before a doctor prescribes a medicine, the doctor will take some blood, have it analyzed at a nearby lab and identify which of, let's say, twelve drugs are most likely to treat the patient effectively with the minimal side-effects."[18] By making its DNA sequence information freely available, the Consortium members were able to cast themselves as acting in the service of the public good. Meanwhile, the Consortium was explicitly designed to undercut efforts such as Genset's to patent and license information on genetic variation.

Genset initially reacted confidently to the prospect of competition from the SNP Consortium. As the *Journal* reported: "Genset's Chief Executive Pascal Brandys says he is aware of the proposed consortium, but it won't affect his plans because Genset has already been finding snips [sic] for two years." However, the Consortium's strategy turned out to be effective in diverting projected value away from patented genomic data, and the value of Genset's stock soon began a precipitous decline, from forty dollars per share in June 1998 to fifteen in 1999, winding up below four dollars per share in 2001.[19]

It was not actual technological development that was driving these sharp changes in valuation, but rather an amorphous process of "market anticipation." A *Nature* article cited stock analysts who explained the basis of the market's judgment: "Genset's change in fortune has – according to several analysts – been largely prompted by market anticipation of the recent creation of a private–public sector consortium that would map and make freely available variations in the human genetic code linked to diseases."[20] In the ensuing months, Genset tried to redefine itself as a drug development company, but failed to generate interest among investors. The company was finally bought by Serono, a large Swiss biotech firm, for 107.4 million euros in June 2002.

The SNP Consortium effectively ensured that valued intellectual property would remain at the level of the drug, downstream in the research process, rather than upstream, at the site of genetic variation. This did not in itself make the potential new health technologies emerging from the Human Genome Project any more publicly accessible. The Consortium's effort to subvert the biotechnology industry's plans to profit from sites of genetic variation was a strategy for protecting current sources of pharmaceutical profit, rather than a gift to the public. Initially posed as a possible solution to the threats facing the pharmaceutical industry in the late 1990s, personalized medicine eventually became a more generalized convention for understanding where genomic research was headed. In turn, this convention directed research – though in precisely what direction remained uncertain.

## Diagnostic "truing"

While most publicity around pharmacogenomics was focused on the long-term vision of personalized medicine, in the short-term, drug companies were interested in a more immediate application: the use of pharmacogenomics as part of a drug development program, geared to increase productivity by bringing drugs more quickly to market. In order to meet Wall Street growth expectations, analysts estimated that the major pharmaceutical companies had to introduce three to five new chemical entities per year.[21] But research pipelines seemed to be running dry, and new drug applications were slowing. The pharmaceutical industry claimed that it was spending five to eight hundred million dollars and eight to ten years per new drug. The difficulty of demonstrating efficacy through clinical trials was one widely cited reason why drug development was a slow and expensive process. Clinical trials for new drugs required tremendous numbers of patients to demonstrate safety and efficacy, and had a high failure rate – which was in part blamed on the heterogeneity of patient populations in these trials. Given limited patent lifetimes, companies calculated the cost of delays in market approval in the millions of dollars per day.

In this context, genomics firms pitched pharmacogenomics to pharmaceutical companies as a technical solution to the problem of the inefficiency of the clinical trial process. The potential usefulness of pharmacogenomics in drug development was a result of the centrality of the specificity model to pharmaceutical circulation. Here pharmacogenomics responded to a need for better ways of stratifying populations in clinical trials. By using pharmacogenomics to forge populations for experiment, drug developers could screen patients in terms of potential drug response before the trial began. This would cut down on adverse reactions and improve the odds of running a successful trial. As one analyst envisioned: "Pharmacogenomic profiling can be used to stratify trials based on patients who are most likely to benefit from therapy" or else to exclude the "poor metabolizer type" from trials.[22] In other words, if one only knew beforehand which patients were likely to respond to the drug, the trial would have much better chances of success.

This was especially the case in developing medications for psychiatric illness. As Allen Roses wrote: "Patient groups who have vaguely defined phenotypes that are more difficult to categorize by objective criteria, such as depression, could be studied more efficiently using medicine response profiles as selection variables."[23] As a tool for gathering homogeneous populations for clinical drug research, the development of pharmacogenomics followed a similar logic to that which animated initial diagnostic standardization efforts in psychiatry, such as the Research Diagnostic Criteria.[24] The regulatory demand for evidence of specific efficacy was helping to drive a series of efforts to more directly couple pharmaceutical intervention and diagnostic target, as key to lock.

Even if the specificity model is not an adequate description of how psychopharmaceuticals work in relation to mental illnesses as they are currently defined, genomics technology seeks to make the model more accurate. Pharmacogenomics serves as a mechanism of adjustment between drug and disease entity – a way of calibrating intervention more closely to illness. In this sense, it is exemplary of the logic of pharmaceutical reason. Here, the adjustment between the drug's effects and the characteristics of its target population is not due to the development of more directly targeted drugs. Rather, the crucial element of the adjustment process occurs at the diagnostic level. The drug remains stable while the target shifts in relation to it. In other words, the specificity model is being built into the technological platform: the model is in a sense being *made* more accurate, not by finding the perfect pharmacological key to fit the illness but by changing the very nature of the lock into that which, by definition, matches the key.[25] This process of adjustment can be thought as "truing" the diagnostic entity – making it more closely fit the intervention.[26]

The technology is especially intriguing in the case of psychiatric disorders because, while it poses the possibility of delineating a physiological basis for these amorphous conditions, it bypasses the question of the coherence of classical illness entities such as bipolar disorder and schizophrenia. The delineation of these new sub-populations has the potential to transform the practice of diagnosis. In a world of gene-chip-based diagnostic tests in the clinic, the broad categories that govern psychiatric practice might be broken down in terms of medication response, so that diagnostic questions would appear no longer as – "is it bipolar disorder or schizophrenia?" but as – "is it a lithium or an olanzapine response profile?"

## Pharmacogenomic norms

The Genset patent did not refer to the distinctive issues raised by genomic research into disorders having to do with human behavior and thought. Nonetheless it seems that questions specifically human were at stake in the research. In a 2002 lecture on his company's recent findings, Genset's scientific director, Daniel Cohen, described the behavioral pathologies of one of their gene knockout mice, but noted: "It's very difficult to know what a schizophrenic mouse is."[27] The technical challenge of linking psychiatric phenotypes to genetic substrates was thus related to the broader questions we have been investigating concerning the problems posed by psychiatric disorder: What are the boundaries of mental illness? Can abstract information gleaned from a blood test be used to distinguish normal from pathological behavior and thought? Is delusion identifiable outside of a social milieu?

Here the reflections of the philosopher of the life sciences Georges Canguilhem may serve to frame the implications of findings such as Genset's. Canguilhem criticized the notion that the violation of norms of human conduct could be understood through the methods of the natural sciences. Such a claim, he thought, would imply that individuals by nature have to submit to contingent social constraints. For Canguilhem this was both empirically suspect and politically dangerous. He argued that the difference between biological and social norms could be found in the site of their respective regulatory apparatuses. Whereas the norms of life were immanent to the organism and oriented to survival, for Canguilhem, social norms were external to organic life and their aims contingent on political decision.[28] If the goal of organs of biological regulation was self-preservation, the *telos* of society remained unclear. "In the case of society," he wrote, "regulation is a need in search of its organ and its norms of exercise," whereas in an organism "the fact of need expresses the existence of a regulatory apparatus."[29] While the living being was able to normatively regulate itself in relation to a changing environment, social organization required the invention of regulatory apparatuses.

What to make, then, of the projected applications of Genset's findings – the prospect of locating bodily markers indicating potential responsiveness to psychotropic medications? Such markers would indicate an internal relationship of potentiality to an external substance already in circulation, or one still to be invented. One is incorporating genomic information into a technology for guiding pharmacological intervention. This seems to disrupt the distinction Canguihlem makes between organic and social norms. At the same time, pharmacogenomics transforms the need that medication addresses. The target of the drug is no longer an illness per se but rather an inherited capacity to respond to the drug.

In a set of reflections on relations between humans and technology, Canguilhem provided a possible model for thinking in simultaneously biological and social terms about such a device. For Canguilhem the invention of technologies was a response to the particular situation of humans, who are distinguished by their need for external supplements for self-preservation.[30] Instead of understanding technology as dehumanizing, Canguilhem's proposal was to reverse the Cartesian analogy in which the living being is seen as a machine: it is more helpful, he suggested, to view the tool or machine as a human organ. If it is constructed to serve human needs, we may see technology as an adaptive organ, a response to human incompleteness. In this sense, the device that links genome to drug intervention is simultaneously external and internal, social and vital.

Thus the development and application of genomic knowledge does not necessarily lead to a biological determinism. In this case, an apparatus for defining and treating illness incorporates biological knowledge into its inventions. Pharmacogenomics technologizes – functionally simplifies – the strategic logic I have called pharmaceutical reason. That is, it is a device that links chemical intervention to diagnostic representation according to the norm of disease specificity. The incorporation of this logic into psychiatry – as we have seen in the case of DSM – reconfigures the role of expertise. The task of the expert is not to interpret signs of psychic distress in terms of a trajectory of subject formation; nor is it to point to the deleterious effects of the social milieu on the ties that bind self to collective. Rather, the psychiatrist's role is limited, if still ambitious: to manage the neurochemical imbalance that disrupts normal behavior. Not surprisingly, such a transformation occasions resistance among recalcitrant experts, as we have seen in the *mundo-psi* of Buenos Aires.

The hunt for bipolar patients in Argentina was a small episode in the larger story of the "informationalization" of life at the turn of the twenty-first century, at the intersection of the burgeoning life sciences industry, a changing politics of health provision, and rising ethical anxiety in both secular and religious circles. Given the marginal status of psychiatry within medicine, and the peripheral position of Argentina in global circuits of knowledge and commerce, the case raised a number of distinctive issues: could knowledge of the psyche be assimilated into the new molecular sciences? What would such an effort mean for the politics of mental health? And what new position would the process imply for the subject of psychic distress?

While a small group of "neural activists" in Argentina sought to shift professional norms in the direction of cosmopolitan biomedicine, the milieu remained structured by a number of factors that militated against the adoption of the new biomedical psychiatry: an entrenched psychoanalytic culture, an anti-capitalist politics of health, and historical memory that linked social activism to psychodynamic epistemology. Experts with investments in interpreting psychic structure or designing social interventions were loathe to admit the placeless, simplifying protocols linked to pharmaceutical reason to the setting. And without professional regulatory mechanisms in place to enforce the use of such protocols, it was unlikely that a significant epistemic shift would take place anytime soon. In the meantime, a heterogeneous set of practitioners – psychoanalysts, neuroscientific psychiatrists, drug marketers, patient activists, and others – creatively assimilated multiple techniques into their work of expertise.

# Notes

## Introduction: specific effects

1. Luhmann 1990: 117.
2. Deleuze and Guattari 1994: 28.
3. Latour 1987.
4. Ian Hacking argues that psychiatric identity is an example of the type of classification he calls "interactive kinds." As opposed to "indifferent kinds" like trees, these are classifications that interact with the thing being classified. Hacking 1999.
5. Rose 1996a. Ian Hacking, "Making Up People," in Hacking 2003.
6. For an optimistic vision of novel medications as self-making techniques, see Kramer 1993; a darker view is articulated by Francis Fukuyama (2002).
7. For an example of such an assemblage in contemporary France, see Rabinow 1999.
8. Swain 1994: 274.
9. See Scull 1989.
10. Canguilhem, "Qu'est-ce que la psychologie?" in Canguilhem 1968.
11. Andreasen 1997.
12. Andreasen 1997: 592.
13. For the description of how drugs attain their effects in relation to the *dispositifs* in which they are used, see Gomart 2002.
14. Healy 1998.
15. See Grob 1991.
16. See Hale, Jr. 1995. Michel Foucault describes the introduction of such techniques in terms of a process of the "depsychiatrization" of madness. See Foucault 1997c.
17. Psychodynamic therapists integrated the new substances into their ongoing practices: "The new drugs have only a symptomatic effect on psychic disorders and ... cannot replace psychotherapy; all they accomplish is to render the patient more amenable to psychotherapy." Association for the Advancement of Psychotherapy, 1955, cit. in Grob 1991: 148.
18. As Swain writes, "the correlation is striking. The intellectual breakthrough of psychoanalysis on the front of psychosis accompanies the breakthrough of neuroleptics and the arrival of anti-depressants on the market (1958)." Swain 1994: 271.
19. Kline 1959: 18.

20. Kline 1959: 309.
21. Kline 1959: 312.
22. Kline 1959: 484.
23. Marks 1997.
24. Hughes 1987.
25. Rosenberg 2002.
26. See Timmermans and Berg 2003.
27. Rosenberg 2002: 23. For critical analyses of biomedicine as a cultural system that excludes the role of narrative and meaning in structuring illness experience, see Good 1994 and Kleinman 1995.
28. Spitzer, Endicott, and Robins 1978, 774.
29. As David Healy writes, "after 1962 a standardization of diagnostic practice was all but inevitable." Healy 1998: 100.
30. See Chapter 1.
31. Wilson 1995.
32. For histories of the formation of DSM-III, see also Kirk and Kutchins 1992; Young 1996.
33. Collier and Ong 2005.
34. Ewald 1990: 148.
35. Macherey 1992: 178–9.
36. Bowker and Star 1999: 16.
37. Weber 1946: 144.
38. Rabinow 2003; Lakoff and Collier 2004.
39. Halperin 1998.
40. Sarlo 1988.
41. Borges 1962: 181.
42. Borges 1962: 181.
43. Borges 1962: 183.
44. Sarlo 1993: 28.
45. Shapin and Schaffer 1986.
46. See Rabinow 1996.

## 1 Diagnostic liquidity

1. Regalado 1999: 49.
2. Foucault 1997a.
3. A project conducted in rural China by Millennium Pharmaceuticals in collaboration with Harvard University and seeking genes linked to asthma provoked a scandal after an investigative report appeared in the *Washington Post*. Pomfret and Nelson 2000: A1.
4. As a 1996 article about a Genset research collaboration in China put it, quoting Genset's president: "China's population is a gold mine of genetic information. The country's rural populations have remained relatively static this century, so each region has a unique blend of genes and diseases. This makes it much easier to trace hereditary diseases back to defective genes, which are unusually abundant where the disease is prevalent. 'You can treat regional local populations almost like single families,' says Brandys.'" Coghlan 1996.
5. Boyle 1997: 9.
6. For the example of organ donation, see Hogle 1995; for the case of evidence-based protocols, see Timmermans and Berg 1997.
7. Carruthers and Stinchcombe 1999: 356.

8. Cronon 1991. Michel Callon (1998) describes the process whereby objects are "disentangled" from their immediate surroundings and made calculable as one of "enframing."
9. Regalado 1999: 45.
10. American Psychiatric Association 1994.
11. Jamison 1997.
12. As an article in *La Nación* put it: "Currently, the hospital needs more sporadic patients to complete the sample that is awaited in France." Navarra 1998: 4.
13. Unlike patient groups in the US, FUBIPA and similar groups are a relatively marginal phenomenon in Argentina, and are typically run by local experts in the disorder rather than by patients and family members. See Chapter 4.
14. One highly publicized example was the Wistar Institute's 1986 field trial of a recombinant rabies vaccine in cattle outside of Buenos Aires, in which no Argentine authorities were informed of the experiment. See Dixon 1988.
15. It appeared, for instance, via the UNESCO Bioethics initiative, represented in Argentina by legal scholar Salvador Bergel (1998), who opposed the licensing of genetic material.
16. To the extent that imagery of a dystopian genetic future entered the popular imagination, it was via the film *Gattaca*, rather than through warnings from "ethics" experts. This can be contrasted with the deCode case in Iceland. See Palsson and Rabinow 1999. On the other hand, Argentina was one of the first countries to ban cloning in the aftermath of Dolly, a result of the power of the Argentine Catholic Church to define the boundaries of reproduction.
17. Goobar 1998: 66.
18. Rabinow 1995; Jasanoff 1995.
19. Doll 1998: 690. See also Boyle 1997.
20. Indeed, a group of major pharmaceutical companies, in partnership with the Wellcome Trust, was able to circumvent the biotech effort to patent and license SNPs – markers of human genetic variation – by forming a consortium in 1999 to make such markers publicly available, significantly hindering the business strategy of companies like Genset. Database companies were then forced to shift into drug development, an even more treacherous and uncertain field.
21. See Palsson and Rabinow 1999. Another difference was that the Argentine subjects of Genset's study were not prospective consumers of the technologies under development, whereas the deCode project guaranteed Icelanders access to Hoffman-LaRoche products developed from the research.
22. Meek 2000.
23. *Genetic Engineering News* 2000.
24. Source: IMS Health. See www.imshealth.com.
25. Herrera 2001.
26. Housman and Ledley 1998.
27. Thayer 1999.
28. Barondes 1999.
29. "Washington Post Health Talk", 28 December 1999.
30. MacKinnon, Jamison, and DePaulo 1997: 368–9.
31. Rose 1996b: 13.
32. Rabinow, 1996: 102. This phenomenon has now been well documented by social scientific observers in Western Europe and the United States. See Callon and Rabeharisoa 2004; Rapp 1999.
33. World Health Organization 2001b. Typical estimates in the bipolar genetics literature were around 1 percent. But some experts thought it was as high as

5 percent. Much depended on the criteria of inclusion, and the means of distinguishing BPD from overlapping syndromes such as schizophrenia, unipolar depression, and attention deficit disorder.

34. For a description of how certain mental disorders come to thrive in specific political, cultural, and professional niches, see Hacking 1998. Bruno Latour (2000) discusses the ontological question of whether tuberculosis can be said to have existed in ancient Egypt.
35. Though discovered in 1949, lithium was not widely adopted until its effectiveness was confirmed in the early 1970s – in part because it was not a proprietary compound and so there was little marketing incentive for conducting the requisite clinical trials, but also because of lack of interest in biological treatment of manic depression among psychodynamic psychiatrists, then predominant in US psychiatry. Jacobsen 1986.
36. See Foucault 1961; also Dreyfus and Rabinow 1983.
37. See Goldstein 1987. Berrios 1988.
38. Berrios 1988.
39. Kraepelin 1904: 12.
40. Cooper *et al.* 1972: 125; see also Healy 1998: 47.
41. Cooper *et al.* 1972: 12.
42. Cooper *et al.* 1972: 130.
43. For a lucid analysis of questions of reliability and validity in psychiatric diagnosis, see Young 1996.
44. Kopnisky and Hyman 2002.
45. Navarra 1998.
46. A key question was whether both bipolar type I and type II were included, as they were in the Genset study. See Kessler *et al.* 1997; Angst 1998.
47. For example, psychiatrist Timothy Crow (1986) wrote, "The psychoses constitute a genetic continuum rather than two unrelated diatheses."
48. Akiskal 1996; some experts also argued that many cases of attention deficit disorder were in fact bipolar disorder.
49. MacKinnon *et al.* 1997: 356.
50. Leboyer *et al.* 1998; Risch and Botstein 1996.
51. Risch and Botstein 1996: 351.
52. Bradbury 2001: 1596.
53. Escamilla *et al.* 1999. In another paper, the UCSF group placed blame on the uncertainty of the relation between phenotype and genotype, on the seemingly multiple ways the "underlying disease" expressed itself: "Genetic studies of psychiatric disorders in humans have been inconclusive owing to the difficulty in defining phenotypes and underlying disease heterogeneity." McInnes *et al.* 1998.
54. "We believe the explanation lies elsewhere [than genetic heterogeneity], namely that the genetic mechanism underlying the disease in these families is more complicated than postulated, leading to a reduction in [statistical] power." Risch and Botstein 1996.
55. Leboyer *et al.* 1998.
56. Wildenauer *et al.* 1999.
57. Wildenauer *et al.* 1999.
58. Wildenauer *et al.* 1999.
59. Lakoff 2000.
60. Gelernter 1995: 1762, 1766.
61. Lawrence Cohen (1998) describes a similar problem as he began a study on old age in India: an apparent lack of patients with senile dementia. In response to

his queries, the argument initially made to him was that there was "no aging in India," that dementia was a disorder of modernity, of the "bad family."
62. See Chapter 2.
63. I describe this setting in detail in Chapter 3.
64. Alder 1998: 501.
65. Sassen 2000; Brenner 1999.
66. I discuss this attempt and responses to it in Chapter 4.
67. Regalado 1999: 49.

## 2 Medicating the symptom

1. Grob 1991.
2. Rose 1999: 133.
3. Romero 2002: 111.
4. For a discussion of the Peronist discourse of democracy as social justice, see Romero 2002: 98.
5. James 1988.
6. For the classic articulation of "social rights" and "social citizenship," see T. H. Marshall, "Citizenship and Social Class," in Marshall 1963.
7. Vezzetti 2003.
8. Cit. in Vezzetti 2003: 159.
9. Plotkin 2001: 140.
10. Vidal 1957: 286.
11. Pichon-Rivière 1983.
12. Vidal 1960.
13. Rodrigue 1965.
14. Social psychiatry developed in England during the Second World War after successes with the use of group dynamics in treating shellshock. Shorter 1997: 229. For its relation to liberal democracy, see Rose 1996b. For the US case, see Grob 1991: 144.
15. Cit. in Shorter 1997: 236.
16. As Hugo Vezzetti writes, the therapeutic community was not only a psychiatric innovation, but also "a laboratory of social research capable of producing knowledge extendable to groups, institutions, and society." Vezzetti 1995: 32.
17. Goldenberg 1958: 402.
18. This strategy of decentralization and community care was modeled on reforms in Great Britain and the United States, where deinstitutionalization was underway, and was also based on recommendations from the WHO. Plotkin, 2003: 201.
19. Grimson 1999.
20. Feitlowitz 1998.
21. I describe this set of exchange relations in detail in Chapter 5.
22. Vezzetti 1997a.
23. Barry, Osborne, and Rose 1996.
24. Per capita health spending rose from $827 to $1291 in this period, according to the World Bank's standardized units of calculation. World Bank 1997. See also World Health Organization 2001b.
25. Borón 1999.
26. Ferrer 1999: 21.

27. Mireille Abelin has noted Nestor Kirchner's appropriation of this freighted term in articulating a new social alternative to neoliberalism, and thus reasserting the (masculine) agency of Argentina in international affairs. See Abelin 2004.
28. In the early seventies, the APA lost its status as the central site of Argentine psychoanalytic thought as rival political and theoretical factions led to a splintering of the psychoanalytic movement. See Chapter 3.
29. Galende 1993: 236.
30. Espelund and Stevens 1998: 314, 322.
31. Ricón 2001: 24.
32. Ricón 2001: 24.
33. Vezzetti 1997a: 431.
34. Visacovsky points out that despite the participants' emphasis on the centrality of psychoanalysis in the legendary Lanús service, Goldenberg himself was not a psychoanalyst. Nonetheless, stories of his relationships with legendary analysts such as Enrique Pichon-Rivière enable contemporary activists to place Goldenberg under the rubric of a socially oriented psychoanalysis. Visacovsky 1998.
35. Vezzetti 1997b, "Sobre los origines de salud mental en la Argentina." Thus Enrique Pichon-Rivière and Mauricio Goldenberg were both members of the *Liga Argentina de Higiene Mental* (LAHM) in the 1930s.
36. Jorge Halperin, "La sociedad exasperada," in *Tres Puntos*, 29 December 1998.
37. Ricón 2001.
38. Kesselman 1999: 34–5.
39. Giorgi 1997.

## 3 The Lacan ward

1. I describe this institutional reform movement in Chapter 2.
2. Plotkin 2001; Vezzetti 1996.
3. Romero 2002; Terán 1991.
4. Sherry Turkle discusses the relation between the emergence of psychoanalytic cultures and political movements in a comparative context, arguing for a link between democratization and popular interest in psychoanalysis. "Preface," in Turkle 1992.
5. Sigal 2002.
6. Plotkin 2001: 124.
7. Plotkin 2001: 138.
8. The *Cordobazo* was a transformative historical event for the Argentine left, linking nascent rights movements to a broader critique of modern bureaucratic institutions, such as the hospital, the prison, and the school. See O'Donnell 1999.
9. Vezzetti 2003.
10. Sigal 2002: 108.
11. The psychiatrist Enrique Pichon-Rivière had met Lacan while in France and introduced his work to his friend, the literary critic Oscar Masotta. For elements of this history, see Garcia 1980; Juan Jose Sebreli, "El Joven Masotta," in Sebreli 1997; Oscar Masotta, "Epilogo," in Masotta 1976.
12. Balán 1991.
13. Rhodes 1991; See also Luhrmann 2000 for a description of pressures towards increasingly short in-patient stays in US hospitals.

14. The oft-mentioned reference for this term was the book by French critic Jean Clavreul (Clavreul 1978).
15. See Peter Kramer's classic discussion of the use of anti-depressants to make people feel "better than well." Kramer 1993.
16. Lacan 1981.
17. As Lacan put it, humans are "an animal at the mercy of language." Lacan, "Direction of the Treatment," in Lacan 1977: 264. Elisabeth Roudinesco emphasizes that for structuralist psychoanalysis, to say that man was at the mercy of language was not to place the human subject at the center of inquiry, but to make logic and language the site of analysis. Roudinesco 1997: 332.
18. Forrester 1996. For neither Freud nor Lacan was psychoanalysis best understood as a science of the individual. While his metaphors are drawn from various nineteenth-century sciences, it seems clear that Freud hoped his science would rejoin neurology as new knowledge emerged, whereas Lacan used linguistics, structural anthropology, and mathematics as models. See Sulloway 1979; Roustang 1990.
19. Here Forrester cites Foucault's work on disciplinary practices and the making of individuals. See Foucault 1977.
20. In June 1955, navy planes dropped bombs on thousands of workers and trade unionists who were gathered in the Plaza de Mayo in Buenos Aires in support of the Perón government, killing several hundred people. Rock 1985: 316. In September the army rebelled as well, eventually forcing Perón from power.
21. Ginzburg points to a group of disciplines that are characterized by certain similarities of method. They take seemingly marginal and irrelevant details as clues that point towards a deeper underlying reality that is not immediately visible. These disciplines are individualizing rather than generalizing; they attend to the concrete rather than the abstract. Whereas the "Galilean" sciences can say nothing about the individual, these "conjectural" sciences are qualitative, and testify only about the specific case, situation, or document. Ginzburg 1983.
22. Foucault 1997d. Mario Biagioli glosses this argument with respect to the sciences: individual authorship may be important for receiving credit, but it is the world itself that testifies to the validity of what is said. Biagioli 1999; Biagioli and Galison 2003.
23. To understand why Foucault was interested in this particular type of discourse it is helpful to remember the context of the talk: Paris, 1969, the height of French Marxism and structuralist psychoanalysis. Indeed, Foucault's discussion of the inevitable necessity of a "return" to the origin was a reference to the work of Jacques Lacan, who was in the audience at the French philosophic society that day. Roudinesco 1997.
24. Foucault 1997d: 117.
25. Freud 1917a: 285.
26. Stengers 1990.
27. Foucault 1997b: 279.
28. Stengers 1997: 90.
29. Stengers 1997: 91. An interesting analogy to the psychoanalytic claim that one must have been successfully analyzed in order to be authorized to speak about psychoanalysis might be Galileo's insistence that philosophers should not criticize his arguments unless they understand mathematics. Mario Biagioli describes the study of such ways of marking distinctions as the "anthropology of incommensurability." Biagioli 1993: 224.

30. Roudinesco 1997: 338.
31. Freud 1923–1925: 149.
32. Cit. in Bowie 1991: 108–9.
33. And in the United States, as Emily Martin has noted, to CEOs. Martin 1999.
34. Freud 1917b: 255.
35. The validity of this category was also subject to debate. Some Argentine psychiatrists dismissed it as a "*bolso de gatos*," a grab bag. One widely read North American bipolar disorder expert recommended treating such cases as bipolar patients. See Akiskal 1996.

## 4 Living with neuroscience

1. Although it spent twice as much per capita on public health as neighboring Chile, Argentina's infant mortality rate was almost two times that of Chile in 1997. United Nations Development Program 1999.
2. Pichot 1997.
3. Kandel 1998.
4. Kandel 1998: 284.
5. Luhrmann 2000.
6. Luhrmann 2000: 276.
7. Luhrmann 2000: 271.
8. Foucault 1961.
9. Rose 1998.
10. For the case of disputed disorders such as Chronic Fatigue Syndrome and Attention Deficit Disorder, see Dumit 2000.
11. Nikolas Rose, "Governing 'Advanced' Liberal Democracies," in Barry, Osbourne, and Rose 1996: 53.
12. Barry *et al.*: 52.
13. Expert-advocates such as Kay Redfield Jamison bring all of these tendencies together. See Jamison 1997.
14. See Chapter 3.
15. Rose 1996b: 15.
16. In the residents' lounge one morning, Pablo worked with a resident on a genealogical chart of bipolars in Lord Tennyson's family. The chart was copied from Jamison 1993.
17. Castel 1988: 127.
18. Max Weber, "Science as a Vocation," in Gerth and Mills 1946.
19. As the Pan American Health Organization reported of Argentina, "information on the prevalence of mental illness is very scant." Pan American Health Organization 1998. As for spending, in its "Atlas" of global mental health, the World Health Organization notes of Argentina: "Details about expenditure on mental health are not available." World Health Organization 2001a: 148.
20. Timmermans and Berg 2003.
21. Robert Castel, "From Dangerousness to Risk," in Burchell, Gordon, and Miller 1991: 281.
22. Burchell *et al.* 1991: 281.
23. World Bank 1993.
24. As the report stated: "Greater competition and accountability are two of the main objectives of current proposals for reforming social insurance in Argentina." World Bank 1993: 160.
25. World Bank 1993: 171.

26. For an analysis of neoliberal reform as the reinscription of substantive values into formal techniques, see Stephen J. Collier, "Budgets and Biopolitics," in Ong and Collier 2005.
27. See Chapter 1 for a discussion of the role of positive symptoms in high rates of schizophrenia diagnosis in the USA during the era of psychodynamic psychiatry.

## 5 The private life of numbers

1. Cecchi 2001: 19.
2. "El Consumo de Tranquilizantes creció entre un 8 y un 9 por ciento," *Clarín*, 3 October 2001.
3. These data come from IMS Health monthly sales figures.
4. IMS Health: www.imshealth.com, accessed December 2001.
5. Ian Hacking describes the "avalanche of printed numbers" produced by nation-states beginning in the Napoleonic era. Hacking 1990.
6. Foucault 2000.
7. Rabinow 1996 [1989].
8. Rose 1999.
9. Rose 1996c.
10. Deleuze, "Post-Script on Control Societies," in Deleuze 1995: 181.
11. Sikkink 1991; Waisman 1987.
12. Martin Hopenhayn (2001) provides an account of this process from the perspective of Latin American intellectuals and policy-makers.
13. Bergel and Correa 1996: 9.
14. www.phrma.org, accessed April 2001.
15. Campanario 1999.
16. See Chapter 2.
17. PhRMA 2001.
18. Fundación ISALUD 1999.
19. Thus in a 1998 newspaper article on new anti-depressants, a Buenos Aires psychiatrist assured the public that happiness cannot be obtained from a pill, while ensuring that medication decisions would be a matter of expertise: "They are very good, I would say excellent, and their cost is accessible, around seventy pesos per month. But they have to be controlled by specialists." Giubellino 1998: 44.
20. As Steven Shapin (1994) has shown, relations of trust and socially sanctioned authority have underpinned scientific knowledge from the earliest moments of what came to be known as the Scientific Revolution.
21. Sabel 1997.
22. Dana and Loewenstein 2003.
23. Healy 2001.
24. For an anthropological reading of the distinction between gifts and commodities, see Appadurai 1986.
25. Fundación ISALUD 1999.
26. Data on the number of sales reps comes from the union of *agentes de propaganda médica* (APMs). Their website, which features an animated suitcase-bearing rep, can be found at www.apm.org.ar, accessed April 2002.
27. For the history of the use of "territory" measures in sales management, see Spears 1995.

28. Michel Callon (1998) has emphasized the central role that tools from accounting and marketing play in organizing the structure of markets.
29. Power 1997.
30. The course was part of Lilly's efforts to promote Zyprexa as Prozac went off patent.
31. As Van der Geest *et al.* (1996: 166) argue, "pharmaceuticals are often recast in another knowledge system and used very differently from the way they were intended in the 'regime of value' where they were produced."
32. BBC 2002.
33. Arie 2001.
34. BBC 2002.
35. Palomar 1996.
36. Gattari, et al. 2001.
37. What is important to note here is the much higher use of tranquilizers than anti-depressants. While the gap was narrowing, anxiolytics were still sold at nearly six times the rate of anti-depressants. I am grateful to Nikolas Rose for obtaining and sharing these most valuable data.
38. Unofficial data: over the two and a half year period, Paxil sales revenue had gone from an annual $6.2 million to $11.5 million. Unit sales of Paxil and Zoloft had also increased markedly.
39. World Health Organization 2001a.
40. Healy 1998.
41. Ehrenberg 1988.
42. Healy 1998; Borch-Jacobsen 2002.
43. Cit. in Borch-Jacobsen 2002.
44. Borch-Jacobsen 2002.

## 6 The segmented phenotype

1. Cohen *et al.* 2003.
2. Chumakov *et al.* 2002; Hattori *et al.* 2003.
3. Sydney Brenner (2000) has argued that the term "open reading frame" is a more accurate rendering of the key informational unit in post-genomics than the gene.
4. Keller 2003.
5. Freud and Breuer 1991: 65, emphasis added. Charcot too had used hypnotic suggestion as a therapeutic trial to confirm a diagnosis of hysteria.
6. Borch-Jacobsen 1996: 82.
7. Healy 1998. See also Pignarre 2001 and Borch-Jacobsen 2002.
8. Roses 2000: 860. An industry analyst writes that pharmacogenomics heralds "the therapeutic management of individual patients." Sadee 1998.
9. See Luhmann (1998) for the distinction between the "present future" and "future presents."
10. Thrift 1998.
11. O'Shea and Madigan 1997.
12. O'Shea and Madigan 1997. It might also be noted that Ira Magaziner, the architect of the failed Clinton health care plan, was a BCG consultant before taking on national health care reform in the early 1990s.
13. In situations of ignorance about the future, Luhmann (1998) writes, "there exists only a 'provisional' foresight, and its value lies not in the certainty that it

provides but in the quick and specific adjustment to a reality that comes to be other than what was expected."

14. Koselleck 1985.
15. Boston Consulting Group 1999.
16. John Maragnore, senior VP of strategic product development, Millennium (BioIT World, n.d.).
17. Michel Foucault defined biopolitics as the effort "to rationalize the problems presented to governmental practice by the phenomena characteristic of a group of living beings constituted as a population." Foucault 1997a: 73.
18. *Wall Street Journal*, 4 March 1999.
19. *Wall Street Journal*, 4 March 1999.
20. Declan Butler, "Big Boost Demanded for France's Life Sciences," *Nature* 399, 20 May 1999: 185.
21. Norton 2001.
22. Norton 2001: 183, 182.
23. Roses 2000: 863. For a description of this vision in psychiatric disorders, see Persidis and Copen 1999.
24. Spitzer, Endicott, and Robins 1978.
25. See Waldby 2001: 779–91, for a similar argument with respect to the technical efficacy of the "central dogma" in molecular biology.
26. The OED defines the verb "to true" as follows: "To make true, as a piece of mechanism or the like; to place, adjust, or shape accurately; to give the precise required form or position to; to make accurately or perfectly straight, level, round, smooth, sharp, etc. as required." *Oxford English Dictionary*, on-line edition: www.oed.com.
27. Cohen also noted that the susceptibility genes that the company had identified seemed to be "human-specific" or at least specific to higher primates. Conference: "Pharmacogenomics and the Practice of Medicine." New York Academy of Medicine, 3 October 2002.
28. "As far as health and disease are concerned, and consequently as far as setting accidents right, correcting disorders or, as it is popularly said, remedying ills are concerned, there is a difference between an organism and a society, in that the therapist of their ills, in the case of the organism, knows in advance and without hesitation, what normal state to establish, while in the case of society, he does not know." Canguilhem 1991: 257.
29. Canguilhem 1991: 252.
30. He cited André Leroi-Gourhan, who wrote that as opposed to animal evolution, "all human evolution converges to place outside of man what in the rest of the animal world corresponds to a specific adaptation." Canguilhem 1991: 255.

# References


Abelin, Mireille. 2004. "The Subversions of Sincerity." Unpublished manuscript.

Akiskal, Hagop S. 1996. "The Prevalent Clinical Spectrum of Bipolar Disorders: Beyond DSM-IV." *Journal of Clinical Psychopharmacology* 16: 2, suppl. 1, 4S–14S.

Alder, Ken. 1998. "Making Things the Same: Representation, Tolerance and the End of the Ancien Régime in France." *Social Studies of Science* 28: 4.

American Psychiatric Association. 1994. *Diagnostic and Statistical Manual of Mental Disorders: DSM-IV*. Washington, DC: American Psychiatric Association.

Andreasen, Nancy. 1997. "What is Psychiatry?" *American Journal of Psychiatry* 154: 5.

Angst, J. 1998. "The emerging epidemiology of hypomania and bipolar II disorder." *Journal of Affective Disorders* 50: 2–3.

Appadurai, Arjun. 1986. *The Social Life of Things*. Cambridge University Press.

Arie, Sophie. 2001. "Argentina Hits Rock Bottom." *The Observer*, 9 December: http://observer.guardian.co.uk.

Balán, Jorge. 1991. *Cuéntame tu vida: una biografía colectiva del psicoanálisis argentino*. Buenos Aires: Planeta.

Barondes, Samuel H. 1999. "An Agenda for Psychiatric Genetics." *Archives of General Psychiatry* 56.

Barry, Andrew, Thomas Osborne, and Nikolas Rose (eds.). 1996. *Foucault and Political Reason: Liberalism, Neo-Liberalism and the Rationalities of Government*. Chicago: University of Chicago Press.

BBC. 2002. "Los Argentinos se sienten devaluados." *BBC online* 24 January.

Bergel, Salvador 1998. "Patentamiento de genes y secuencias de genes." *Revista de Derecho y Genoma Humano* 8: 31–59.

Bergel, Salvador, and Carlos Correa (eds.). 1996. *Patentes y Competencia*. Buenos Aires: Rubinzal-Culzoni: Buenos Aires.

Berrios, German E. 1988. "Depressive and Manic States during the Nineteenth Century." In Anastasius Georgotas and Robert Cancro (eds.), *Depression and Mania: A Comprehensive Textbook*. New York: Elsevier.

Biagioli, Mario. 1993. *Galileo, Courtier: The Practice of Science in the Culture of Absolutism*. Chicago: University of Chicago Press.

1999. "Aporias of Scientific Authorship: Credit and Responsibility in Contemporary Biomedicine." In Biagioli (ed.), *The Science Studies Reader*. New York: Routledge.

Biagioli, Mario, and Peter Galison (eds.). 2003. *Scientific Authorship: Credit and Intellectual Property in Science*. New York: Routledge.

Borch-Jacobsen, Mikkel. 1996. *Remembering Anna O.: A Century of Mystification* New York: Routledge, 1996.

2002. "Prozac Notion," *London Review of Books*, 9 July.

Borges, Jorge Luis. 1962. "The Argentine Writer and Tradition." In Donald A. Yates and James E. Irby (eds.), *Labyrinths: Selected Stories and Other Writings*. New York: New Directions.

Borón, Atilio A. 1999. " 'Pensamiento unico' " y resignación política: los limites de una falsa coartada." In Borón, *Tiempos Violentos: Neoliberalismo, globalización y desigualdad en America Latina*. Buenos Aires: Eudeba.

Boston Consulting Group. 1999. "The Pharmaceutical Industry into its Second Century: From Serendipity to Strategy."

Bowie, Malcolm. 1991. *Lacan*. Cambridge, MA: Harvard University Press.

Bowker, Geoffrey, and Susan Leigh Star. 1999. *Sorting Things Out: Classification and its Consequences* Cambridge, MA: MIT Press.

Boyle, James. 1997. *Shamans, Software and Spleens: Law and the Construction of the Information Society*. Cambridge, MA: Harvard University Press.

Bradbury, Jane. 2001. "Teasing out the genetics of bipolar disorder." *The Lancet* 357, 19 May.

Brenner, Neil. 1999. "Globalization as Reterritorialisation: The Re-scaling of Urban Governance in the European Union." *Urban Studies* 36: 3.

Brenner, Sydney. 2000. "Genomics: The End of the Beginning." *Science* 287 (5461): 2173, 24 March.

Burchell, Graham, Colin Gordon, and Peter Miller (eds.). 1991. *The Foucault Effect: Studies in Governmentality*. Chicago: University of Chicago Press.

Callon. Michel. 1998. "The Embeddedness of Economic Markets in Economics." In Callon (ed.), *The Laws of the Markets*. Oxford and Malden, MA: Blackwell.

Callon, Michel, and Vololona Rabeharisoa. 2004. "Gino's Lesson on Humanity: Genetics, Mutual Entanglements and the Sociologist's Role." *Economy and Society* 33: 1.

Campanario, Sebastian. 1999. "Recrudece la guerra por las patentes." *Clarín*, 9 May.

Canguilhem, Georges. 1968. *Études d'histoire et de philosophie des sciences*. Paris: J. Vrin.

1991. *The Normal and the Pathological*. New York: Zone Books.

Carruthers, Bruce, and Arthur Stinchcombe. 1999. "The Social Structure of Liquidity: Flexibility, Markets, and States," *Theory and Society* 28: 3.

Castel, Robert. *The Regulation of Madness: The Origins of Incarceration in France*. 1988. Berkeley and Los Angeles: The University of California Press.

Cecchi, Horacio. 2001. "Una notícia para Comerse las uñas." *Página* 12, 16 August.

Chumakov, Ilya *et al.* 2002. "Genetic and Physiological Data Implicating the New Human Gene G72 and the Gene for D-amino Acide Oxidase in Schizophrenia." *Proceedings of the National Academy of Sciences* 99: 21, 15 October.

*Clarín*. 2001. "El Consumo de Tranquilizantes creció entre un 8 y un 9 por ciento." *Clarín*, 3 October.

Clavreul, Jean. 1978. *L'ordre Médicale*. Paris: Seuil.

Coghlan, Andy. 1996. "Chinese Deal Sparks Eugenics Protests." *The New Scientist*, 16 November.

Cohen, *et al.* 2003. "Schizophrenia Associated Gene, Proteins, and Biallelic Markers." United States Patent # 6,555,316, 29 April.

Cohen, Lawrence. 1998. *No Aging in India: Alzheimer's, The Bad Family, and Other Modern Things*. Berkeley: University of California Press.

Collier, Stephen J., and Aihwa Ong. 2005. "Global Assemblages, Anthropological Problems." In Aihwa Ong and Stephen J. Collier (eds.), *Global Assemblages: Technology, Politics and Ethics as Anthropological Problems*. New York: Blackwell.

Cooper, J. E., R. E. Kendell, B. J. Gurland, L. Sharpe, J. R. M. Copeland, and R. Simon. 1972. *Psychiatric Diagnosis in New York and London: A Comparative Study of Mental Hospital Admissions*. Institute of Psychiatry, Maudsley Monographs, Number Twenty. London: Oxford University Press.

Cronon, William. 1991. *Nature's Metropolis: Chicago and the Great West*. New York: W. W. Norton.

Crow, T. J. 1986. "The Continuum of Psychosis and its Implication for the Structure of the Gene." *British Journal of Psychiatry* 149.

Dana, Jason, and George Loewenstein. 2003. "A Social Science Perspective on Gifts to Physicians from Industry." *Journal of the American Medicine Association* 290: 2, 9 July.

Deleuze, Gilles. 1995. *Negotiations*. New York: Columbia University Press.

Deleuze, Gilles and Félix Guattari. 1994. *What is Philosophy?* New York: Columbia University Press.

Dixon, Bernard. 1988. "Genetic Engineers Call for Regulation." *The Scientist* 2: 8.

Doll, John J. 1998. "The Patenting of DNA." *Science* 280.

Dreyfus, Hubert, and Paul Rabinow. 1983. *Michel Foucault: Beyond Structuralism and Hermeneutics*. Chicago: University of Chicago Press.

Dumit, Joseph. 2000. "When Explanations Rest: 'Good-Enough' Brain Science and the New Socio-Medical Disorders." In Margaret Lock, Allan Young, and Alberto Cambrosio (eds.), *Living and Working with the New Medical Technologies*. Cambridge: Cambridge University Press.

Ehrenberg, Alain. 1988. *La Fatigue d'Etre Soi: Dépression et Société*. Paris: Odile Jacob.

Escamilla M. A., L. A. McInnes, M. Spesny, V. I. Reus, S. K. Service, N. Shimayoshi, D. J. Tyler, S. Silva, J. Molina, A. Gallegos, L. Meza, M. L. Cruz, S. Batki, S. Vinogradov, T. Neylan, J. B. Nguyen, E. Fournier, C. Araya, S. H. Barondes, P. Leon, L. A. Sandkuijl, and N. B. Freimer. 1999. "Assessing the Feasibility of Linkage Disequilibrium Methods for Mapping Complex Traits: An Initial Screen for Bipolar Disorder Loci on Chromosome 18." *American Journal of Human Genetics* 64.

Espelund, Wendy Nelson, and Mitchell L. Stevens. 1998. "Commensuration as a Social Process." *Annual Reviews in Sociology* 24.

Ewald, Francois. 1990. "Norms, Discipline and the Law." *Representations* 30.

Feitlowitz, Marguerite. 1998. *A Lexicon of Terror: Argentina and the Legacies of Torture*. New York: Oxford University Press.

Ferrer, Aldo. 1999. "Interview." *Clarín*, 21 March.

Forrester, John. 1996. "If *p*, then what? Thinking in Cases." *History of the Human Sciences* 9: 3.

Foucault, Michel. 1961. *Madness and Civilization: A History of Insanity in the Age of Reason*. Trans. Richard Howard. New York: Vintage.

1977. *Discipline and Punish: The Birth of the Prison*. Trans. Alan Sheridan. New York: Pantheon Books.

1997a. "The Birth of Biopolitics." In *Ethics: Subjectivity and Truth*. Vol. I, *Essential Works of Foucault, 1954–1984*. Ed. Paul Rabinow. New York: The New Press.

1997b. "On the Genealogy of Ethics." In *Ethics: Subjectivity and Truth*. Vol. I, *Essential Works of Foucault, 1954–1984*. Ed. Paul Rabinow. New York: The New Press.

1997c. "Psychiatric Power." In *Ethics: Subjectivity and Truth*. Vol. I, *Essential Writings of Foucault*. Ed. Paul Rabinow. New York: The New Press.

1997d. "What is an Author?" In *Ethics: Subjectivity and Truth*. Vol. I, *Essential Works of Foucault*. Ed. Paul Rabinow. New York: The New Press.

2000. "'*Omnes et Singulatim*': Toward a Critique of Political Reason." In *Power*. Vol. III, *The Essential Works of Foucault*. Ed. James D. Faubion. New York: The New Press.

Freud, Sigmund. 1917a. "A Difficulty in the Path of Psychoanalysis." In *The Standard Edition of the Complete Psychological Works of Sigmund Freud*. Vol. XVI. Trans. and ed. James Strachey. London: The Hogarth Press.

1917b. "Mourning and Melancholia." In *The Standard Edition of the Complete Psychological Works of Sigmund Freud*. Vol. XIV. Trans. and ed. James Strachey. London: The Hogarth Press.

1923–1925. "Neurosis and Psychosis." In *The Standard Edition of the Complete Psychological Works of Sigmund Freud*. Vol. XIX. Trans. and ed. James Strachey. London: The Hogarth Press.

1991. (with Marcel Breuer). *Studies on Hysteria*. London: Penguin.

Fukuyama, Francis. 2002. *Our Posthuman Future: Consequences of the Biotechnology Revolution*. New York: Farrar, Strauss & Giroux.

Fundación ISALUD. 1999. "El Mercado de Medicamentos en la Argentina." *Estudios de la Economía Real*, No. 13. Buenos Aires: Fundación ISALUD.

Galende, Emiliano. 1993. *Psicoanálisis y salud mental: Para una critica de la razón psiquiátrica*. 2nd Edn. Buenos Aires: Editorial Paidos.

Garcia, German L. 1980. *Oscar Masotta y el psicoanálysis del castellano*. Barcelona: Editorial Argonauta.

Gattari, Miriam, Susana Scarpatti, Inés Bignone, Ricardo Bolaños, and Ulises Romeo. 2001. "Estudio de utilización de ansiolíticos y antidepresivos en cuatro entidades de la seguridad social de la Argentina, periodo 1997–2000." Unpublished Manuscript.

Gelernter, J. 1995. "Editorial: Genetics of Bipolar Affective Disorder: Time for Another Reinvention?" *American Journal of Human Genetics* 56.

Gerth, H. H., and C. Wright Mills. 1946. *From Max Weber: Essays in Sociology*. New York: Oxford University Press.

Ginzburg, Carlo. 1983. "Clues: Morelli, Freud, and Sherlock Holmes." In Umberto Eco and Thomas A. Sebeok (eds.), *The Sign of Three: Dupin, Holmes, Pierce*. Bloomington: Indiana University Press.

Giorgi, Victor. 1997. "Neoliberalismo, subjectividad y salud." *Vertex*.

Giubellino, Gabriel. 1998. "Los expertos ponen reparos a las nuevas 'pildoras mágicas." *Clarín*, 26 October.

Goldenberg, Mauricio. 1958. "Estado Actual de la Asistencia Psiquiátrica en el País." *Acta Neuropsiquiátrica Argentina* 4.

Goldstein, Jan. 1987. *Console and Classify: The French Psychiatric Profession in the Nineteenth Century*. New York: Cambridge University Press.

Gomart, Emilie. 2002. "Methadone: Six Effects in Search of a Substance." *Social Studies of Science* 32: 1.

Goobar, Walter. 1998. "De quien es esa naricita?" *Siglo XXI*, 27 August.

Good, Byron. 1994. *Medicine, Rationality, and Experience: An Anthropological Perspective*. Cambridge: Cambridge University Press.

Grimson, Dicky. 1999. "Hacia lo social." *Página* 12.

Grob, Gerald N. 1991. *From Asylum to Community: Mental Health Policy in Modern America*. Princeton: Princeton University Press.

Hacking, Ian. 1990. *The Taming of Chance*. Cambridge University Press.

1998. *Mad Travelers: Reflections on the Reality of Transient Mental Illnesses*. Charlottesville: University of Virginia Press.

1999. *The Social Construction of* What? Cambridge, MA: Harvard University Press.

2003. *Historical Ontology*. Cambridge, MA: Harvard University Press.

Hale, Jr., Nathan G. 1995. *The Rise and Crisis of Psychoanalysis in the United States: Freud and the Americans, 1917–1985*. New York: Oxford University Press.

Halperin, Jorge. 1998. "Crisis en Villa Freud." *Trespuntos*. 22 December.

Hattori, E. *et al.* 2003. "Polymorphisms at the G72/G30 Gene Locus, on 13q33, are Associated with Bipolar Disorder in Two Independent Pedigree Series." *American Journal of Human Genetics* 72.

Healy, David. 1998. *The Anti-Depressant Era*. Cambridge, MA: Harvard University Press.

2001. "The Dilemmas Posed by New and Fashionable Treatments." *Advances in Psychiatric Treatment* 7.

Herrera, Stephan. 2001. "The Biotech Boom: Revenge of the Neurons." *Red Herring*, 1 October.

Hogle, Linda. 1995. "Standardization across Non-standard Domains: The Case of Organ Procurement." *Science, Technology and Human Values* 20: 4.

Hopenhayn, Martin. 2001. *No Apocalypse, No Integration: Modernism and Postmodernism in Latin America*. Durham, NC: Duke University Press.

Housman, David, and Fred D. Ledley. 1998. "Why Pharmacogenomics? Why Now?" *Nature Biotechnology* 16.

Hughes, Thomas P. 1987. "The Evolution of Large Technological Systems." In Wiebe E. Bijker, Thomas P. Hughes, and Trevor J. Pinch (eds.), *The Social Construction of Technology*. Cambridge, MA: MIT Press.

Jacobsen, Erik. 1986. "The Early History of Psychotherapeutic Drugs." *Psychopharmacology* 89: 138–44.

James, Daniel. 1988. *Resistance and Integration: Peronism and the Argentine Working Class, 1946–1976*. New York: Cambridge University Press.

Jamison, Kay Redfield. 1993. *Touched with Fire: Manic-Depressive Illness and the Artistic Temperament*. New York: Free Press.

1997. *An Unquiet Mind: A Memoir of Moods and Madness*. New York: Vintage.

Jasanoff, Sheila. 1995. *Science at the Bar: Law, Science, and Technology in America*. Cambridge, MA: Harvard University Press.

Kandel, Eric R. 1998. "A New Intellectual Framework for Psychiatry." *American Journal of Psychiatry* 155: 4.

Keller, Evelyn Fox. 2003. *Making Sense of Life: Explaining Biological Development With Models, Metaphors, and Machines*. Cambridge, MA: Harvard University Press.

Kesselman, Hernan. 1999. "Solitarios, asustados gladiadores contemporáneos: Facetas del 'daño psicológico' en la Argentina de hoy y su repercusión en la salud mental," *Página 12*, 9 April.

Kessler, R. C., K. A. McGonagle and S. Zhao. 1997. "The Epidemiology of DSM-III-R Bipolar I Disorder in a General Population Survey." *Psychological Medicine* 27:5.

Kirk, Stuart A., and Herb Kutchins. 1992. *The Selling of DSM: The Rhetoric of Science in Psychiatry*. New York: Aldine de Gruyter.

Kleinman, Arthur. 1995. *Writing at the Margin: Discourse Between Anthropology and Medicine*. Berkeley and Los Angeles: University of California Press.

Kline, Nathan S., ed. 1959. *Psychopharmacology Frontiers: Proceedings of the Psychopharmacology Symposium*. London: J. & A. Churchill.

Kopnisky, Kathy L., and Steven Hyman. 2002. "Psychiatry in the Postgenomic Era." *TEN* 4: 1.

Koselleck, Reinhardt. 1985. *Futures Past: On the Semantics of Historical Time*. Trans. Keith Tribe. Cambridge MA: MIT Press.

Kraepelin, Emil. 1904. "Stages of Maniacal-Depressive Insanity." In *Lectures on Clinical Psychiatry*. New York: William Wood.

Kramer, Peter. 1993. *Listening to Prozac: A Psychiatrist Explores Antidepressant Drugs and the Remaking of the Self*. New York: Penguin.

Lacan, Jacques. 1977. *Écrits: A Selection*. Trans. Alan Sheridan. New York: W. W. Norton.

1981. *The Seminar of Jacques Lacan, Book III: The Psychoses 1955–1956*. Ed. Jacques-Alain Miller. Trans. Russell Grigg. New York: W. W. Norton.

Lakoff, Andrew. 2000. "Adaptive Will: The Evolution of Attention Deficit Disorder." *Journal of the History of the Behavioral Sciences* 36: 2.

Lakoff, Andrew, and Stephen J. Collier. 2004. "Ethics and the Anthropology of Modern Reason." *Anthropological Theory* 4: 4.

Latour, Bruno. 1987. *Science in Action*. Cambridge, MA: Harvard University Press.

2000. "On the Partial Existence of Existing *and* Non-Existing Objects." In Lorraine Daston (ed.), *Biographies of Scientific Objects*. Chicago: University of Chicago Press.

Leboyer, M., F. Bellivier, M. Nosten-Bertrand, R. Jouvent, D. Pauls, J. Mallet. 1998. "Psychiatric Genetics: Search for Phenotypes." *Trends in Neurosciences* 21:3.

Luhmann, Niklas. 1990. *Essays on Self-Reference*. New York: Columbia University Press.

1998. *Observations on Modernity*. Stanford: Stanford University Press.

Luhrmann, T. M. 2000. *Of Two Minds: The Growing Disorder in American Psychiatry*. New York: Knopf.

Macherey, Pierre. 1992. "Towards a Natural History of Norms." In T. J. Armstrong (ed.), *Michel Foucault, Philosopher: Essays*. New York: Routledge.

MacKinnon, Dean F. Kay, Redfield Jamison, and J. Raymond DePaulo. 1997. "Genetics of Manic Depressive Illness." *Annual Reviews in Neurosciences* 20.

Marks, Harry M. 1997. *The Progress of Experiment: Science and Therapeutic Reform in the United States, 1900–1990*. New York: Cambridge University Press.

Marshall, T. H. 1963. *Sociology at the Crossroads, and Other Essays*. London: Heinemann.

Martin, Emily. 1999. "Flexible Survivors." *Anthropology Newsletter* 40: 6.

Masotta, Oscar. 1976. *Ensayos Lacanianos*. Buenos Aires: Anagrama.

McInnes, L. A., V. I. Reus, N. B. Freimer. 1998. "Mapping Genes for Psychiatric Disorders and Behavioral Traits." *Current Opinion in Genetics and Development* 8: 3.

Meek, James. 2000. "Why You are First in the Great Gene Race." *The Guardian*, 15 November.

Navarra, Gabriela. 1998. "De la euforia a la depresión." *La Nación*, 22 July, 6: 4.

Norton, Ronald. 2001. "Clinical Pharmacogenomics: Applications in Pharmaceutical R & D." *Drug Development Today* 6: 4 February.

O'Donnell, Guillermo. 1999. *Counterpoints: Selected Essays on Authoritarianism and Democratization*. South Bend, IN: University of Notre Dame Press.

Ong, Aihwa, and Stephen J. Collier. (eds.). 2005. *Global Assemblages: Technology, Politics and Ethics as Anthropological Problems*. New York: Blackwell.

O'Shea, James, and Charles Madigan. 1997. *Dangerous Company: The Consulting Powerhouses and the Businesses They Save and Ruin*. New York: Times Books.

Palomar, Jorge. 1996. "El Ranking de los Remedios." *La Nación On Line*. http://www.lanacion.com.

Pálsson, Gísli, and Paul Rabinow. 1999. "Iceland: The Case of a National Human Genome Project." *Anthropology Today* 15: 5.

Pan American Health Organization. 1998. *Health in the Americas*. Washington, DC: Pan American Health Organization.

Persidis, Aris, and Rachel M. Copen. 1999. "Mental Disorder Drug Discovery." *Nature Biotechnology* 17.

PhRMA. 2001. "Special 301 Submission: Priority Foreign Countries." Accessed at www.phrma.org., January 2002.

Pichon-Rivière, Enrique. 1983. *La Psiquiatría, una Nueva Problemática*. Buenos Aires: Ediciones Nueva Visión.

Pichot, Pierre J. 1997. "DSM-III and its Reception: A European View." *American Journal of Psychiatry*. 154: 6, Suppl. (Jun), 47–54.

Pignarre, Philippe. 2001. *Comment la dépression est devenue une épidémie?* Paris: La Découverte.

Plotkin, Mariano Ben. 2001. *Freud in the Pampas: the Emergence and Development of a Psychoanalytic Culture in Argentina.* Stanford, CA: Stanford University Press.

2003. "Psychiatrists and the Reception of Psychoanalysis, 1910s – 1970s." In Mariano Plotkin (ed.), *Argentina on the Couch: Psychiatry, State, and Society, 1880 to the Present.* Albuquerque, NM: University of New Mexico Press.

Pomfret, John, and Deborah Nelson. 2000. "In Rural China, a Genetic Mother Lode." *Washington Post*, 20 December, A1.

Power, Michael. 1997. *The Audit Society: Rituals of Verification.* New York: Oxford University Press.

Rabinow, Paul. 1996 [1989]. *French Modern: Norms and Forms of the Social Environment.* Chicago: University of Chicago Press.

1995. *Making PCR: A Story of Biotechnology.* Chicago: University of Chicago Press.

1996. *Essays on the Anthropology of Reason.* Princeton: Princeton University Press.

1999. *French DNA: Trouble in Purgatory.* Chicago: University of Chicago Press.

2003. *Anthropos Today: Reflections on Modern Equipment.* Princeton: Princeton University Press.

Rapp, Rayna. 1999. *Testing Women, Testing the Fetus: The Social Impact of Amniocentesis in America.* New York: Routledge.

Regalado, Antonio. 1999. "Inventing the Pharmacogenomics Business." *American Journal of Health System Pharmacy* 56: 1.

Rhodes, Lorna A. 1991. *Emptying Beds: The Work of an Emergency Psychiatric Unit.* Berkeley: University of California Press.

Ricón, Lía. 2001. "Crisis de fin de siglo y subjectividad." *Vertex: Revista Argentina de Psiquiatría.*

Risch, Neil, and David Botstein. 1996. "A Manic Depressive History." *Nature Genetics* 12.

Rock, David. 1985. *Argentina, 1516–1987.* Berkeley: University of California Press.

Rodrigué, Emilio. 1965. *Biografía de una comunidad terapéutica.* Buenos Aires: EUDEBA.

Romero, Luis Alberto. 2002. *A History of Argentina in the Twentieth Century.* Trans. James P. Brennan. University Park, PA: The Pennsylvania State University Press.

Rose, Nikolas. 1996a. *Inventing our Selves: Psychology, Power, and Personhood.* Cambridge: Cambridge University Press.

1996b. "Psychiatry as a Political Science: Advanced Liberalism and the Administration of Risk." *History of the Human Sciences* 9: 2.

1996c. "The Death of the Social? Refiguring the Territory of Government." *Economy and Society* 25: 3.

1998. "The Psychiatric Gaze." Unpublished manuscript.

1999. *Powers of Freedom: Reframing Political Thought.* New York: Cambridge University Press.

Rosenberg, Charles. 2002. "The Tyranny of Diagnosis: Specific Entities and Individual Experience." *Milbank Quarterly* 80.

Roses, Allen D. 2000. "Pharmacogenomics and the Practice of Medicine." *Nature* 405: 15 June.

Roudinesco, Elisabeth. 1997. *Jacques Lacan: Outline of a Life, History of a System of Thought*. Trans. Barbara Bray. New York: Columbia University Press.

Roustang, Francois. 1990. *The Lacanian Delusion*. Trans. Greg Sims. New York: Oxford University Press.

Sabel, Charles. 1997. "Constitutional Orders: Trust Building and Response to Change." In J. R. Hollingsworth and R. Boyer (eds.), *Contemporary Capitalism: The Embeddedness of Institutions*. Cambridge: Cambridge University Press.

Sadee, Wolfgang. 1998. "Genomics and Drugs: Finding the Optimal Drug for the Right Patient." *Pharmaceutical Research* 15: 7.

Sarlo, Beatriz. 1993. *Jorge Luis Borges: A Writer on the Edge*. Ed. John King. London; New York: Verso.

1988. *Una modernidad periférica: Buenos Aires 1920 y 1930*. Buenos Aires: Nueva Visión.

Sassen, Saskia. 2000. "Spatialities and Temporalities of the Global: Elements for a Theorization." *Public Culture* 12: 1.

Scull, Andrew. 1989. *Social Order/ Mental Disorder: Anglo-American Psychiatry in Historical Perspective*. Berkeley: University of California Press.

Sebreli, Juan Jose. 1997. *Escritos sobre escritos, ciudades bajo ciudades, 1950–1997*. Buenos Aires: Editorial Sudamericana.

Shapin, Steven. 1994. *A Social History of Truth: Civility and Science in Seventeenth Century England*. Chicago: University of Chicago Press.

Shapin, Steven, and Simon Schaffer. 1986. *Leviathan and the Air-Pump*. Princeton: Princeton University Press.

Shorter, Edward. 1997. *A History of Psychiatry: From the Era of the Asylum to the Age of Prozac*. New York: John Wiley & Sons.

Sigal, Silvia. 2002. *Intelectuales y poder en Argentina: la década del sesenta*. Buenos Aires: Siglo Veintiuno de Argentina.

Sikkink, Kathryn. 1991. *Ideas and Institutions: Developmentalism in Brazil and Argentina*. Ithaca, NY: Cornell University Press.

Spears, Timothy. 1995. *100 Years on the Road: Traveling Salesmen in American Culture*. New Haven: Yale University Press.

Spitzer, R. L., J. Endicott, and E. Robins. 1978. "Research Diagnostic Criteria: Rationale and Reliability." *Archives of General Psychiatry* 35: 6.

Stengers, Isabelle. 1990. "The Deceptions of Power: Psychoanalysis and Hypnosis." *SubStance* 62/63.

1997. *Power and Invention: Situating Science*. Minneapolis: University of Minnesota Press.

Sulloway, Frank J. 1979. *Freud: Biologist of the Mind: Beyond the Psychoanalytic Legend*. New York: Basic Books.

Swain, Gladys. 1994. *Dialogue avec l'insensé: Essais d'histoire de la psychiatrie*. Paris: Gallimard.

Terán, Oscar. 1991. *Nuestros años sesentas: la formación de la nueva izquierda intelectual en la Argentina, 1956–1966*. Buenos Aires: Puntosur.

Thayer, Ann M. 1999. "Deciphering Diseases." *Chemical and Engineering News*, 30 August.

Thrift, Nigel. 1998. "Virtual Capitalism: The Globalization of Reflexive Business Knowledge." In James G. Carrier and Daniel Miller, (eds.), *Virtualism: A New Political Economy*. Oxford University Press.

Timmermans, Stefan, and Marc Berg. 1997. "Standardization in Action: Achieving Local Universality through Medical Protocols." *Social Studies of Science* 27.

2003. *The Gold Standard: The Challenge of Evidence-Based Medicine and Standardization in Health Care*. Philadelphia: Temple University Press.

Turkle, Sherry. 1992. *Psychoanalytic Politics: Jacques Lacan and Freud's French Revolution*. 2nd edn. London: The Guilford Press.

United Nations Development Program. 1999. *Human Development Report 1999*. New York: Oxford University Press.

Van der Geest, Sjaak, Susan Reynolds Whyte, and Anita Hardon. 1996. "The Anthropology of Pharmaceuticals: A Biographic Approach." *Annual Review of Anthropology* 25.

Vezzetti, Hugo. 1995. "Las Ciencias Sociales y el campo de la salud mental en la década del sesenta." *Punto de Vista* 54.

1996. *Aventuras de Freud en el país de los argentinos: de José Ingenieros a Enrique Pichon-Rivière*. Buenos Aires: Paidós.

1997a. *Salud Mental: Profesionales, Curanderos y Acompañantes Quimicos*. In Jorge Halperin (comp.), *Argentina en el Tercer Milenio*. Buenos Aires: Editorial Atlantida.

1997b. "Sobre los origines de salud mental en la Argentina." *Documenta*. Revista de la Dirección de Salud Mental de la Secretaría de Salud del Gobierno de la Ciudad de Buenos Aires, no. 1, Julio.

2003. "From the Psychiatric Hospital to the Street: Enrique Pichon-Rivière and the Diffusion of Psychoanalysis in Argentina." In Mariano Plotkin (ed.), *Argentina on the couch: Psychiatry, State, and Society, 1880 to the Present*. Albuquerque, NM: University of New Mexico Press.

Vidal, Guillermo. 1957. "Trastornos Endocrines y Metabólicas en la Squizofrenia." *Acta Neuropsiquiatría Argentina* 3.

1960. "Neuropsychopharmacology." *Acta Neuropsiquiatría Argentina* 6.

Visacovsky, Sergio Eduardo. 1998. "Genealogias rompidas. Memória, politica e filição no psicanálise argentina." *Mosaico: Revista de Ciências Sociais* 1: 1.

Waisman, Carlos. 1987. *Reversal of Development in Argentina: Postwar Counterrevolutionary Policies and Their Structural Consequences*. Princeton: Princeton University Press.

Waldby, Catherine. 2001. "Code Unknown: Histories of the Gene." *Social Studies of Science* 31: 5.

Weber, Max. 1946. "Science as a Vocation." In H. H. Gerth and C. Wright Mills (trans. and ed.), *From Max Weber: Essays in sociology*. New York: Oxford University Press.

Wildenauer, D. B, S. G. Schwab, W. Maier, and S. D. Detera-Wadleigh. 1999. "Do Schizophrenia and Affective Disorder Share Susceptibility Genes?" *Schizophrenia Research* 39.

Wilson, Mitchell. 1995. "DSM-III and American Psychiatry: A History." *American Journal of Psychiatry* 150: 3.

World Bank. 1993. "An Agenda For Action." *World Development Report 1993: Investing in Health.* New York: Oxford University Press.

World Bank. 1997. *Health, Nutrition, and Population: A Statistical Handbook* Washington, DC: World Bank.

World Health Organization. 2001a. *Atlas: Country Profiles on Mental Health Resources in the World.* Geneva: World Health Organization.

2001b. *World Health Report, 2001.* Geneva: World Health Organization.

Young, Allan. 1996. *The Harmony of Illusions: Inventing Post-Traumatic Stress Disorder.* Princeton: Princeton University Press.

# Index